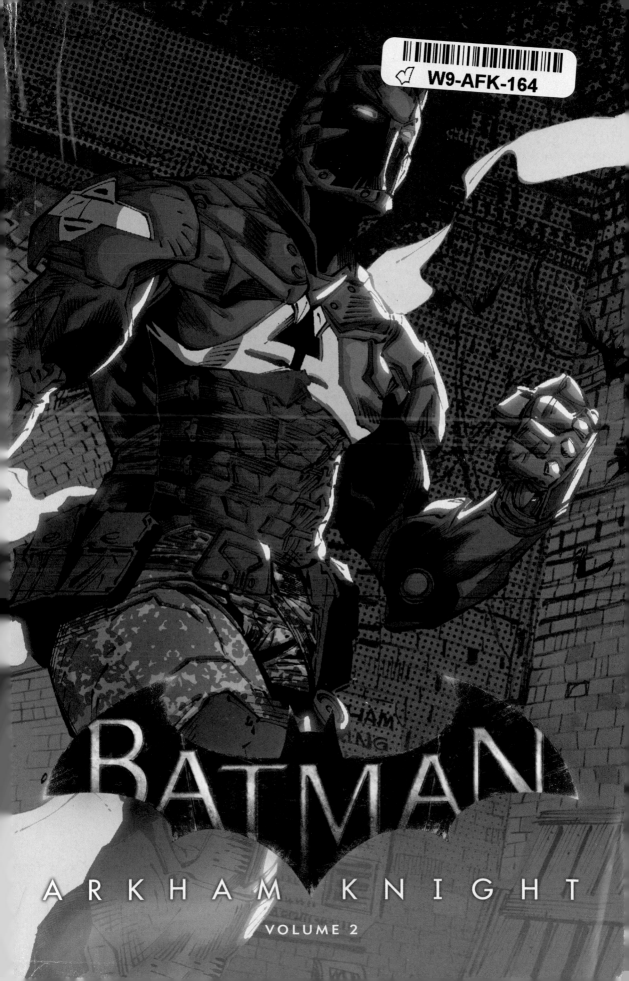

BATMAN

ARKHAM KNIGHT

VOLUME 2

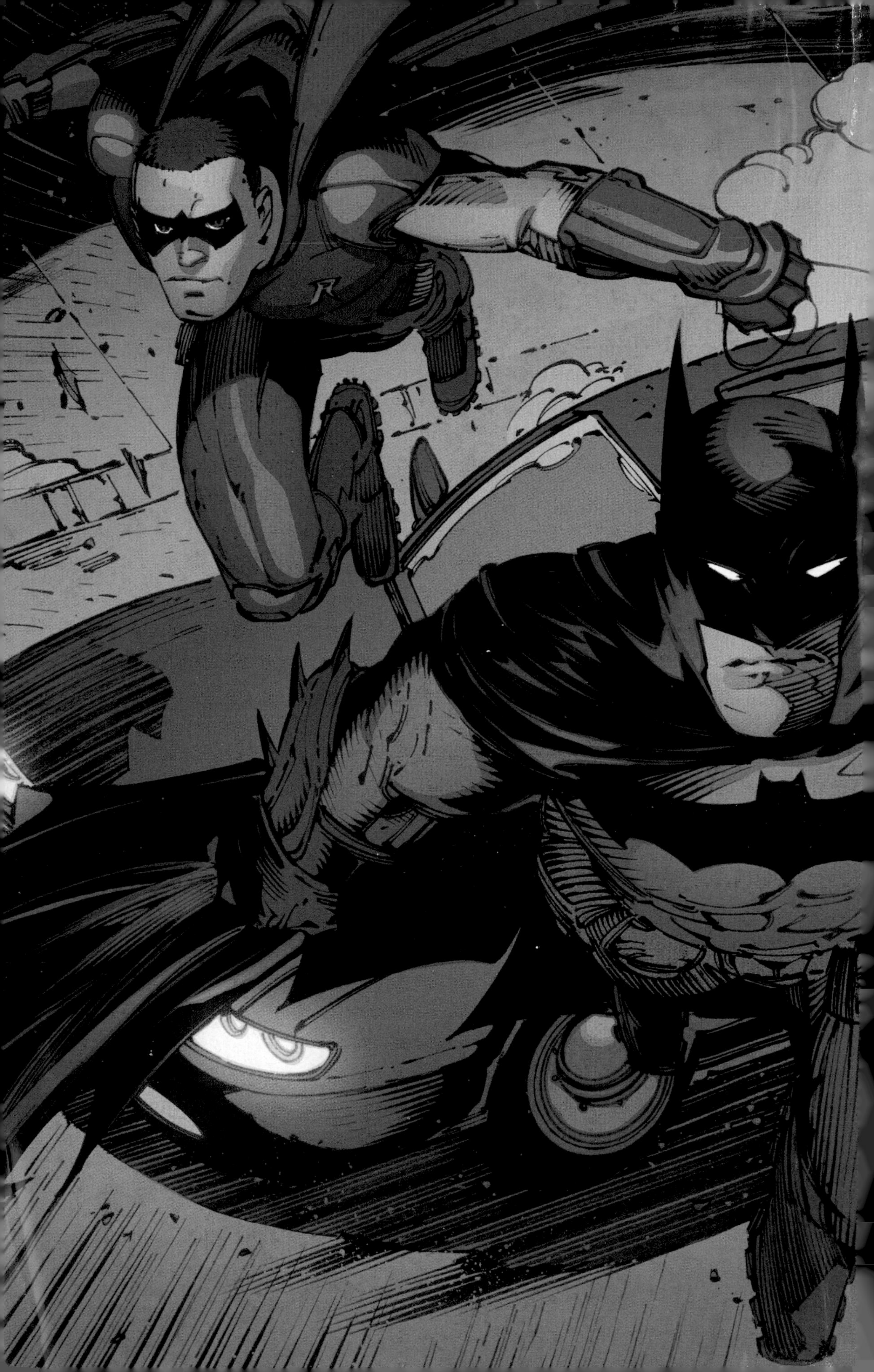

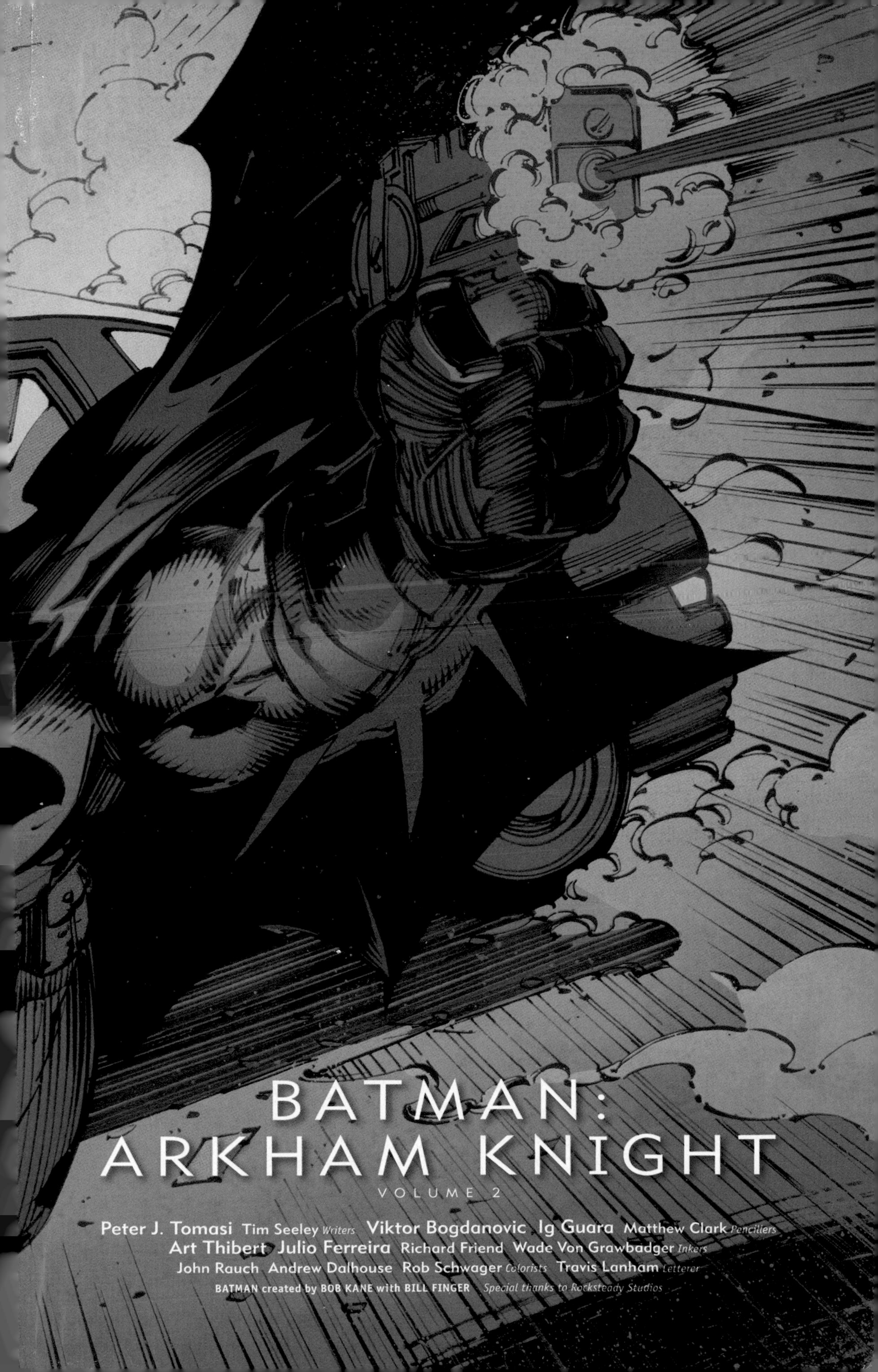

BATMAN: ARKHAM KNIGHT

VOLUME 2

Peter J. Tomasi Tim Seeley *Writers* Viktor Bogdanovic Ig Guara Matthew Clark *Pencillers*
Art Thibert Julio Ferreira Richard Friend Wade Von Grawbadger *Inkers*
John Rauch Andrew Dalhouse Rob Schwager *Colorists* Travis Lanham *Letterer*

BATMAN created by BOB KANE with BILL FINGER *Special thanks to Rocksteady Studios*

Alex Antone *Editor – Original Series*
Brittany Holzherr *Assistant Editor – Original Series*
Jeb Woodard *Group Editor – Collected Editions*
Liz Erickson *Editor – Collected Edition*
Steve Cook *Design Director – Books*
Damian Ryland *Publication Design*

Bob Harras *Senior VP – Editor-in-Chief, DC Comics*

Diane Nelson *President*
Dan DiDio and Jim Lee *Co-Publishers*
Geoff Johns *Chief Creative Officer*
Amit Desai *Senior VP – Marketing & Global Franchise Management*
Nairi Gardiner *Senior VP – Finance*
Sam Ades *VP – Digital Marketing*
Bobbie Chase *VP – Talent Development*
Mark Chiarello *Senior VP – Art, Design & Collected Editions*
John Cunningham *VP – Content Strategy*
Anne DePies *VP – Strategy Planning & Reporting*
Don Falletti *VP – Manufacturing Operations*
Lawrence Ganem *VP – Editorial Administration & Talent Relations*
Alison Gill *Senior VP – Manufacturing & Operations*
Hank Kanalz *Senior VP – Editorial Strategy & Administration*
Jay Kogan *VP – Legal Affairs*
Derek Maddalena *Senior VP – Sales & Business Development*
Jack Mahan *VP – Business Affairs*
Dan Miron *VP – Sales Planning & Trade Development*
Nick Napolitano *VP – Manufacturing Administration*
Carol Roeder *VP – Marketing*
Eddie Scannell *VP – Mass Account & Digital Sales*
Courtney Simmons *Senior VP – Publicity & Communications*
Jim (Ski) Sokolowski *VP – Comic Book Specialty & Newsstand Sales*
Sandy Yi *Senior VP – Global Franchise Management*

BATMAN: ARKHAM KNIGHT VOLUME 2

Published by DC Comics. Compilation and all new material Copyright © 2016 DC Comics. All Rights Reserved.

Originally published in single magazine form in BATMAN: ARKHAM KNIGHT 5-9, BATMAN: ARKHAM KNIGHT: BATGIRL BEGINS and online as BATMAN: ARKHAM KNIGHT Digital Chapters 13-26, BATMAN: ARKHAM KNIGHT: BATGIRL BEGINS Copyright © 2015 DC Comics. All Rights Reserved. All characters, their distinctive likenesses and related elements featured in this publication are trademarks of DC Comics. The stories, characters and incidents featured in this publication are entirely fictional. DC Comics does not read or accept unsolicited ideas, stories or artwork.

DC Comics, 2900 West Alameda Ave., Burbank, CA 91505
Printed by RR Donnelley, Owensville, MO, USA. 6/3/16. First Printing.
ISBN: 978-1-4012-6340-9

Library of Congress Cataloging-in-Publication Data is available.

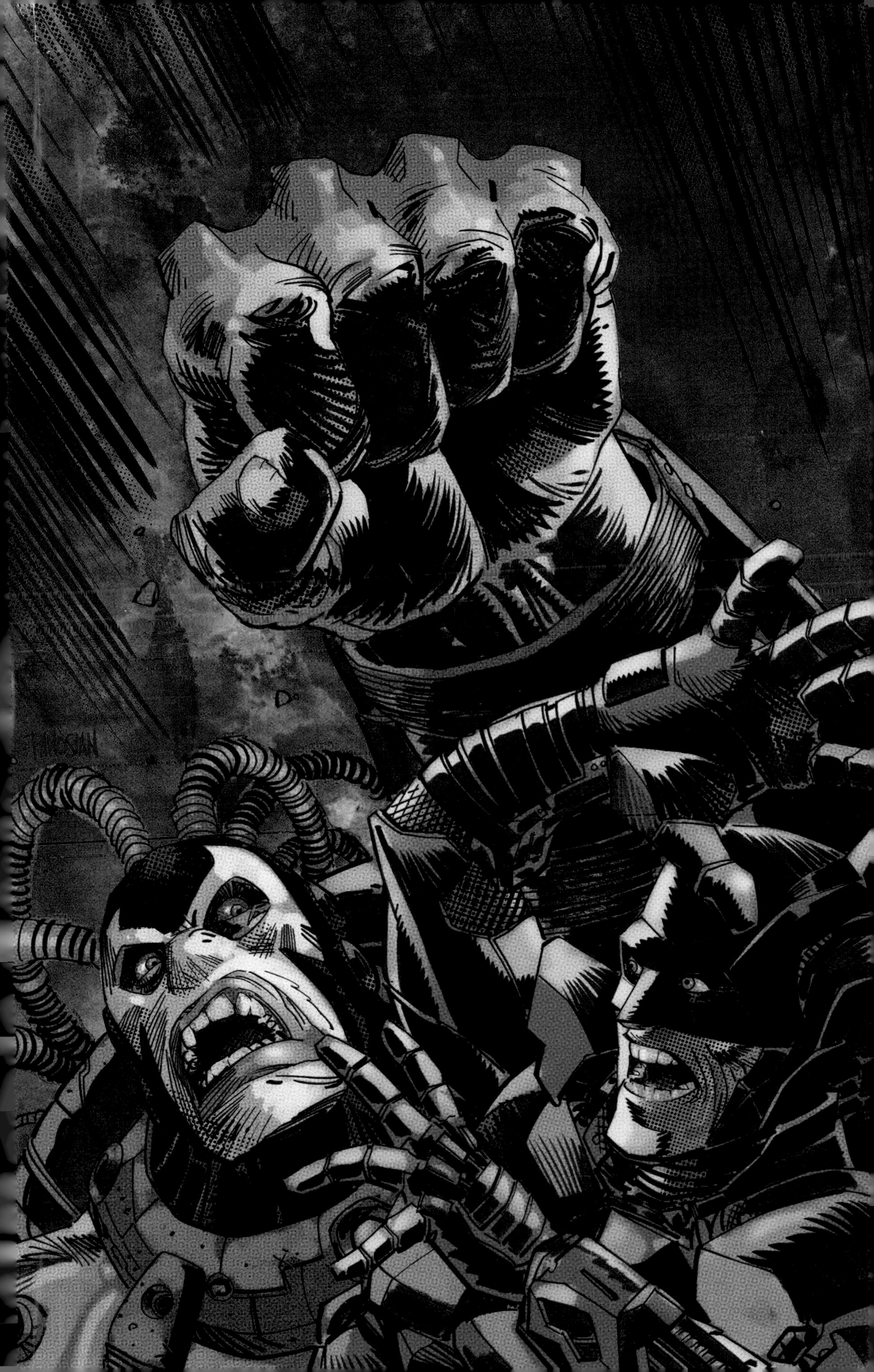

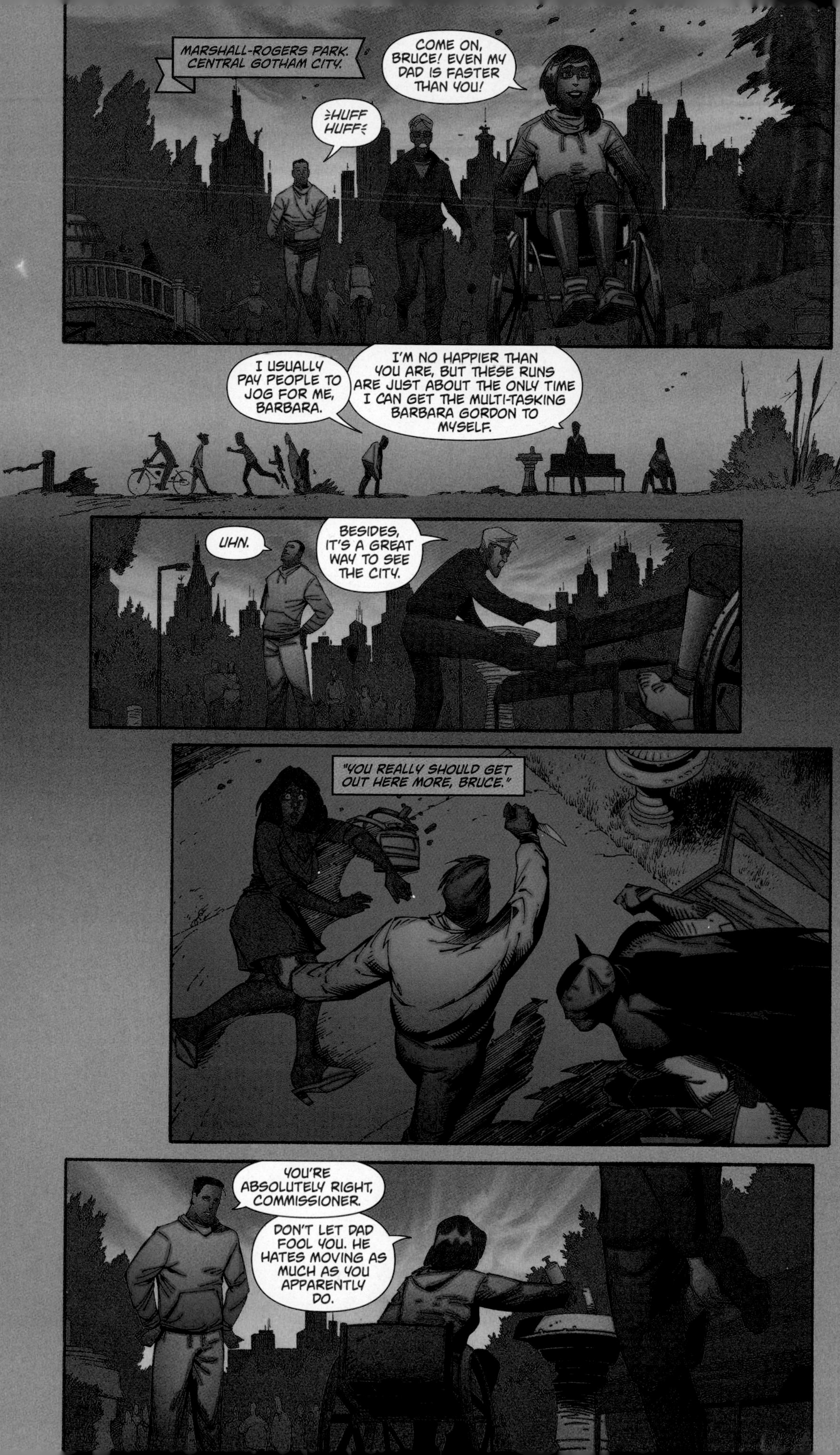
MARSHALL-ROGERS PARK. CENTRAL GOTHAM CITY.
COME ON, BRUCE! EVEN MY DAD IS FASTER THAN YOU!
HUFF HUFF
I USUALLY PAY PEOPLE TO JOG FOR ME, BARBARA.
I'M NO HAPPIER THAN YOU ARE, BUT THESE RUNS ARE JUST ABOUT THE ONLY TIME I CAN GET THE MULTI-TASKING BARBARA GORDON TO MYSELF.
UHN.
BESIDES, IT'S A GREAT WAY TO SEE THE CITY.
"YOU REALLY SHOULD GET OUT HERE MORE, BRUCE."
YOU'RE ABSOLUTELY RIGHT, COMMISSIONER.
DON'T LET DAD FOOL YOU. HE HATES MOVING AS MUCH AS YOU APPARENTLY DO.

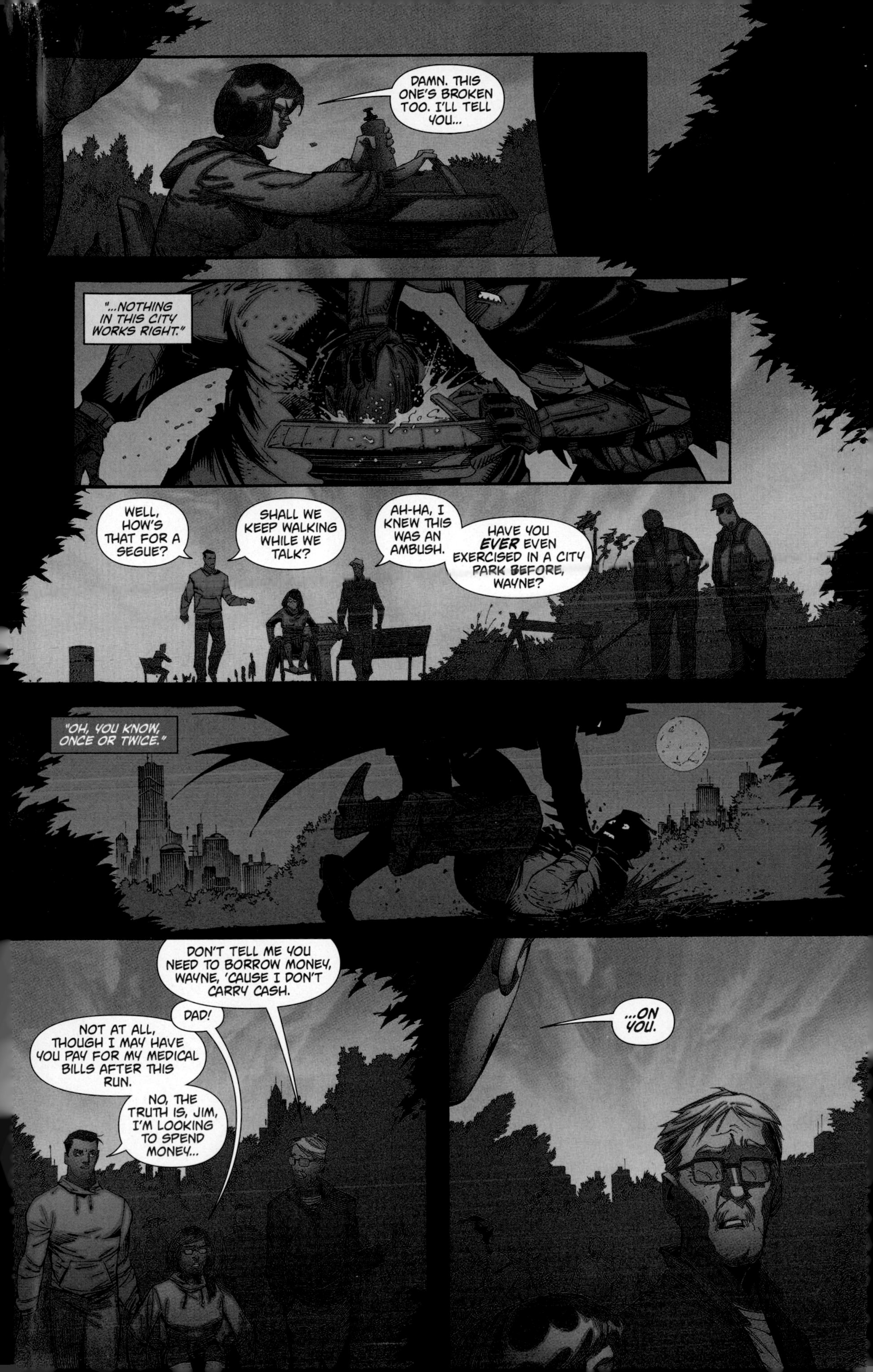
DAMN. THIS ONE'S BROKEN TOO. I'LL TELL YOU...
"...NOTHING IN THIS CITY WORKS RIGHT."
WELL, HOW'S THAT FOR A SEGUE?
SHALL WE KEEP WALKING WHILE WE TALK?
AH-HA, I KNEW THIS WAS AN AMBUSH.
HAVE YOU EVER EVEN EXERCISED IN A CITY PARK BEFORE, WAYNE?
"OH, YOU KNOW, ONCE OR TWICE."
DON'T TELL ME YOU NEED TO BORROW MONEY, WAYNE, 'CAUSE I DON'T CARRY CASH.
DAD!
NOT AT ALL, THOUGH I MAY HAVE YOU PAY FOR MY MEDICAL BILLS AFTER THIS RUN.
NO, THE TRUTH IS, JIM, I'M LOOKING TO SPEND MONEY...
...ON YOU.

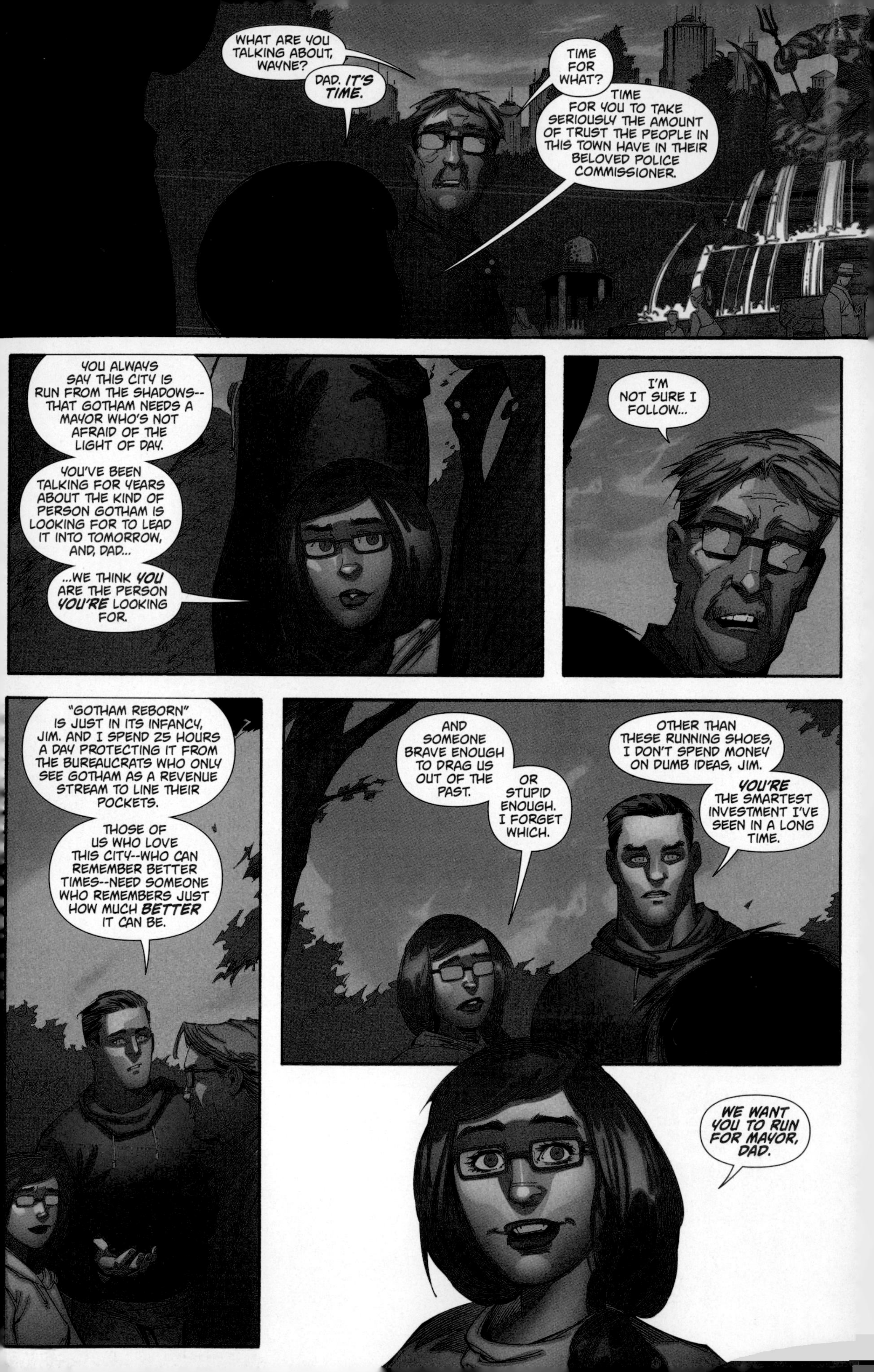
WHAT ARE YOU TALKING ABOUT, WAYNE?
DAD. IT'S TIME.
TIME FOR WHAT?
TIME FOR YOU TO TAKE SERIOUSLY THE AMOUNT OF TRUST THE PEOPLE IN THIS TOWN HAVE IN THEIR BELOVED POLICE COMMISSIONER.
YOU ALWAYS SAY THIS CITY IS RUN FROM THE SHADOWS--THAT GOTHAM NEEDS A MAYOR WHO'S NOT AFRAID OF THE LIGHT OF DAY.
YOU'VE BEEN TALKING FOR YEARS ABOUT THE KIND OF PERSON GOTHAM IS LOOKING FOR TO LEAD IT INTO TOMORROW, AND, DAD...
...WE THINK YOU ARE THE PERSON YOU'RE LOOKING FOR.
I'M NOT SURE I FOLLOW...
"GOTHAM REBORN" IS JUST IN ITS INFANCY, JIM. AND I SPEND 25 HOURS A DAY PROTECTING IT FROM THE BUREAUCRATS WHO ONLY SEE GOTHAM AS A REVENUE STREAM TO LINE THEIR POCKETS.
THOSE OF US WHO LOVE THIS CITY--WHO CAN REMEMBER BETTER TIMES--NEED SOMEONE WHO REMEMBERS JUST HOW MUCH BETTER IT CAN BE.
AND SOMEONE BRAVE ENOUGH TO DRAG US OUT OF THE PAST.
OR STUPID ENOUGH. I FORGET WHICH.
OTHER THAN THESE RUNNING SHOES, I DON'T SPEND MONEY ON DUMB IDEAS, JIM.
YOU'RE THE SMARTEST INVESTMENT I'VE SEEN IN A LONG TIME.
WE WANT YOU TO RUN FOR MAYOR, DAD.

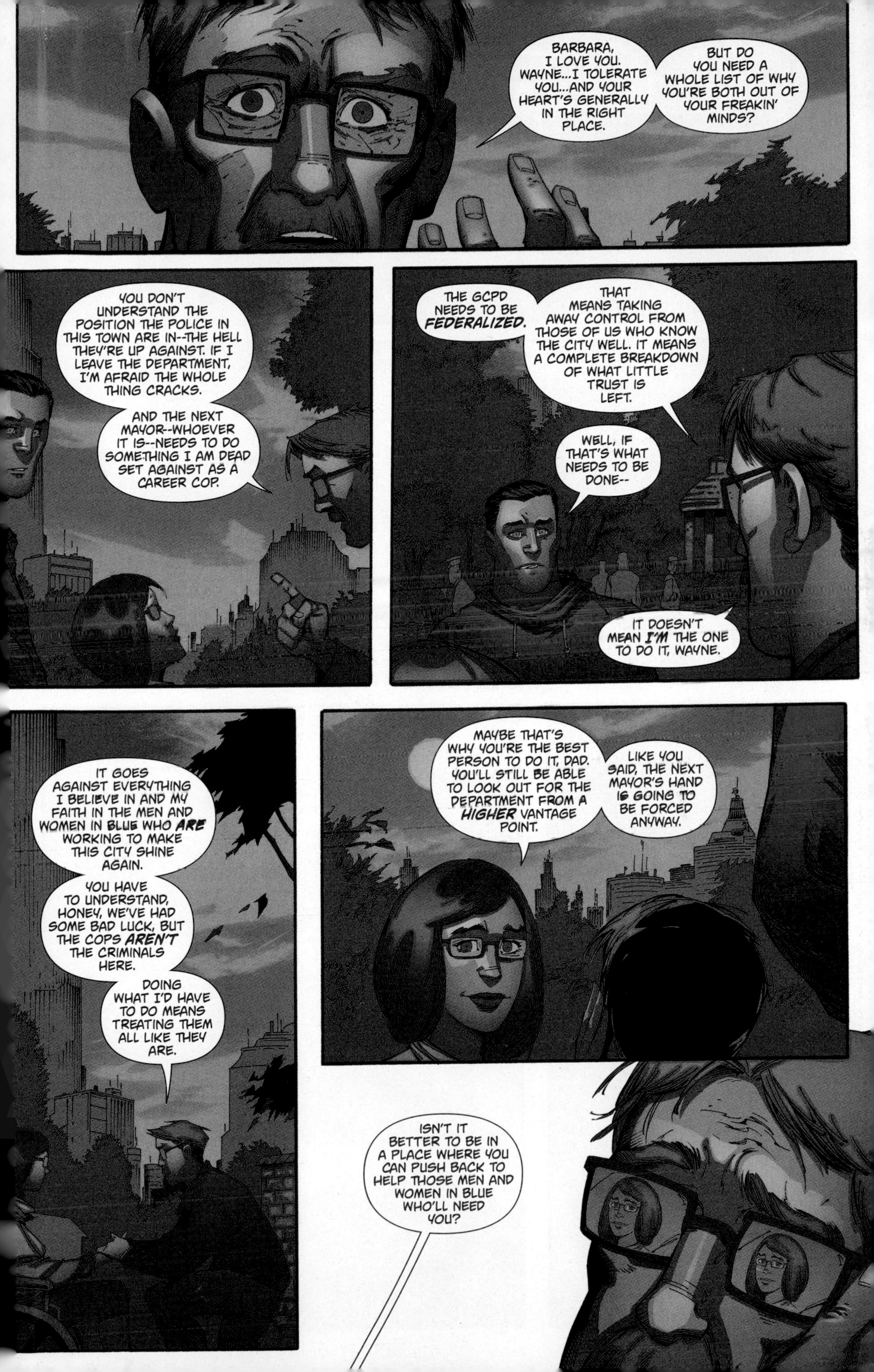
BARBARA, I LOVE YOU. WAYNE...I TOLERATE YOU...AND YOUR HEART'S GENERALLY IN THE RIGHT PLACE.
BUT DO YOU NEED A WHOLE LIST OF WHY YOU'RE BOTH OUT OF YOUR FREAKIN' MINDS?
YOU DON'T UNDERSTAND THE POSITION THE POLICE IN THIS TOWN ARE IN--THE HELL THEY'RE UP AGAINST. IF I LEAVE THE DEPARTMENT, I'M AFRAID THE WHOLE THING CRACKS.
AND THE NEXT MAYOR--WHOEVER IT IS--NEEDS TO DO SOMETHING I AM DEAD SET AGAINST AS A CAREER COP.
THE GCPD NEEDS TO BE FEDERALIZED.
THAT MEANS TAKING AWAY CONTROL FROM THOSE OF US WHO KNOW THE CITY WELL. IT MEANS A COMPLETE BREAKDOWN OF WHAT LITTLE TRUST IS LEFT.
WELL, IF THAT'S WHAT NEEDS TO BE DONE--
IT DOESN'T MEAN I'M THE ONE TO DO IT, WAYNE.
IT GOES AGAINST EVERYTHING I BELIEVE IN AND MY FAITH IN THE MEN AND WOMEN IN BLUE WHO ARE WORKING TO MAKE THIS CITY SHINE AGAIN.
YOU HAVE TO UNDERSTAND, HONEY, WE'VE HAD SOME BAD LUCK, BUT THE COPS AREN'T THE CRIMINALS HERE.
DOING WHAT I'D HAVE TO DO MEANS TREATING THEM ALL LIKE THEY ARE.
MAYBE THAT'S WHY YOU'RE THE BEST PERSON TO DO IT, DAD. YOU'LL STILL BE ABLE TO LOOK OUT FOR THE DEPARTMENT FROM A HIGHER VANTAGE POINT.
LIKE YOU SAID, THE NEXT MAYOR'S HAND IS GOING TO BE FORCED ANYWAY.
ISN'T IT BETTER TO BE IN A PLACE WHERE YOU CAN PUSH BACK TO HELP THOSE MEN AND WOMEN IN BLUE WHO'LL NEED YOU?

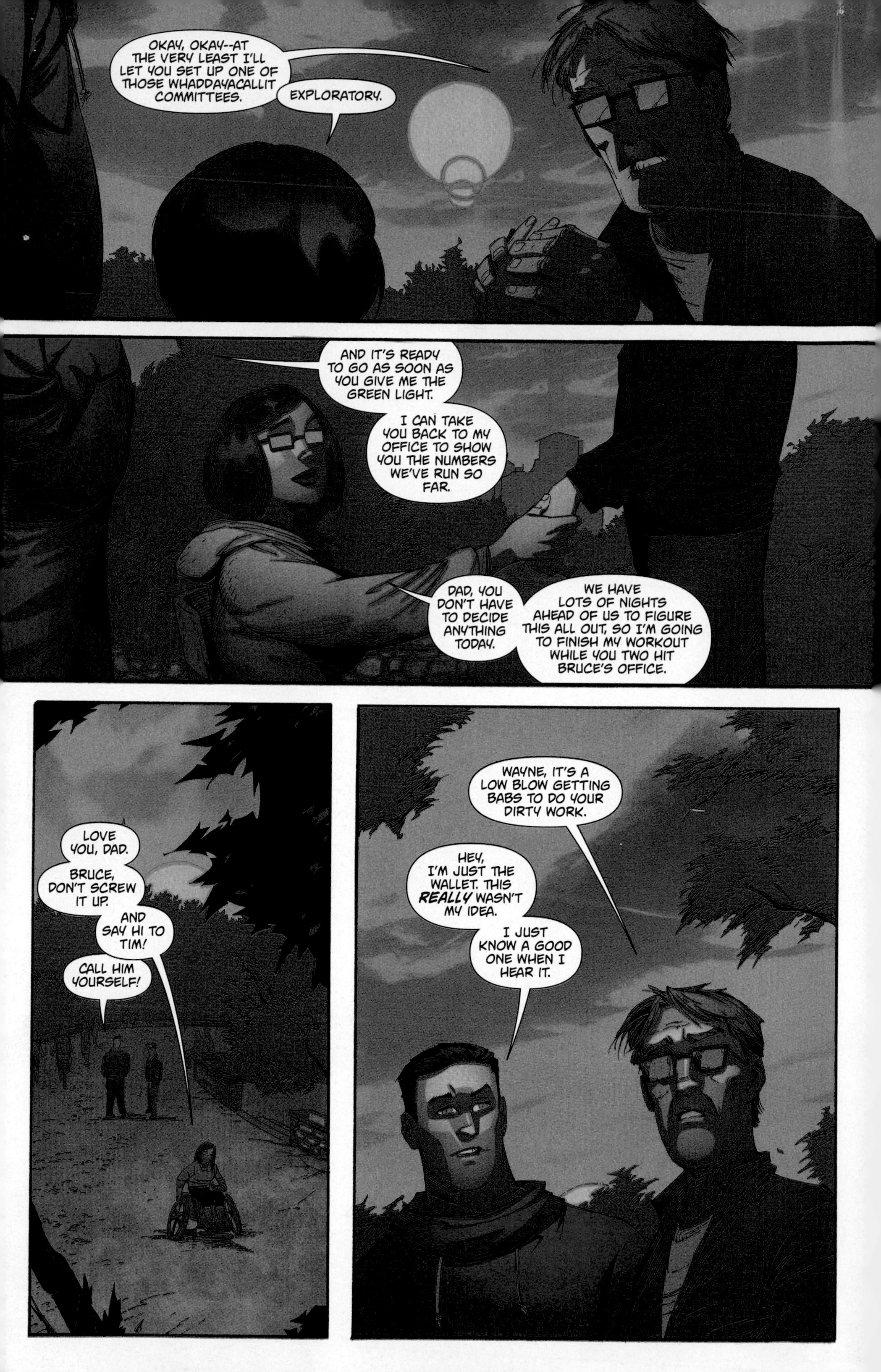
OKAY, OKAY--AT THE VERY LEAST I'LL LET YOU SET UP ONE OF THOSE WHADDAYACALLIT COMMITTEES.
EXPLORATORY.
AND IT'S READY TO GO AS SOON AS YOU GIVE ME THE GREEN LIGHT.
I CAN TAKE YOU BACK TO MY OFFICE TO SHOW YOU THE NUMBERS WE'VE RUN SO FAR.
DAD, YOU DON'T HAVE TO DECIDE ANYTHING TODAY.
WE HAVE LOTS OF NIGHTS AHEAD OF US TO FIGURE THIS ALL OUT, SO I'M GOING TO FINISH MY WORKOUT WHILE YOU TWO HIT BRUCE'S OFFICE.
LOVE YOU, DAD.
BRUCE, DON'T SCREW IT UP.
AND SAY HI TO TIM!
CALL HIM YOURSELF!
WAYNE, IT'S A LOW BLOW GETTING BABS TO DO YOUR DIRTY WORK.
HEY, I'M JUST THE WALLET. THIS REALLY WASN'T MY IDEA.
I JUST KNOW A GOOD ONE WHEN I HEAR IT.

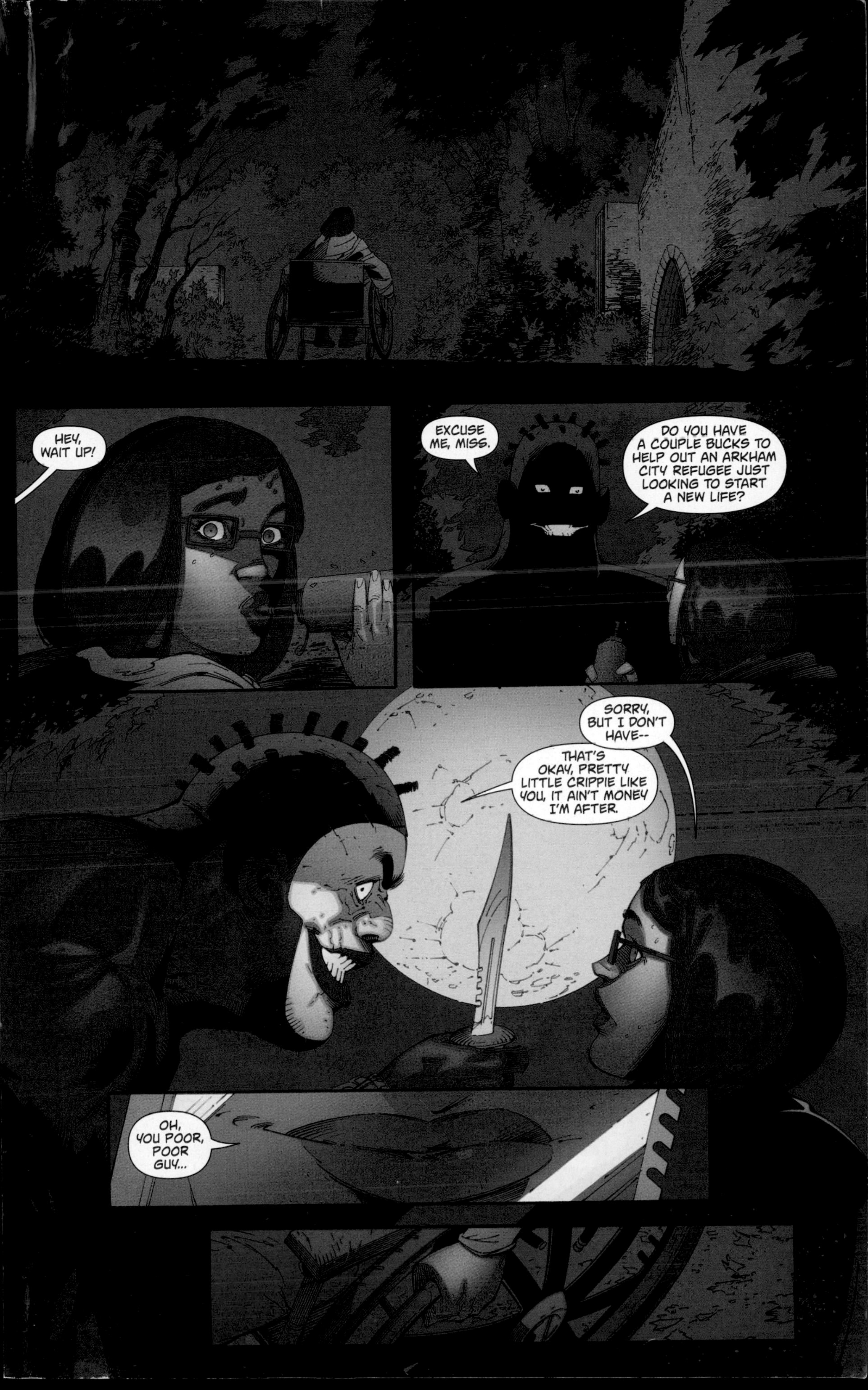
HEY, WAIT UP!
EXCUSE ME, MISS.
DO YOU HAVE A COUPLE BUCKS TO HELP OUT AN ARKHAM CITY REFUGEE JUST LOOKING TO START A NEW LIFE?
SORRY, BUT I DON'T HAVE--
THAT'S OKAY, PRETTY LITTLE CRIPPIE LIKE YOU, IT AIN'T MONEY I'M AFTER.
OH, YOU POOR, POOR GUY...

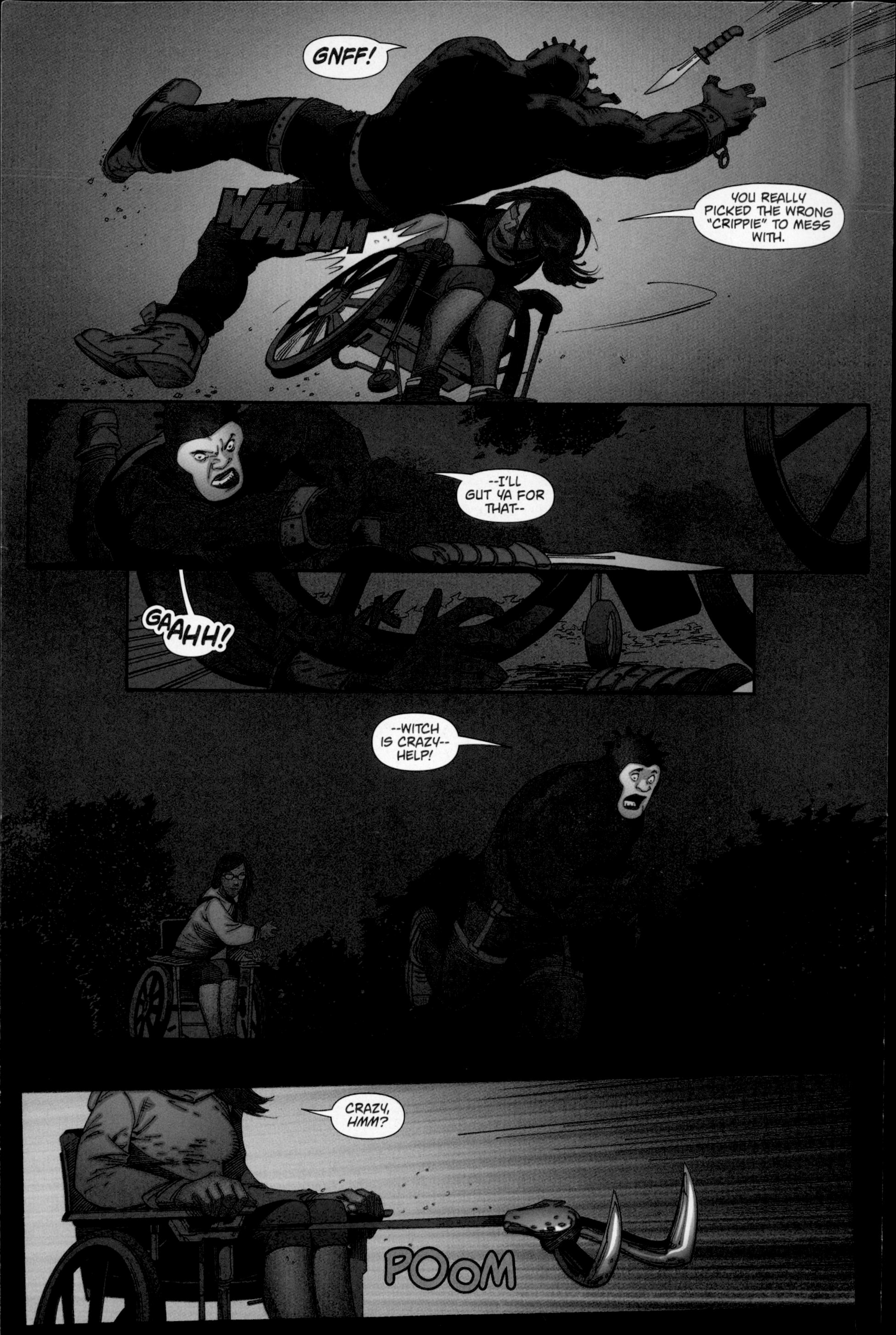
GNFF!
WHAMM
YOU REALLY PICKED THE WRONG "CRIPPIE" TO MESS WITH.
--I'LL GUT YA FOR THAT--
GAAHH!
--WITCH IS CRAZY-- HELP!
CRAZY, HMM?
POOM

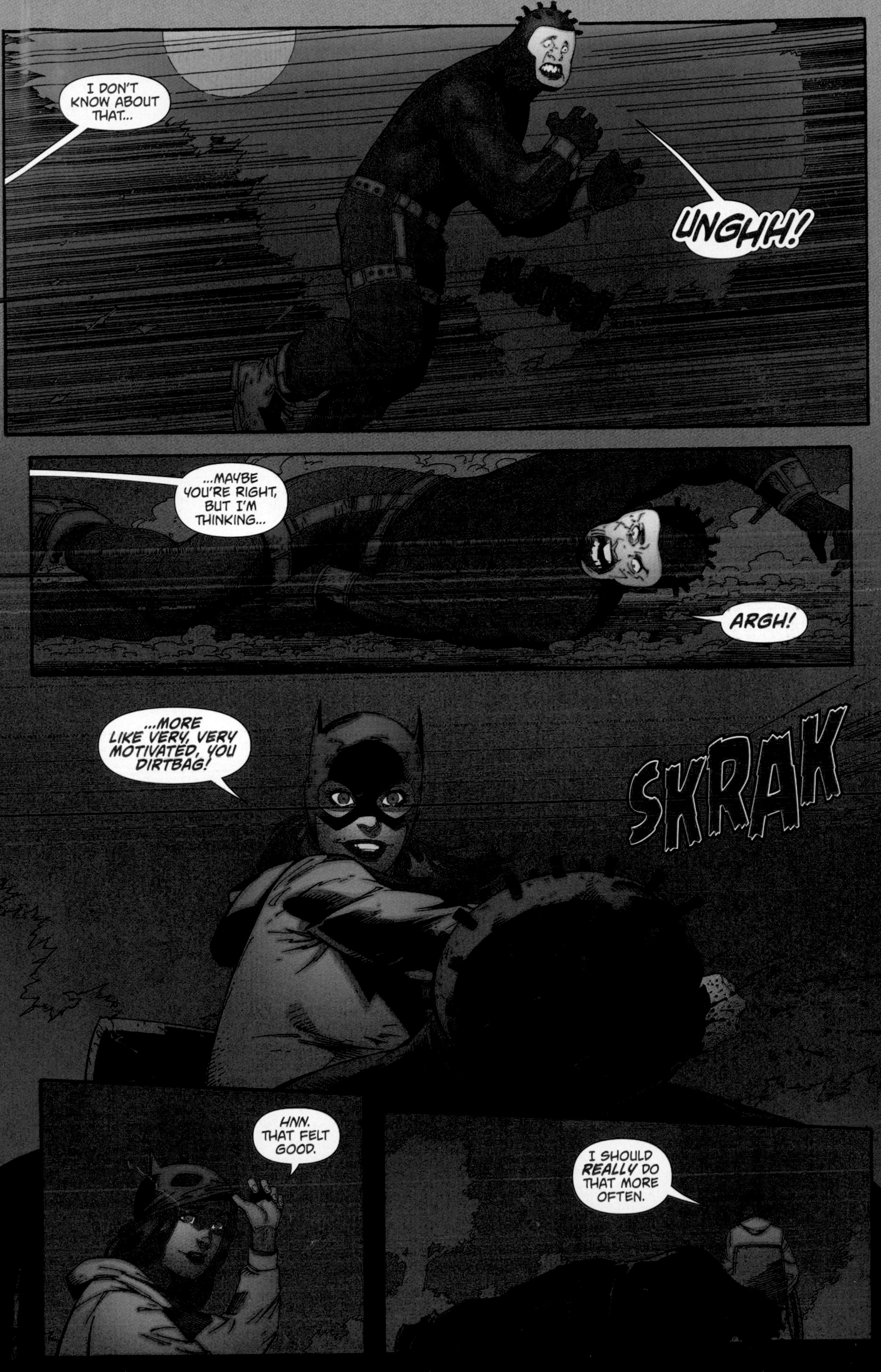
I DON'T KNOW ABOUT THAT...
UNGHH!
...MAYBE YOU'RE RIGHT, BUT I'M THINKING...
ARGH!
...MORE LIKE VERY, VERY MOTIVATED, YOU DIRTBAG!
SKRAK
HNN. THAT FELT GOOD.
I SHOULD REALLY DO THAT MORE OFTEN.

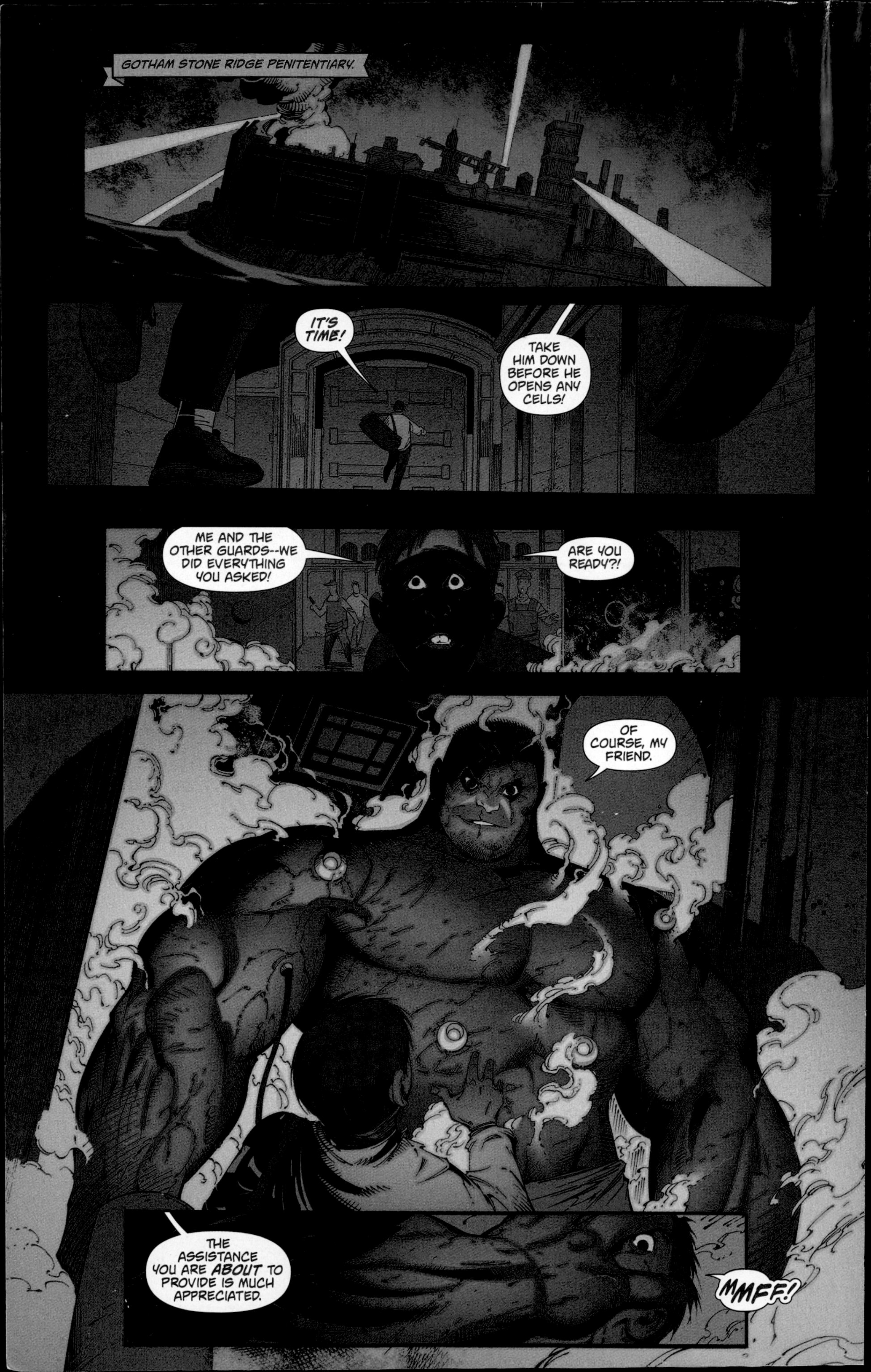
GOTHAM STONE RIDGE PENITENTIARY.
IT'S TIME!
TAKE HIM DOWN BEFORE HE OPENS ANY CELLS!
ME AND THE OTHER GUARDS--WE DID EVERYTHING YOU ASKED!
ARE YOU READY?!
OF COURSE, MY FRIEND.
THE ASSISTANCE YOU ARE ABOUT TO PROVIDE IS MUCH APPRECIATED.
MMFF!

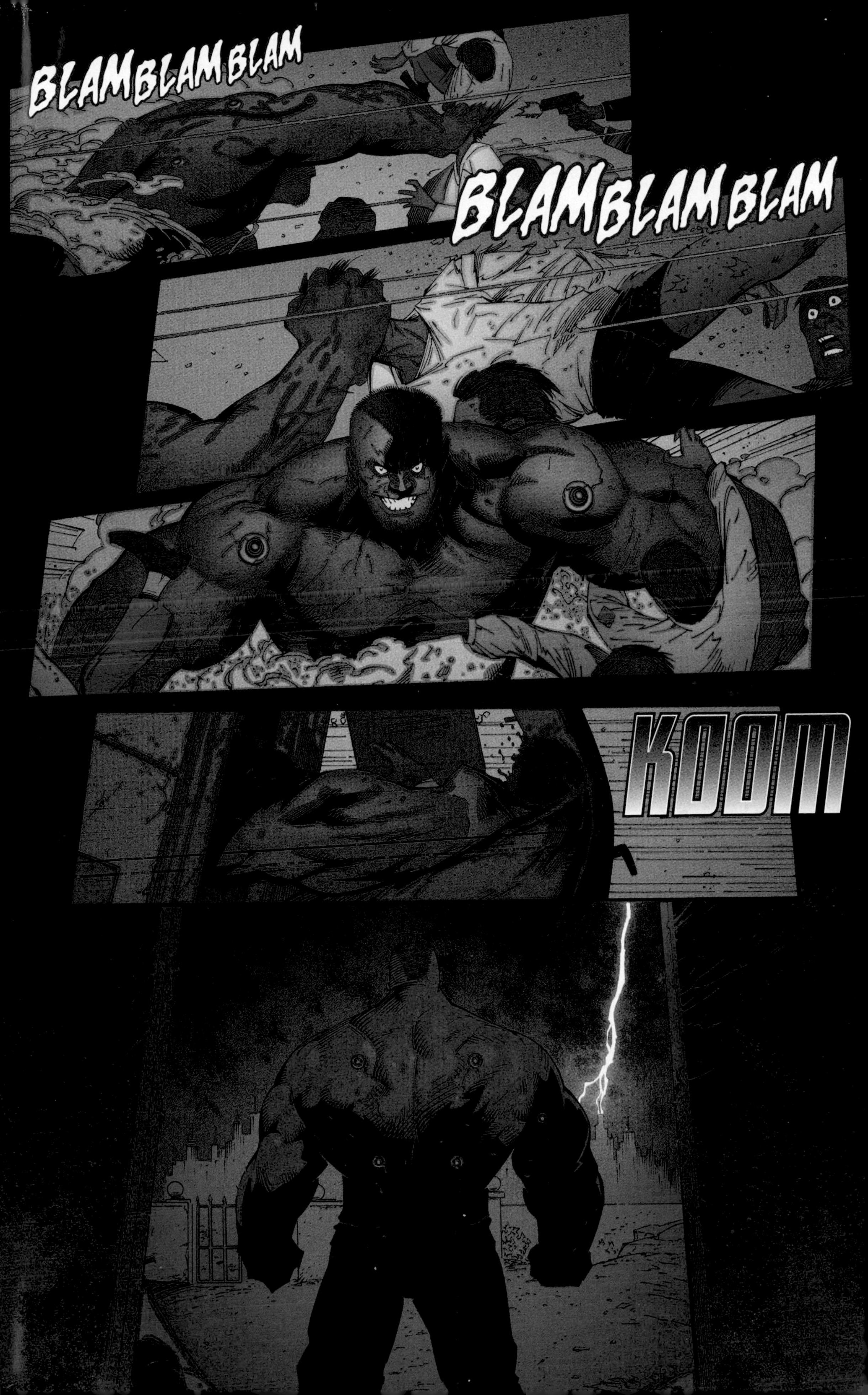
BLAMBLAMBLAM
BLAMBLAMBLAM
KOOM

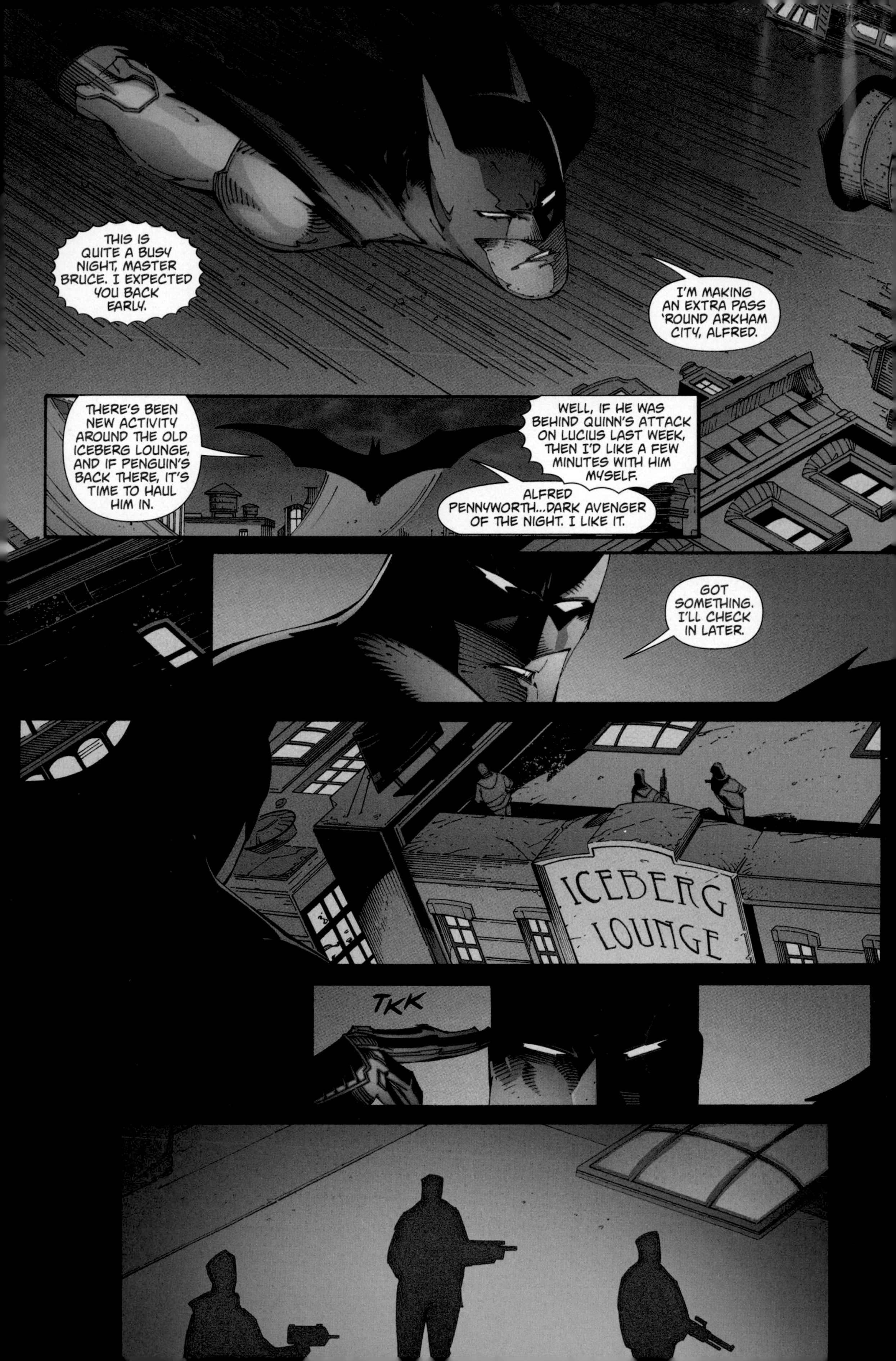

THIS IS QUITE A BUSY NIGHT, MASTER BRUCE. I EXPECTED YOU BACK EARLY.
I'M MAKING AN EXTRA PASS 'ROUND ARKHAM CITY, ALFRED.
THERE'S BEEN NEW ACTIVITY AROUND THE OLD ICEBERG LOUNGE, AND IF PENGUIN'S BACK THERE, IT'S TIME TO HAUL HIM IN.
WELL, IF HE WAS BEHIND QUINN'S ATTACK ON LUCIUS LAST WEEK, THEN I'D LIKE A FEW MINUTES WITH HIM MYSELF.
ALFRED PENNYWORTH...DARK AVENGER OF THE NIGHT. I LIKE IT.
GOT SOMETHING. I'LL CHECK IN LATER.
ICEBERG LOUNGE
TKK

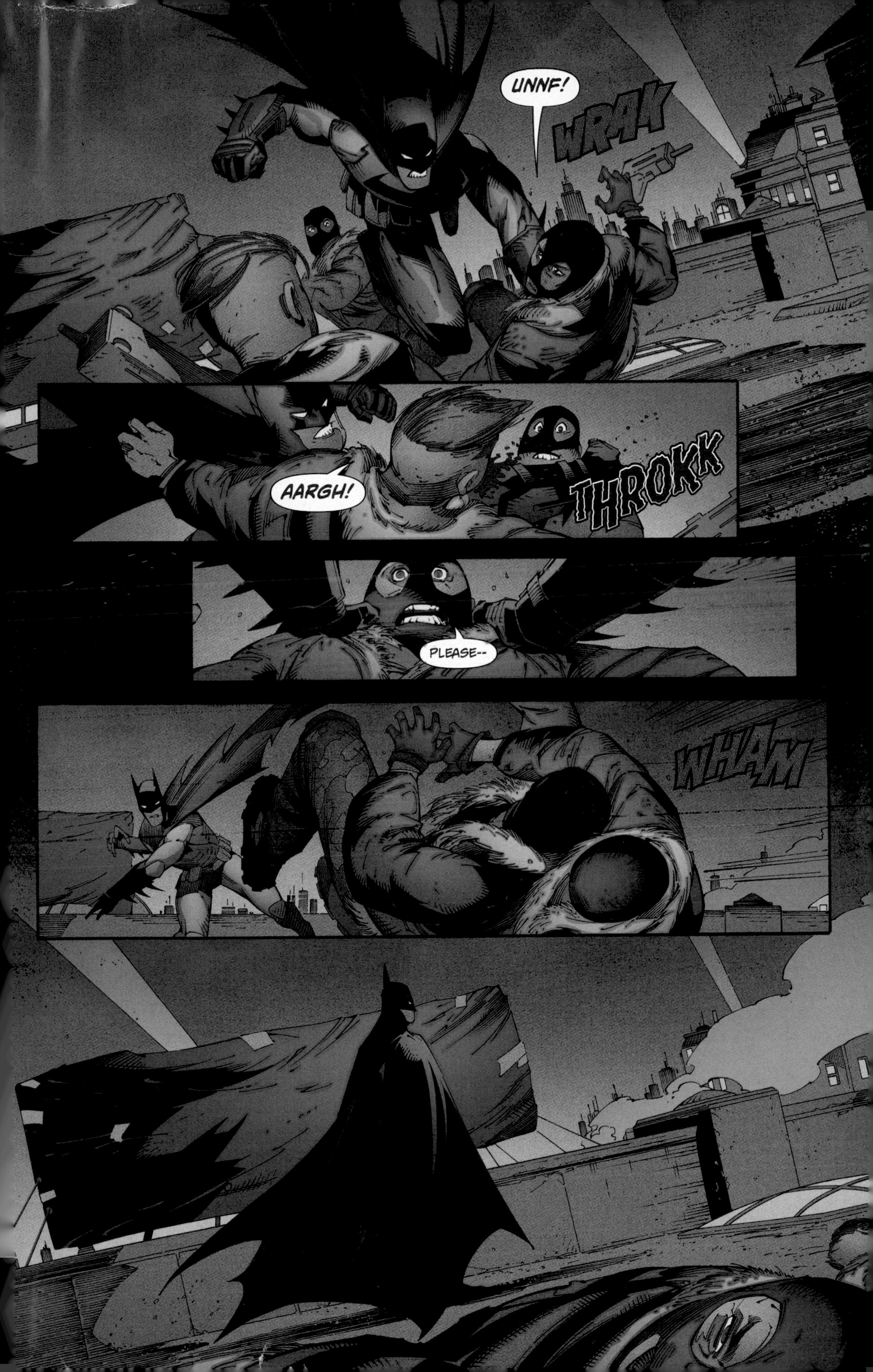
UNNF!
WRAK
AARGH!
THROKK
PLEASE--
WHAM

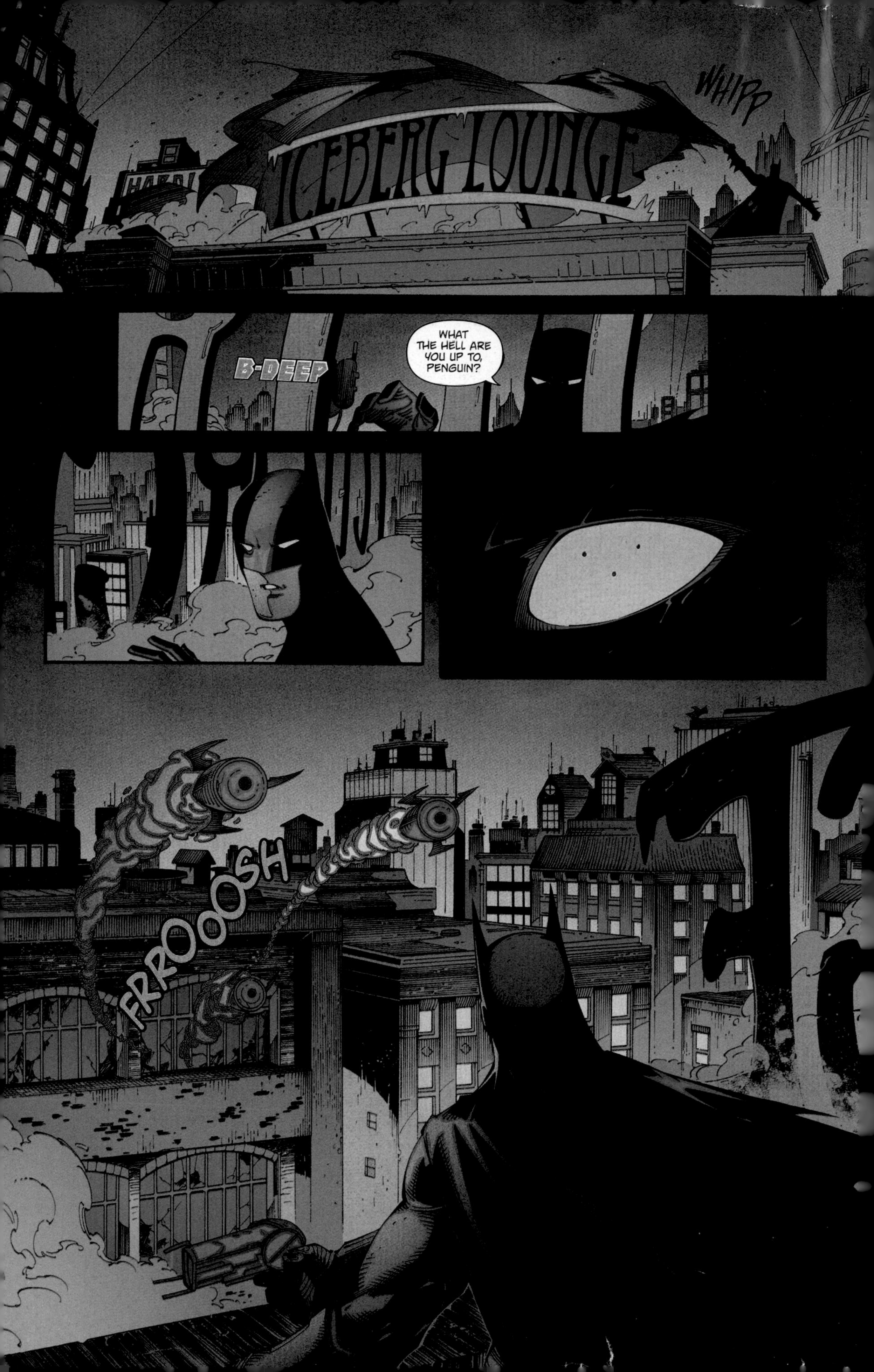

ICEBERG LOUNGE
WHIPP
B-DEEP
WHAT THE HELL ARE YOU UP TO, PENGUIN?
FRROOOSH

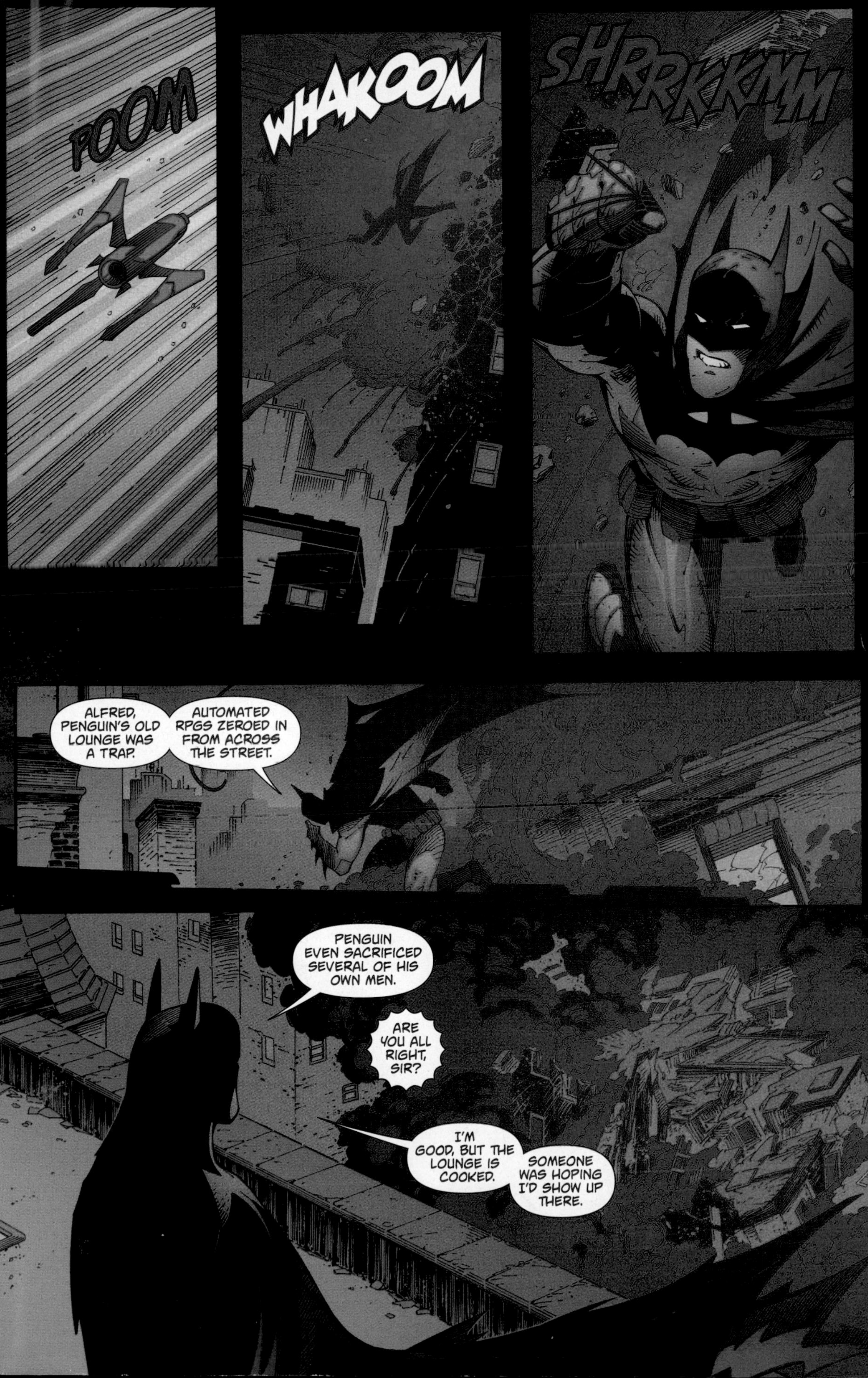
POOM
WHAKOOM
SHRRKKMM
ALFRED, PENGUIN'S OLD LOUNGE WAS A TRAP.
AUTOMATED RPGS ZEROED IN FROM ACROSS THE STREET.
PENGUIN EVEN SACRIFICED SEVERAL OF HIS OWN MEN.
ARE YOU ALL RIGHT, SIR?
I'M GOOD, BUT THE LOUNGE IS COOKED.
SOMEONE WAS HOPING I'D SHOW UP THERE.

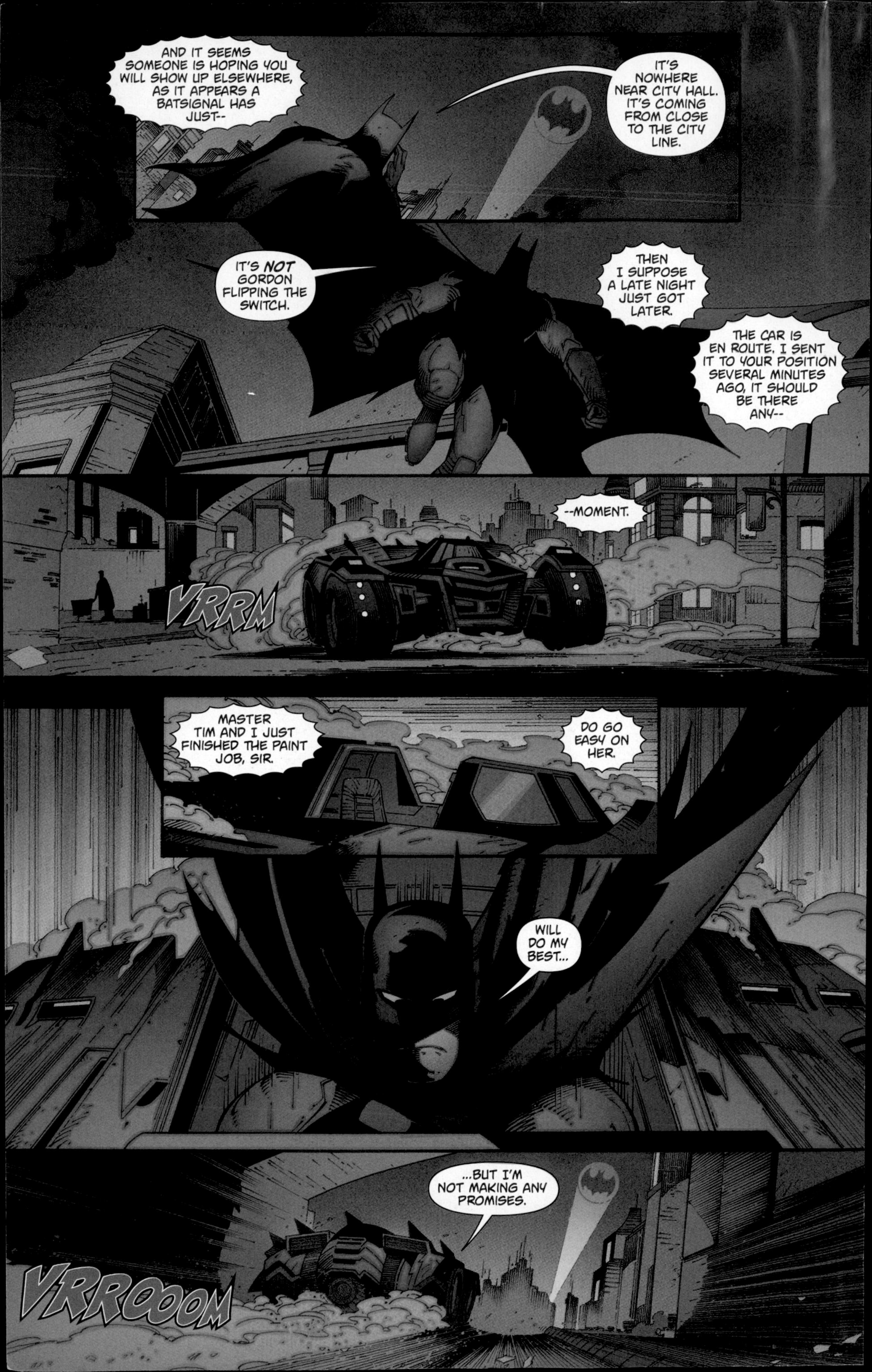
AND IT SEEMS SOMEONE IS HOPING YOU WILL SHOW UP ELSEWHERE, AS IT APPEARS A BATSIGNAL HAS JUST--
IT'S NOWHERE NEAR CITY HALL. IT'S COMING FROM CLOSE TO THE CITY LINE.
IT'S *NOT* GORDON FLIPPING THE SWITCH.
THEN I SUPPOSE A LATE NIGHT JUST GOT LATER.
THE CAR IS EN ROUTE. I SENT IT TO YOUR POSITION SEVERAL MINUTES AGO, IT SHOULD BE THERE ANY--
--MOMENT.
VRRM
MASTER TIM AND I JUST FINISHED THE PAINT JOB, SIR.
DO GO EASY ON HER.
WILL DO MY BEST...
...BUT I'M NOT MAKING ANY PROMISES.
VRROOOM

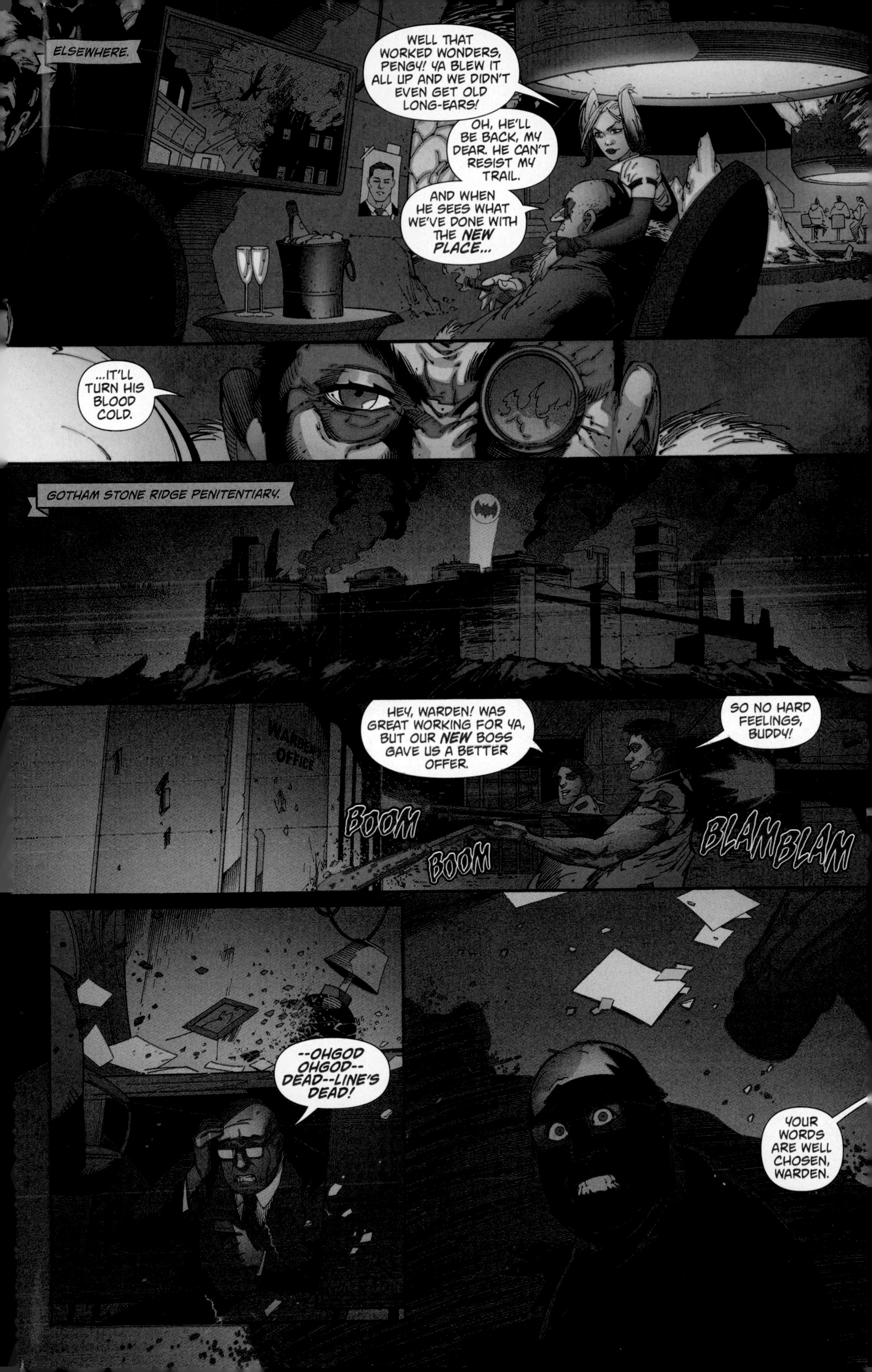
ELSEWHERE.
WELL THAT WORKED WONDERS, PENGY! YA BLEW IT ALL UP AND WE DIDN'T EVEN GET OLD LONG-EARS!
OH, HE'LL BE BACK, MY DEAR. HE CAN'T RESIST MY TRAIL.
AND WHEN HE SEES WHAT WE'VE DONE WITH THE NEW PLACE...
...IT'LL TURN HIS BLOOD COLD.
GOTHAM STONE RIDGE PENITENTIARY.
HEY, WARDEN! WAS GREAT WORKING FOR YA, BUT OUR NEW BOSS GAVE US A BETTER OFFER.
SO NO HARD FEELINGS, BUDDY!
BOOM
BOOM
BLAMBLAM
--OHGOD OHGOD--DEAD--LINE'S DEAD!
YOUR WORDS ARE WELL CHOSEN, WARDEN.

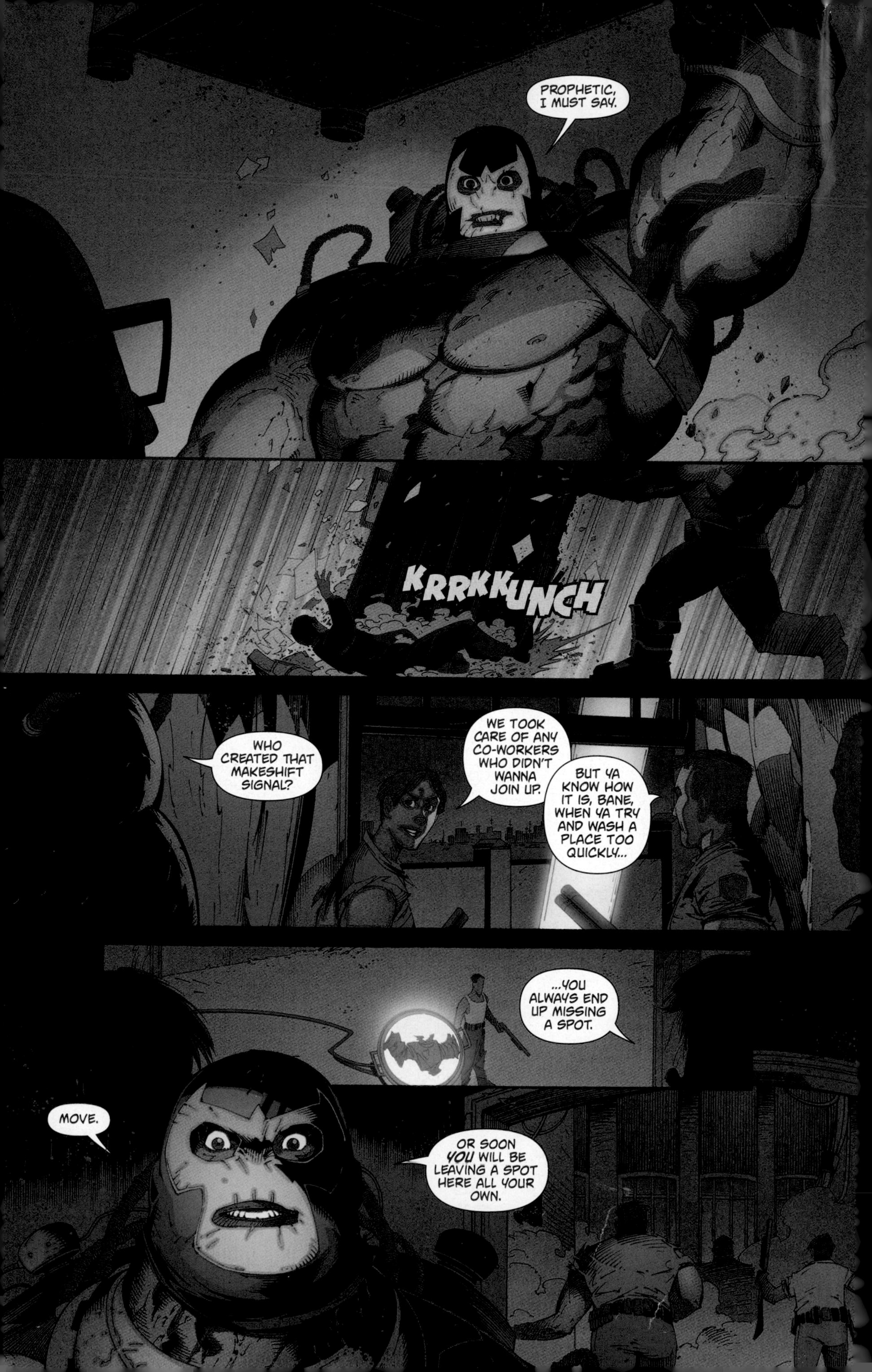
PROPHETIC, I MUST SAY.
KRRKKUNCH
WHO CREATED THAT MAKESHIFT SIGNAL?
WE TOOK CARE OF ANY CO-WORKERS WHO DIDN'T WANNA JOIN UP.
BUT YA KNOW HOW IT IS, BANE, WHEN YA TRY AND WASH A PLACE TOO QUICKLY...
...YOU ALWAYS END UP MISSING A SPOT.
MOVE.
OR SOON YOU WILL BE LEAVING A SPOT HERE ALL YOUR OWN.

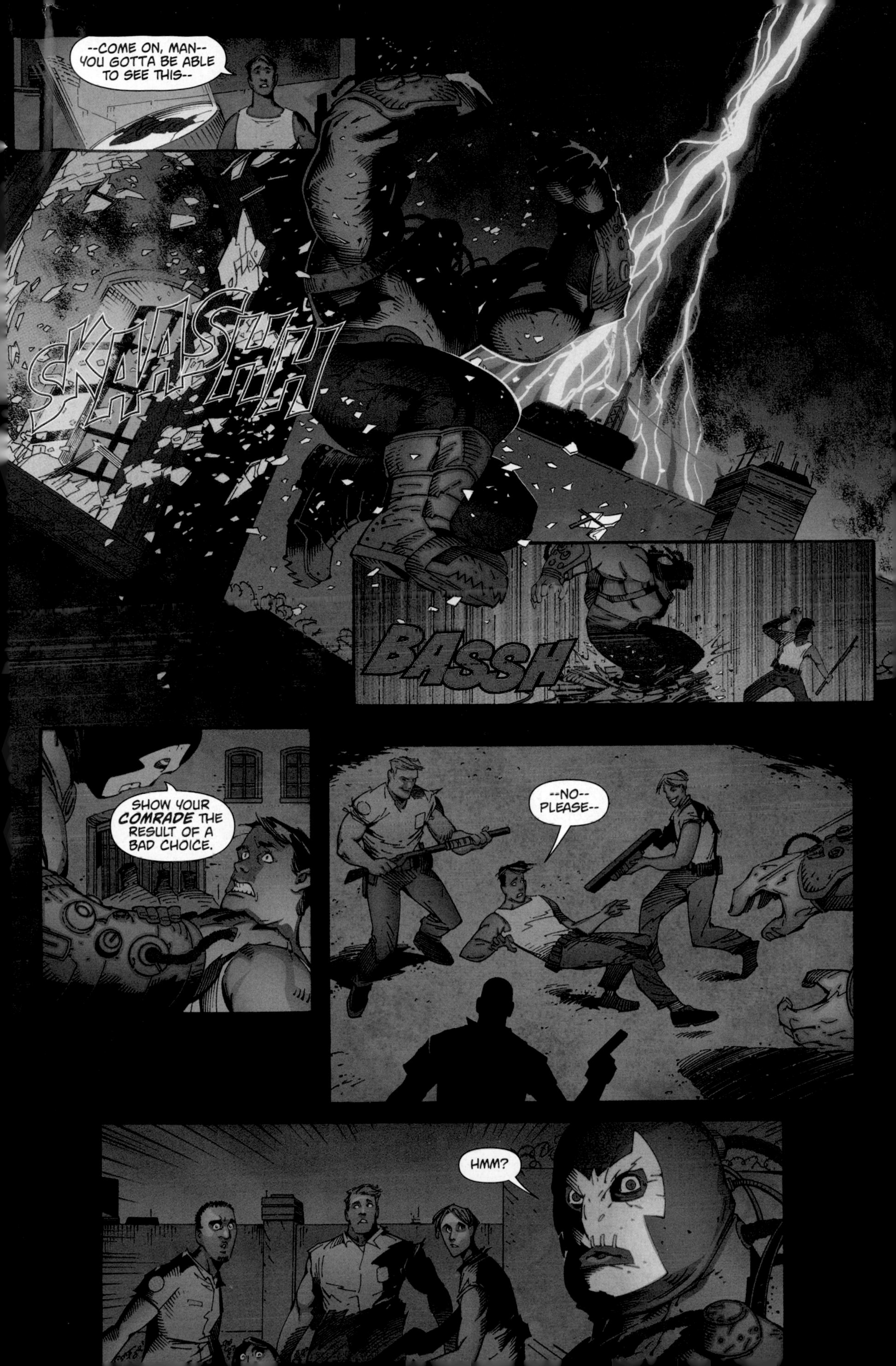
--COME ON, MAN-- YOU GOTTA BE ABLE TO SEE THIS--
SKRASHH
BASSH
SHOW YOUR COMRADE THE RESULT OF A BAD CHOICE.
--NO-- PLEASE--
HMM?

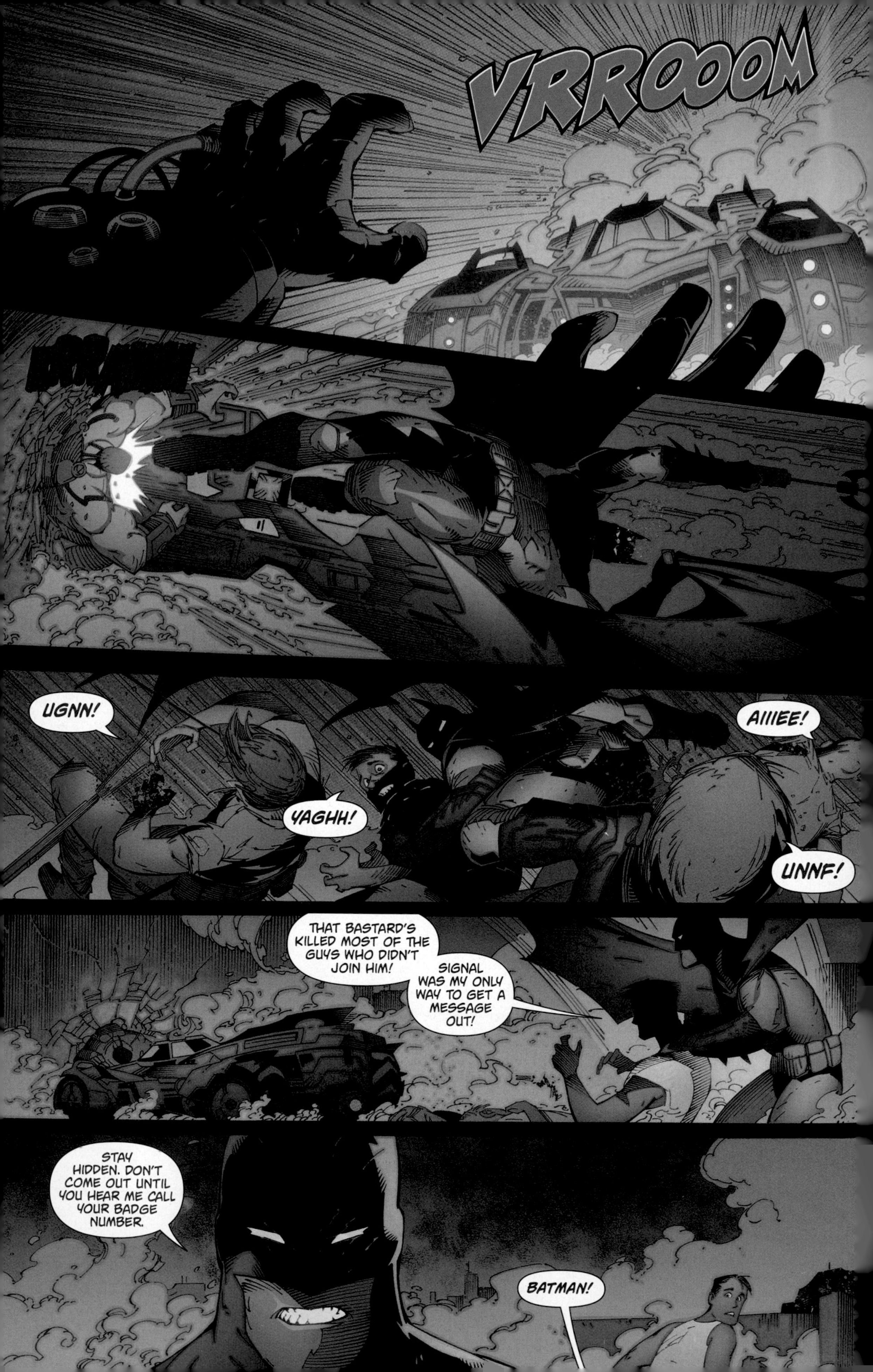
VRROOOM
UGNN!
YAGHH!
AIIIEE!
UNNF!
THAT BASTARD'S KILLED MOST OF THE GUYS WHO DIDN'T JOIN HIM!
SIGNAL WAS MY ONLY WAY TO GET A MESSAGE OUT!
STAY HIDDEN. DON'T COME OUT UNTIL YOU HEAR ME CALL YOUR BADGE NUMBER.
BATMAN!

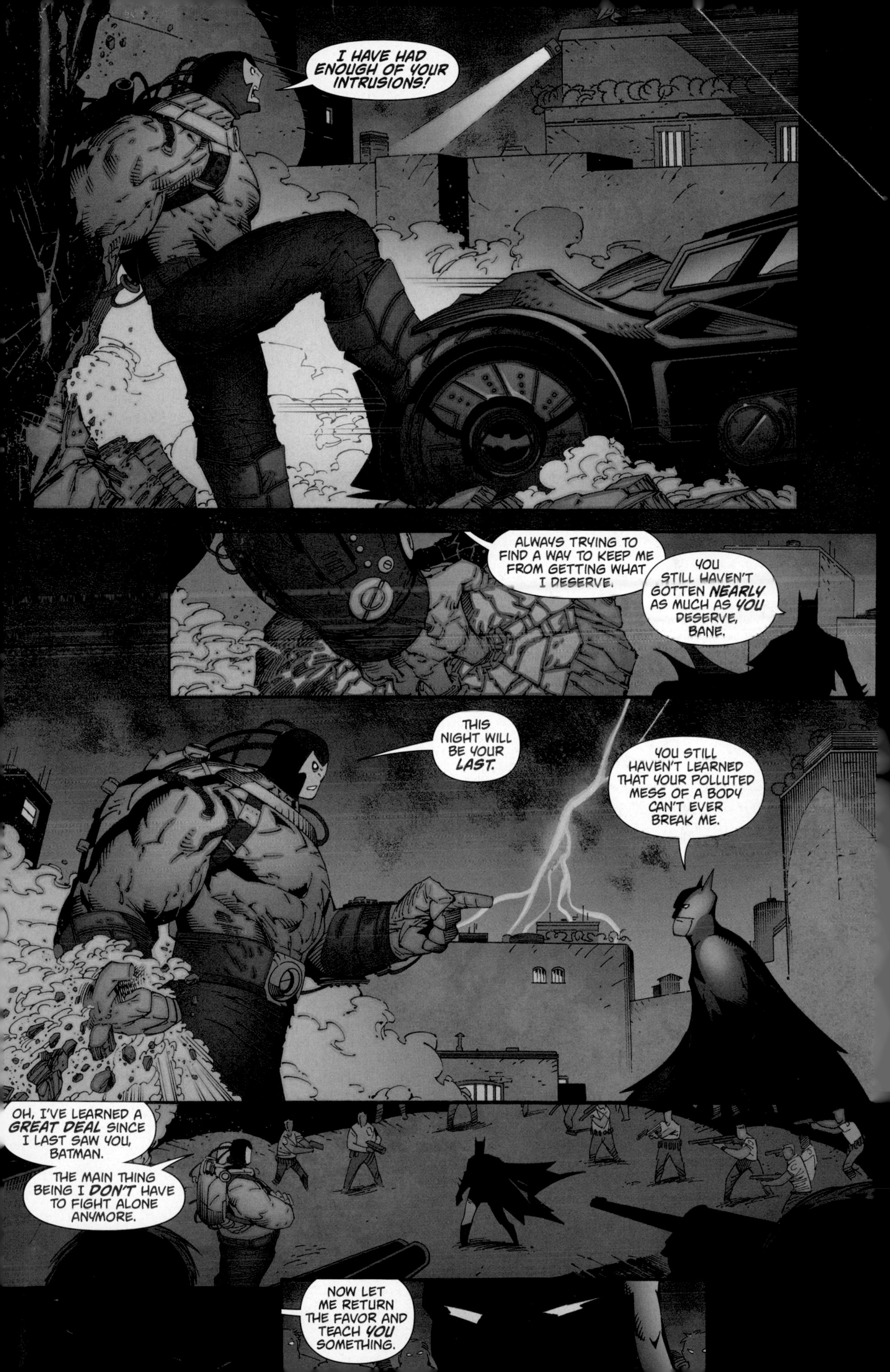

I HAVE HAD ENOUGH OF YOUR INTRUSIONS!
ALWAYS TRYING TO FIND A WAY TO KEEP ME FROM GETTING WHAT I DESERVE.
YOU STILL HAVEN'T GOTTEN NEARLY AS MUCH AS YOU DESERVE, BANE.
THIS NIGHT WILL BE YOUR LAST.
YOU STILL HAVEN'T LEARNED THAT YOUR POLLUTED MESS OF A BODY CAN'T EVER BREAK ME.
OH, I'VE LEARNED A GREAT DEAL SINCE I LAST SAW YOU, BATMAN.
THE MAIN THING BEING I DON'T HAVE TO FIGHT ALONE ANYMORE.
NOW LET ME RETURN THE FAVOR AND TEACH YOU SOMETHING.

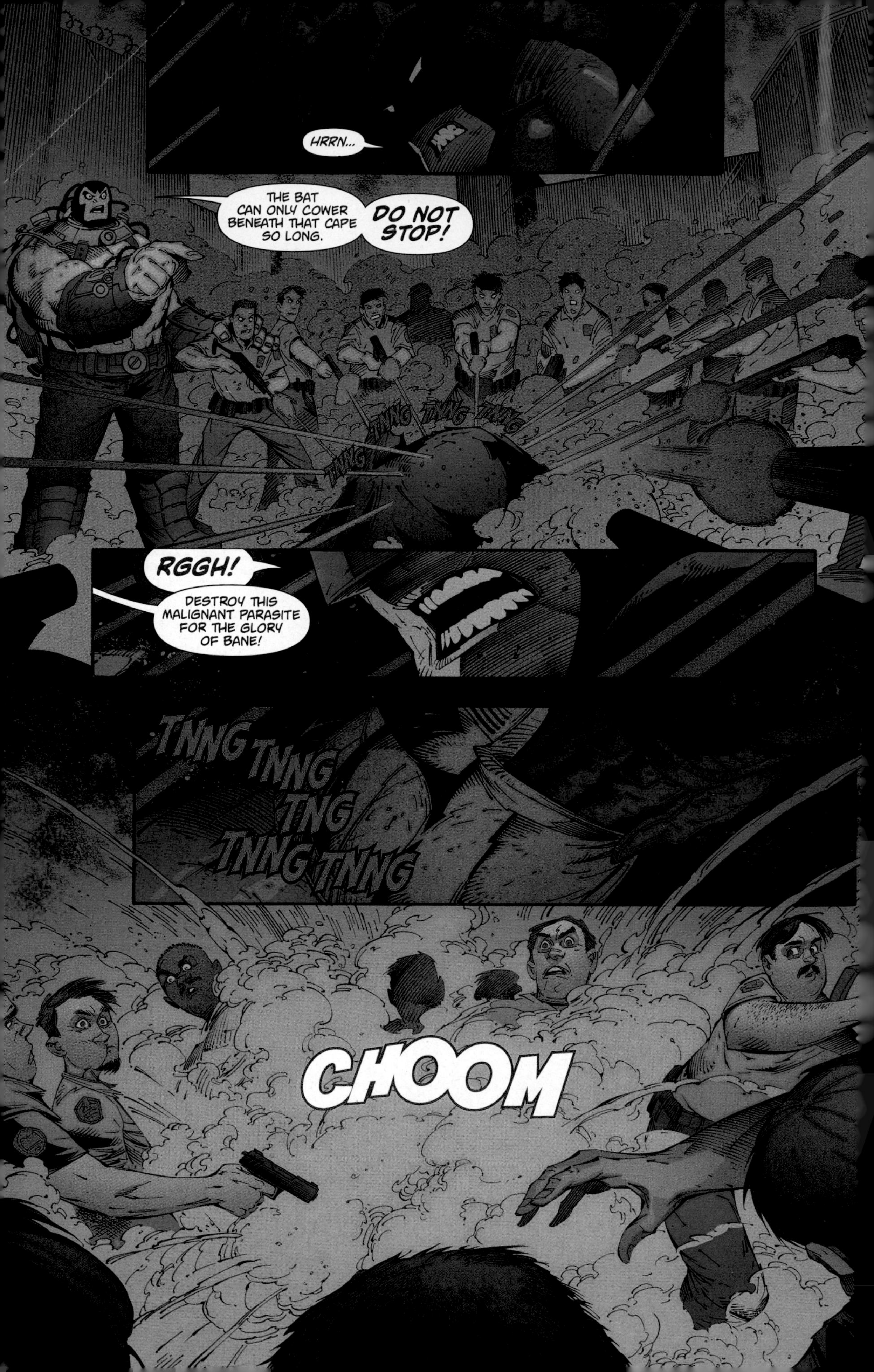
HRRN...
THE BAT CAN ONLY COWER BENEATH THAT CAPE SO LONG.
DO NOT STOP!
TNNG TNNG TNNG TNNG
RGGH!
DESTROY THIS MALIGNANT PARASITE FOR THE GLORY OF BANE!
TNNG TNNG TNG TNNG TNNG
CHOOM

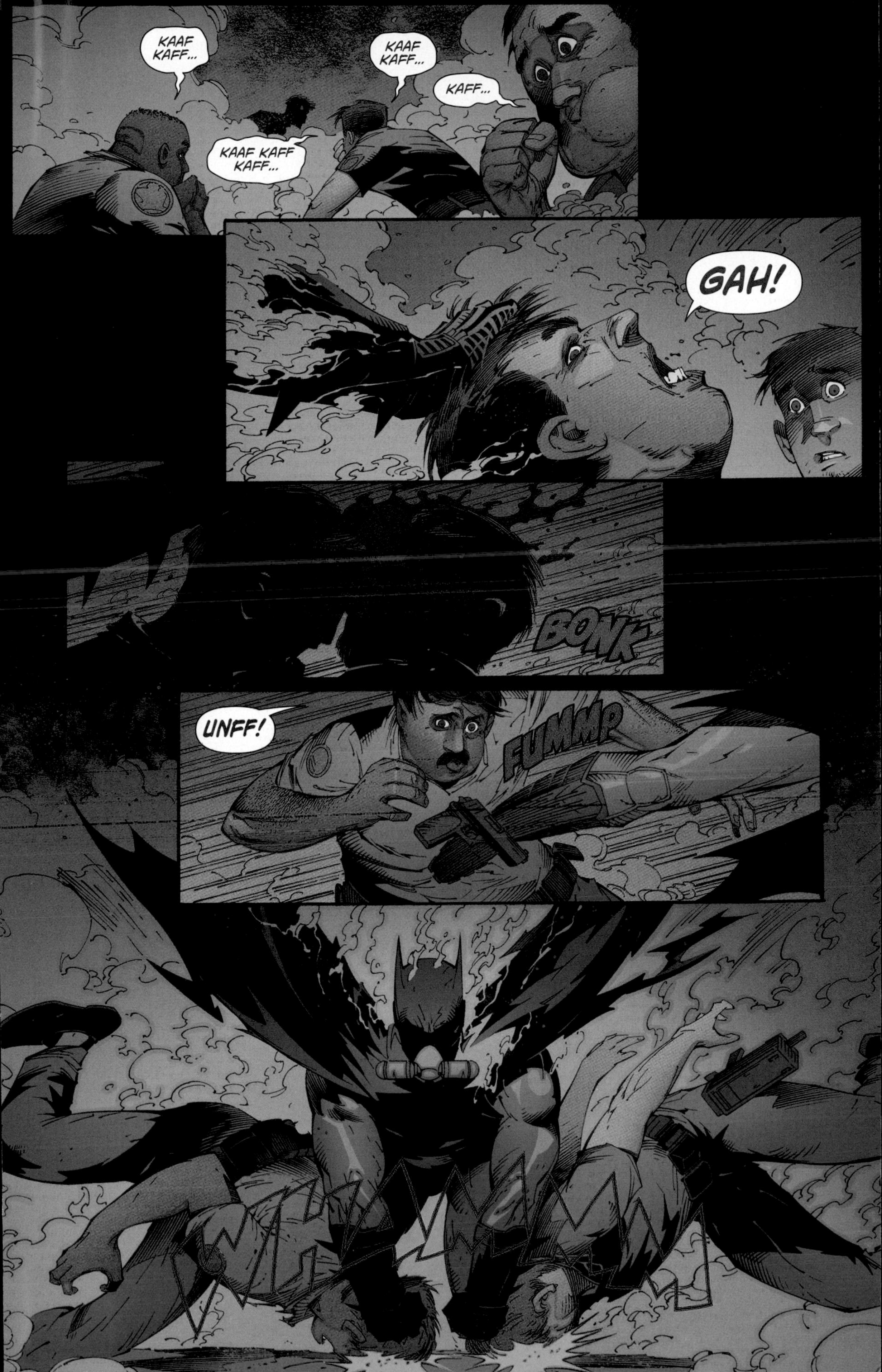
KAAF KAFF...
KAAF KAFF...
KAFF...
KAAF KAFF KAFF...
GAH!
BONK
UNFF!
FUMMP

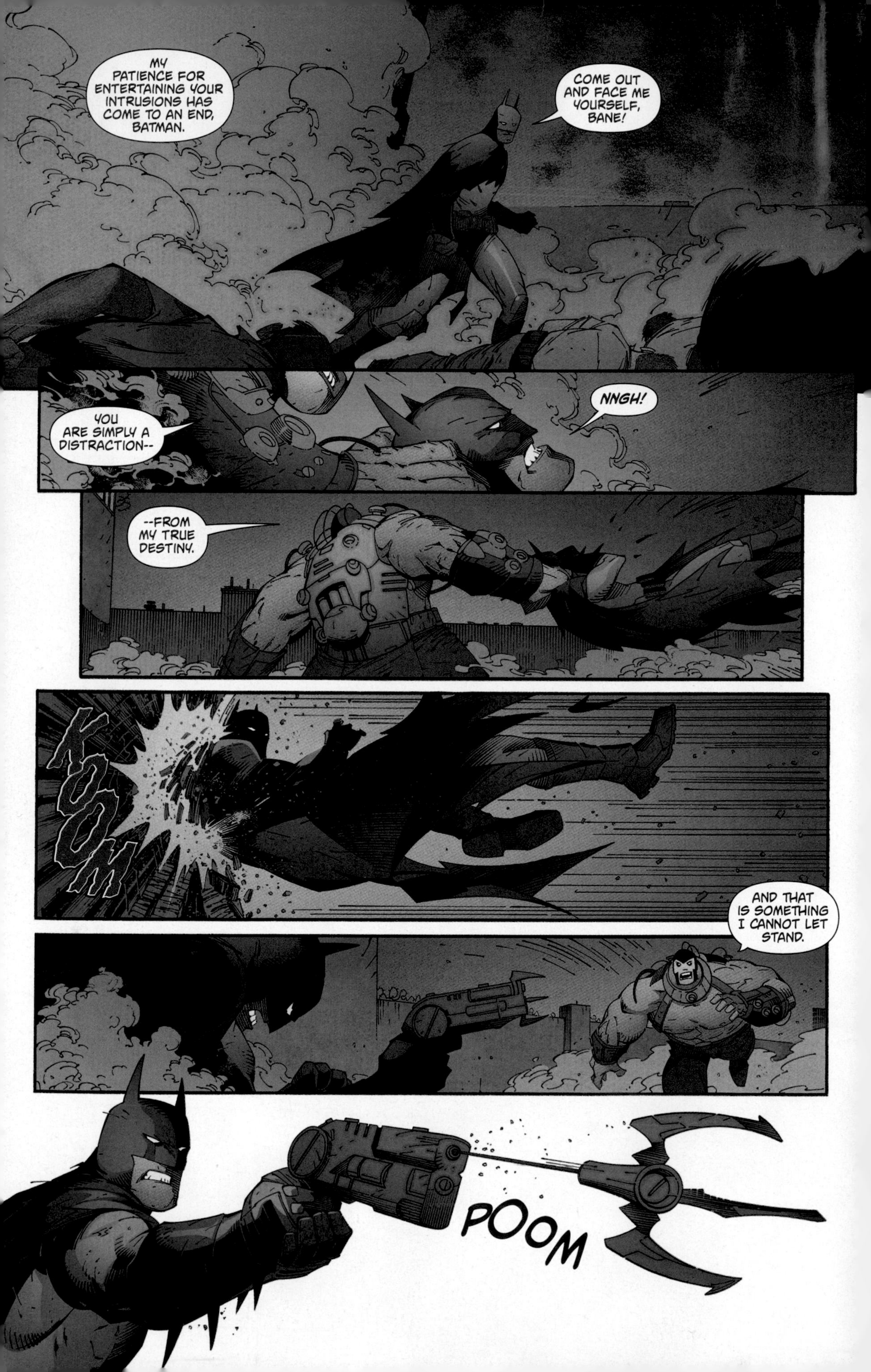
MY PATIENCE FOR ENTERTAINING YOUR INTRUSIONS HAS COME TO AN END, BATMAN.
COME OUT AND FACE ME YOURSELF, BANE!
YOU ARE SIMPLY A DISTRACTION--
NNGH!
--FROM MY TRUE DESTINY.
KOOOM
AND THAT IS SOMETHING I CANNOT LET STAND.
POOM

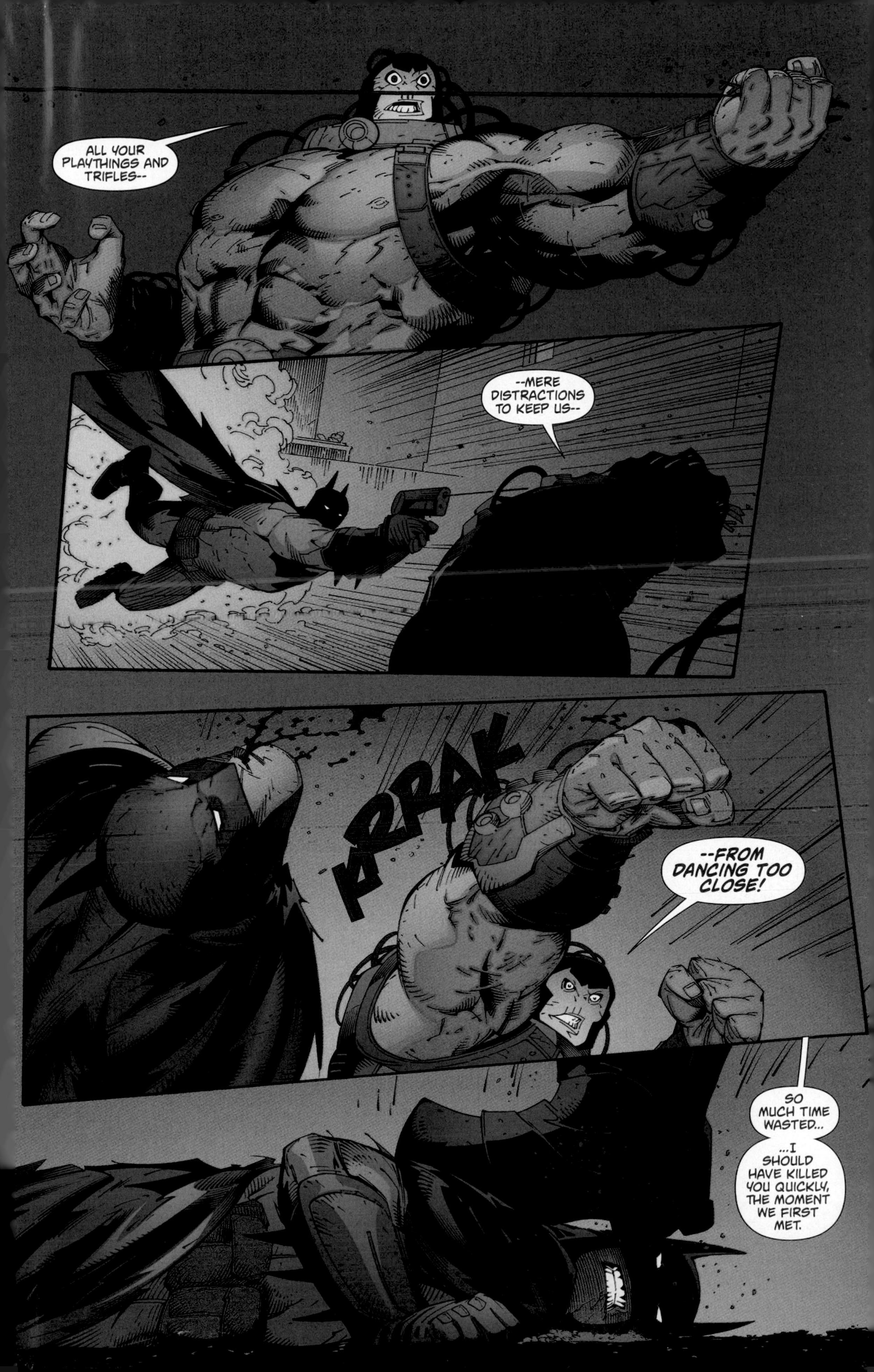
ALL YOUR PLAYTHINGS AND TRIFLES--
--MERE DISTRACTIONS TO KEEP US--
KRRAK
--FROM DANCING TOO CLOSE!
SO MUCH TIME WASTED...
...I SHOULD HAVE KILLED YOU QUICKLY, THE MOMENT WE FIRST MET.

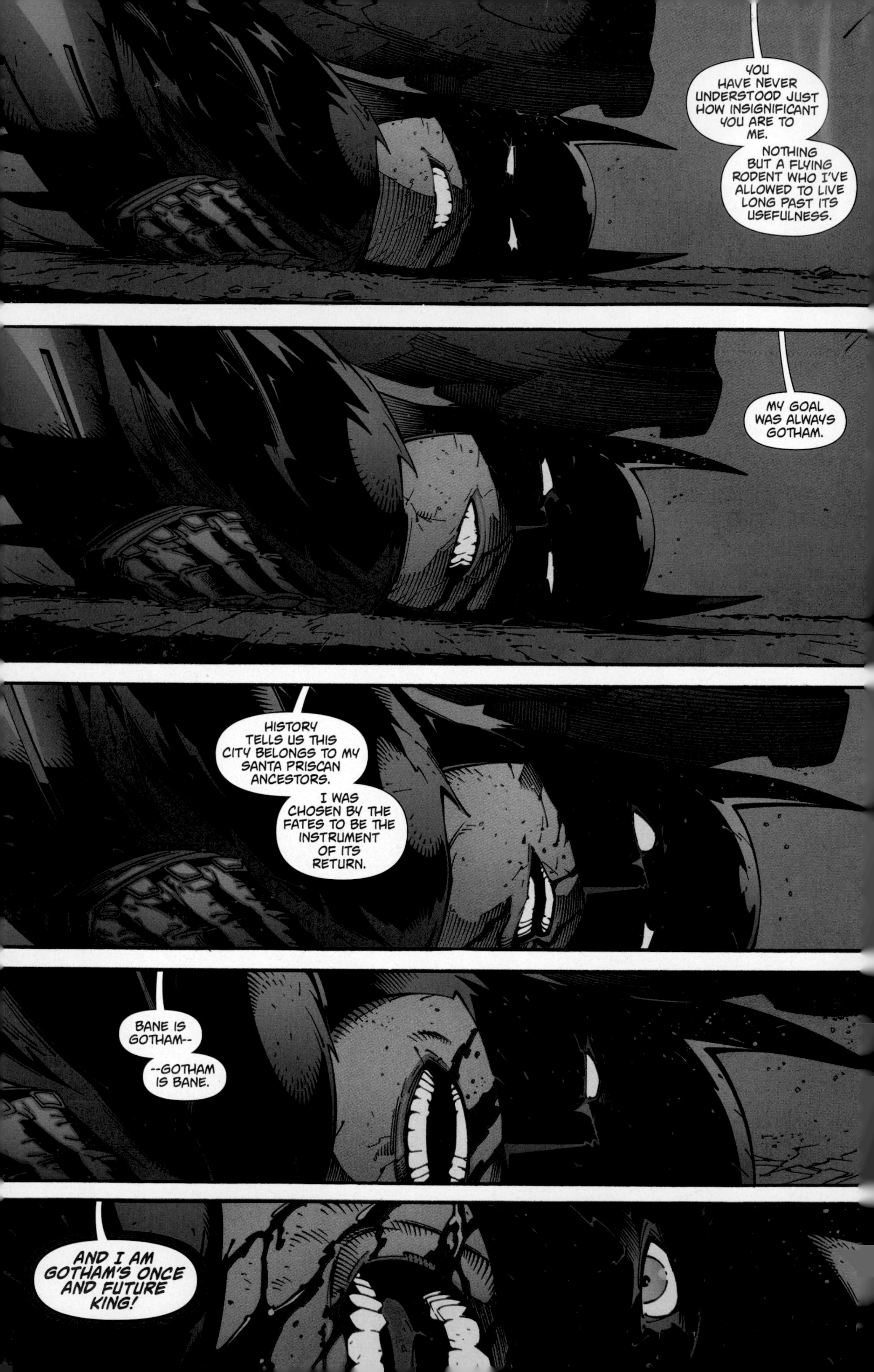
YOU HAVE NEVER UNDERSTOOD JUST HOW INSIGNIFICANT YOU ARE TO ME.
NOTHING BUT A FLYING RODENT WHO I'VE ALLOWED TO LIVE LONG PAST ITS USEFULNESS.
MY GOAL WAS ALWAYS GOTHAM.
HISTORY TELLS US THIS CITY BELONGS TO MY SANTA PRISCAN ANCESTORS.
I WAS CHOSEN BY THE FATES TO BE THE INSTRUMENT OF ITS RETURN.
BANE IS GOTHAM--
--GOTHAM IS BANE.
AND I AM GOTHAM'S ONCE AND FUTURE KING!

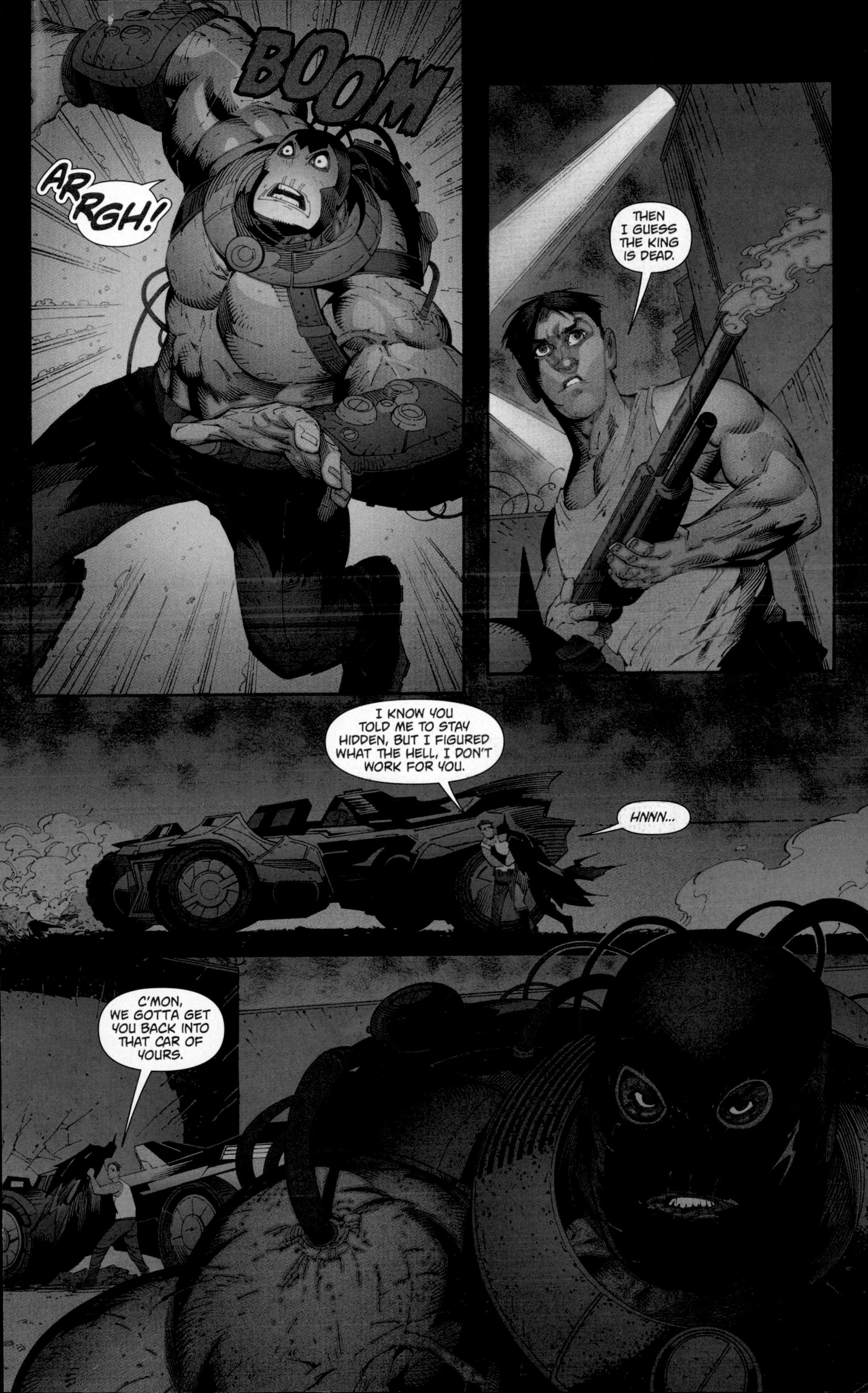
BOOM
ARRGH!
THEN I GUESS THE KING IS DEAD.
I KNOW YOU TOLD ME TO STAY HIDDEN, BUT I FIGURED WHAT THE HELL, I DON'T WORK FOR YOU.
HNNN...
C'MON, WE GOTTA GET YOU BACK INTO THAT CAR OF YOURS.

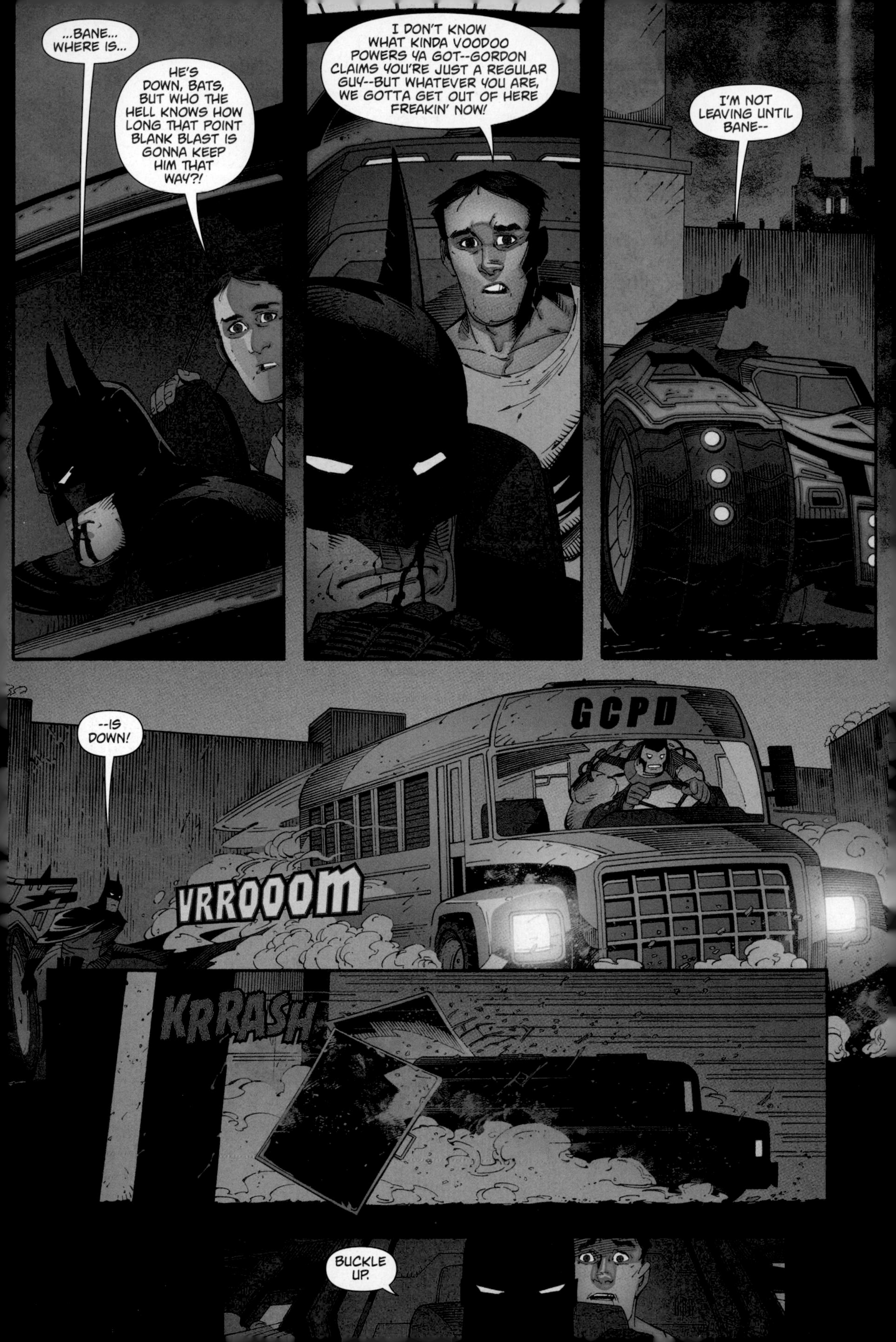
...BANE... WHERE IS...
HE'S DOWN, BATS, BUT WHO THE HELL KNOWS HOW LONG THAT POINT BLANK BLAST IS GONNA KEEP HIM THAT WAY?!
I DON'T KNOW WHAT KINDA VOODOO POWERS YA GOT--GORDON CLAIMS YOU'RE JUST A REGULAR GUY--BUT WHATEVER YOU ARE, WE GOTTA GET OUT OF HERE FREAKIN' NOW!
I'M NOT LEAVING UNTIL BANE--
--IS DOWN!
GCPD
VRROOOM
KRRASH
BUCKLE UP.

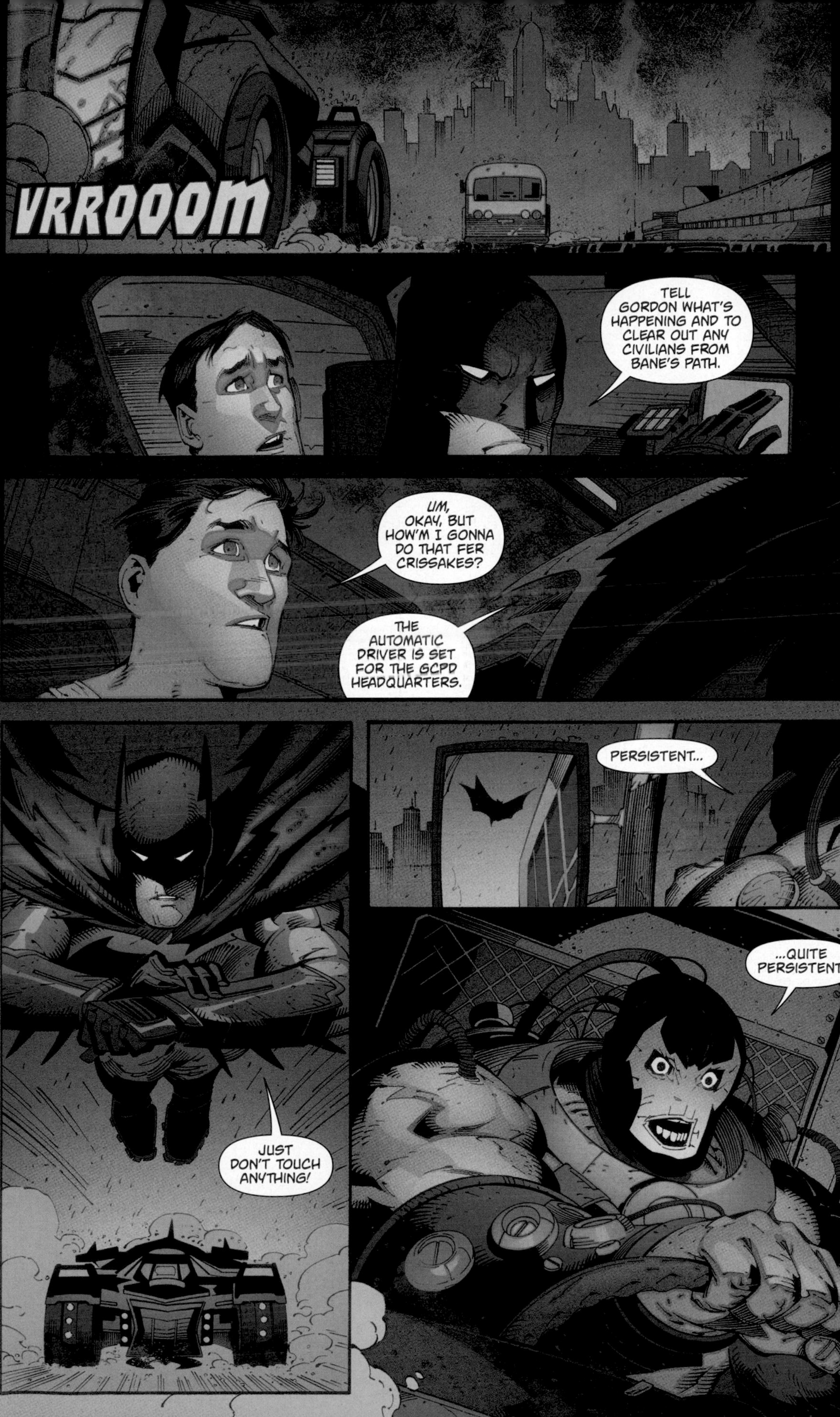
VRROOOM
TELL GORDON WHAT'S HAPPENING AND TO CLEAR OUT ANY CIVILIANS FROM BANE'S PATH.
UM, OKAY, BUT HOW'M I GONNA DO THAT FER CRISSAKES?
THE AUTOMATIC DRIVER IS SET FOR THE GCPD HEADQUARTERS.
JUST DON'T TOUCH ANYTHING!
PERSISTENT...
...QUITE PERSISTENT.

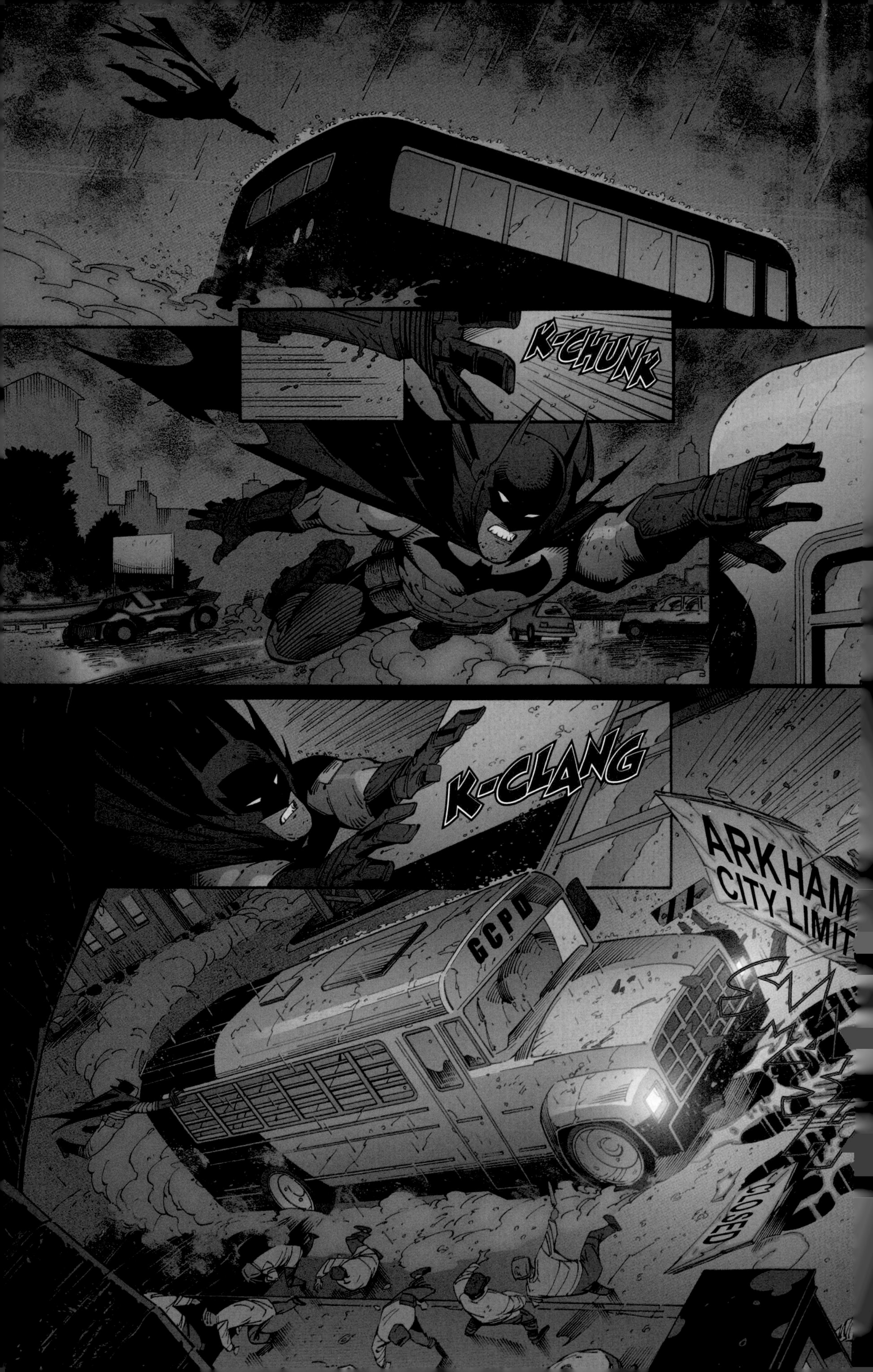
K-CHUNK
K-CLANG
ARKHAM
CITY LIMIT
CLOSED
GCPD

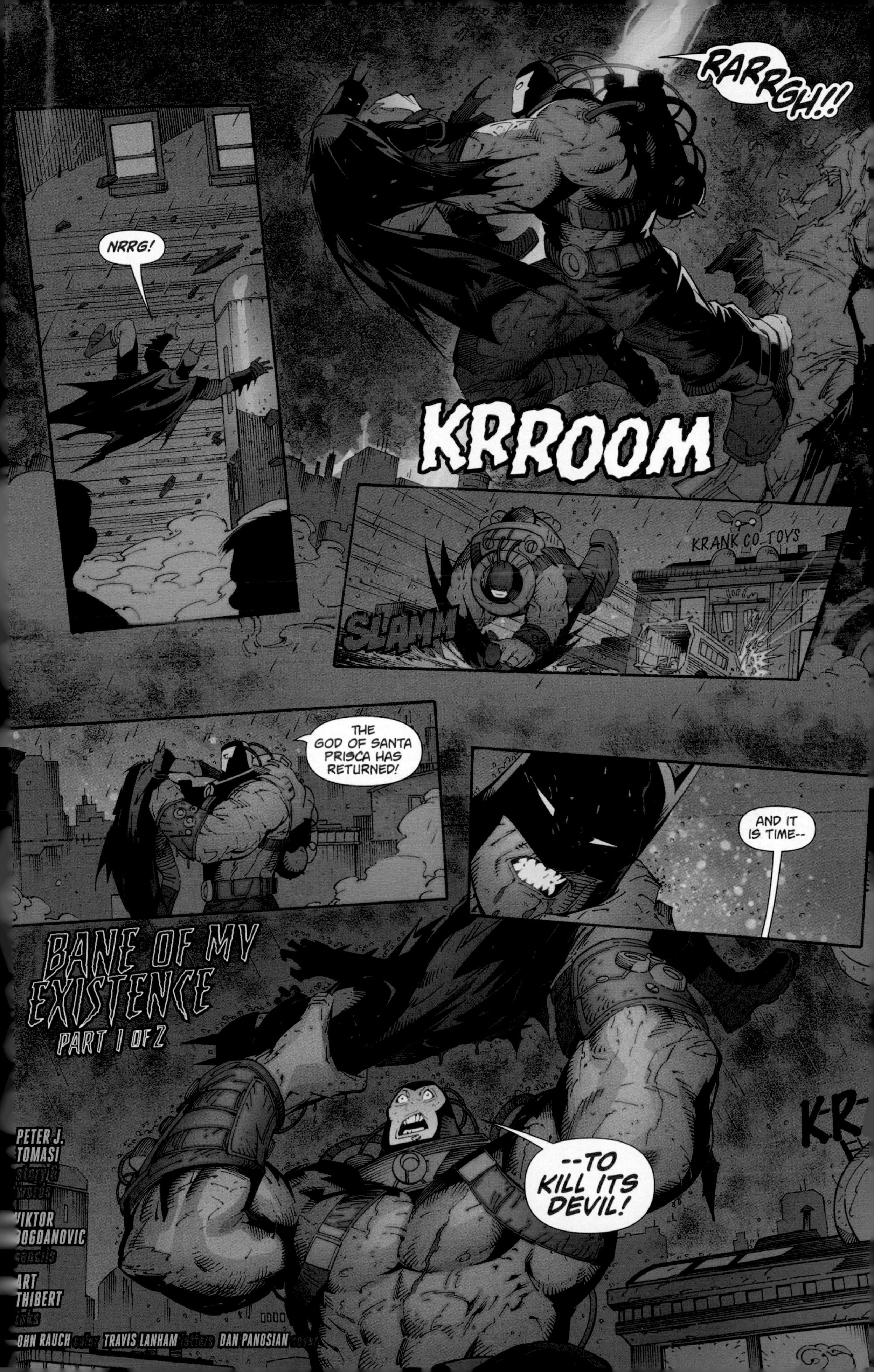
RARRGH!!
NRRG!
KRROOM
KRANK CO. TOYS
SLAMM
THE GOD OF SANTA PRISCA HAS RETURNED!
AND IT IS TIME--
BANE OF MY EXISTENCE
PART 1 OF 2
--TO KILL ITS DEVIL!
K-R
PETER J. TOMASI
VIKTOR BOGDANOVIC
ART THIBERT
OHN RAUCH
TRAVIS LANHAM
DAN PANOSIAN

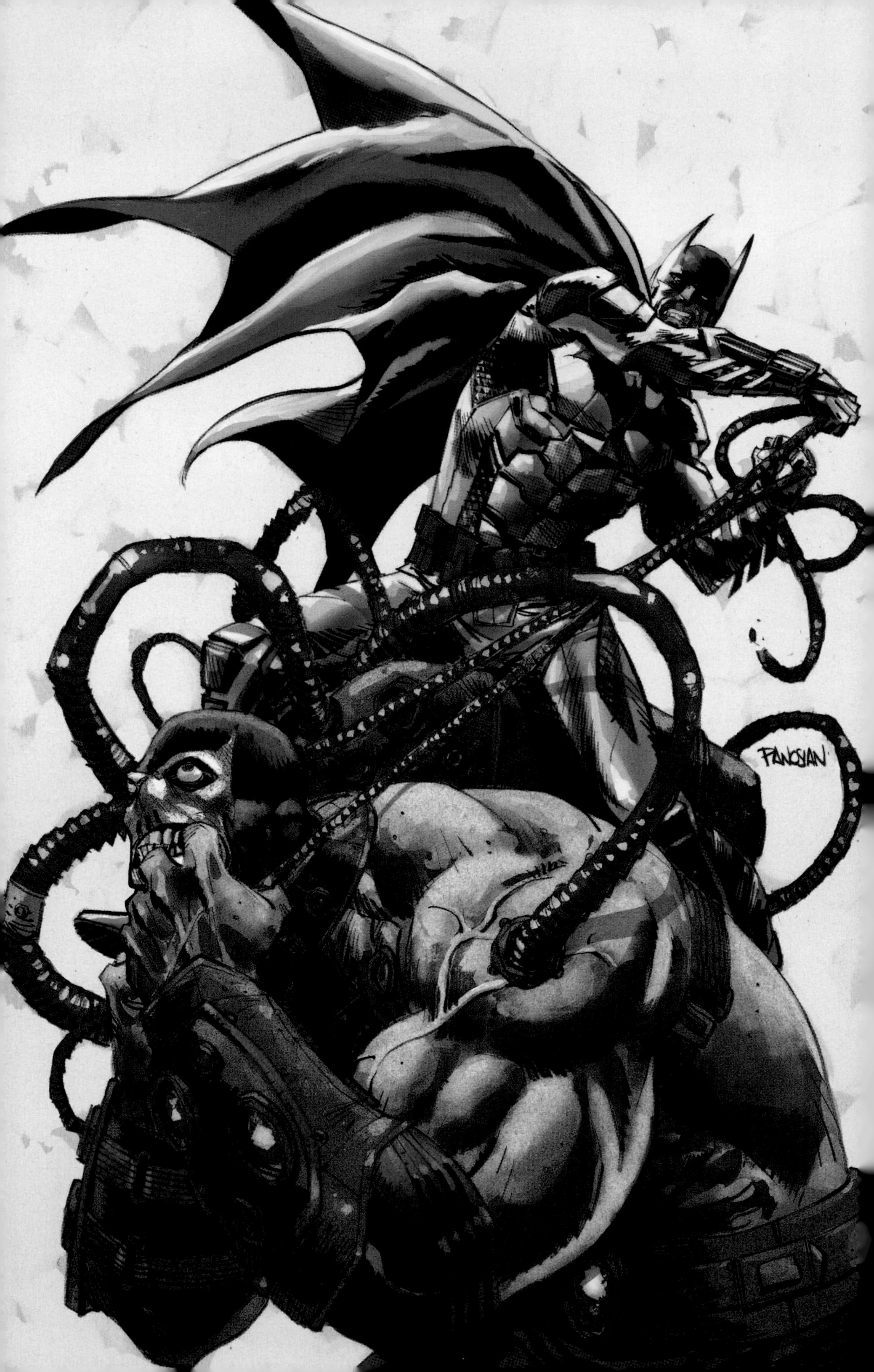
PANOSIAN

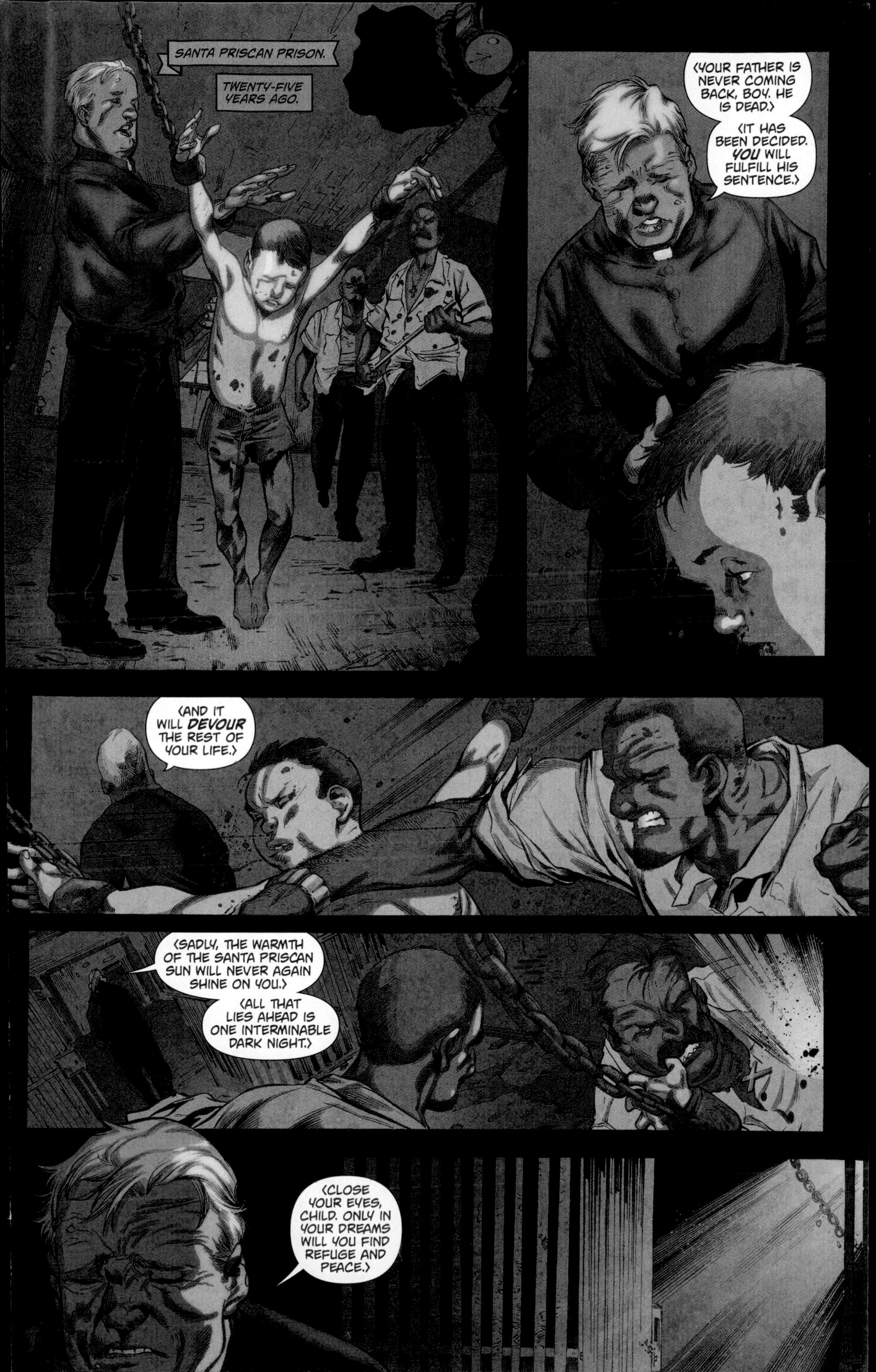
SANTA PRISCAN PRISON.
TWENTY-FIVE YEARS AGO.
<YOUR FATHER IS NEVER COMING BACK, BOY. HE IS DEAD.>
<IT HAS BEEN DECIDED. YOU WILL FULFILL HIS SENTENCE.>
<AND IT WILL DEVOUR THE REST OF YOUR LIFE.>
<SADLY, THE WARMTH OF THE SANTA PRISCAN SUN WILL NEVER AGAIN SHINE ON YOU.>
<ALL THAT LIES AHEAD IS ONE INTERMINABLE DARK NIGHT.>
<CLOSE YOUR EYES, CHILD. ONLY IN YOUR DREAMS WILL YOU FIND REFUGE AND PEACE.>

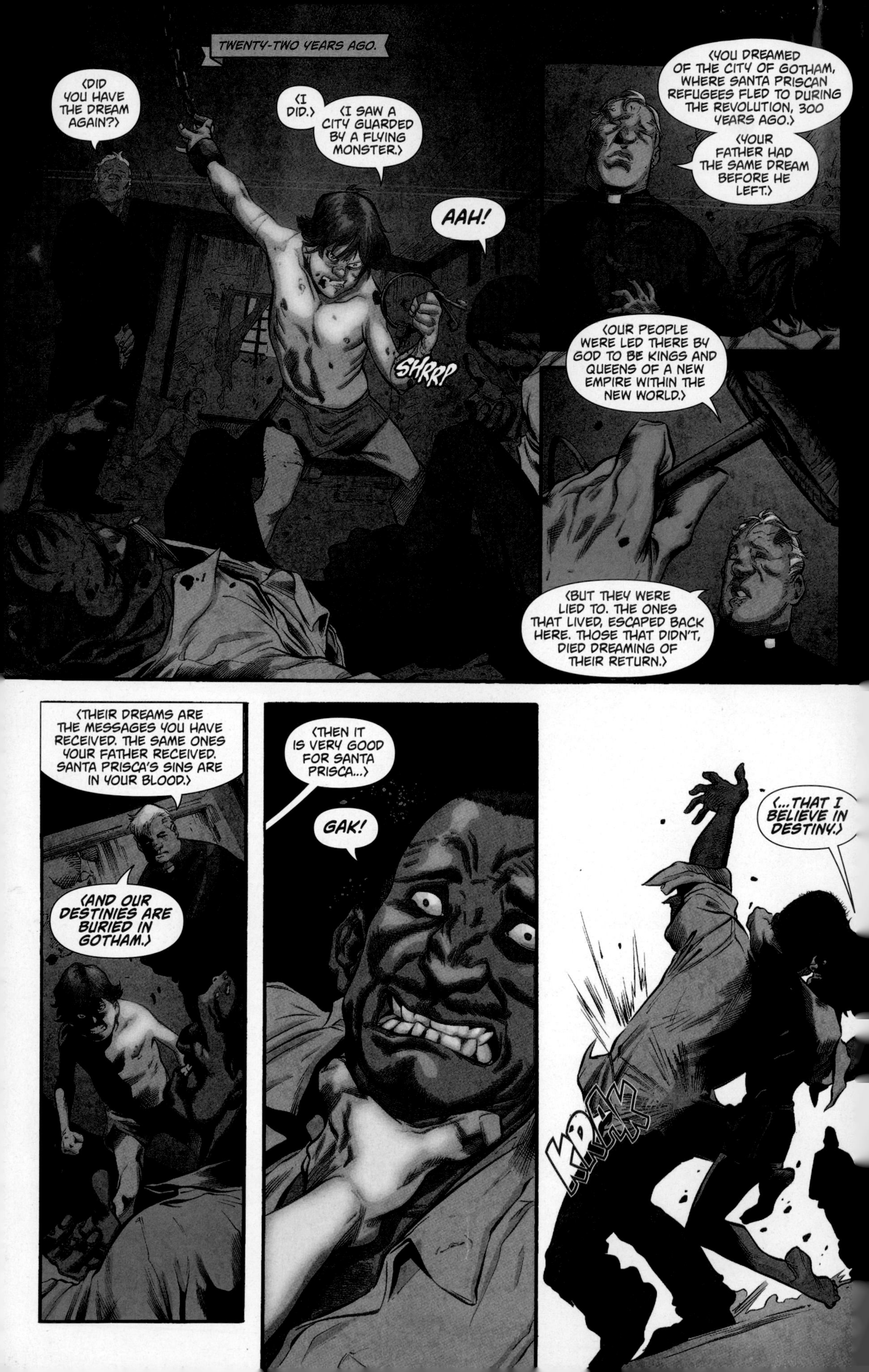
TWENTY-TWO YEARS AGO.
‹DID YOU HAVE THE DREAM AGAIN?›
‹I DID.›
‹I SAW A CITY GUARDED BY A FLYING MONSTER.›
AAH!
SHRRP
‹YOU DREAMED OF THE CITY OF GOTHAM, WHERE SANTA PRISCAN REFUGEES FLED TO DURING THE REVOLUTION, 300 YEARS AGO.›
‹YOUR FATHER HAD THE SAME DREAM BEFORE HE LEFT.›
‹OUR PEOPLE WERE LED THERE BY GOD TO BE KINGS AND QUEENS OF A NEW EMPIRE WITHIN THE NEW WORLD.›
‹BUT THEY WERE LIED TO. THE ONES THAT LIVED, ESCAPED BACK HERE. THOSE THAT DIDN'T, DIED DREAMING OF THEIR RETURN.›
‹THEIR DREAMS ARE THE MESSAGES YOU HAVE RECEIVED. THE SAME ONES YOUR FATHER RECEIVED. SANTA PRISCA'S SINS ARE IN YOUR BLOOD.›
‹AND OUR DESTINIES ARE BURIED IN GOTHAM.›
‹THEN IT IS VERY GOOD FOR SANTA PRISCA...›
GAK!
‹...THAT I BELIEVE IN DESTINY.›
KRAK

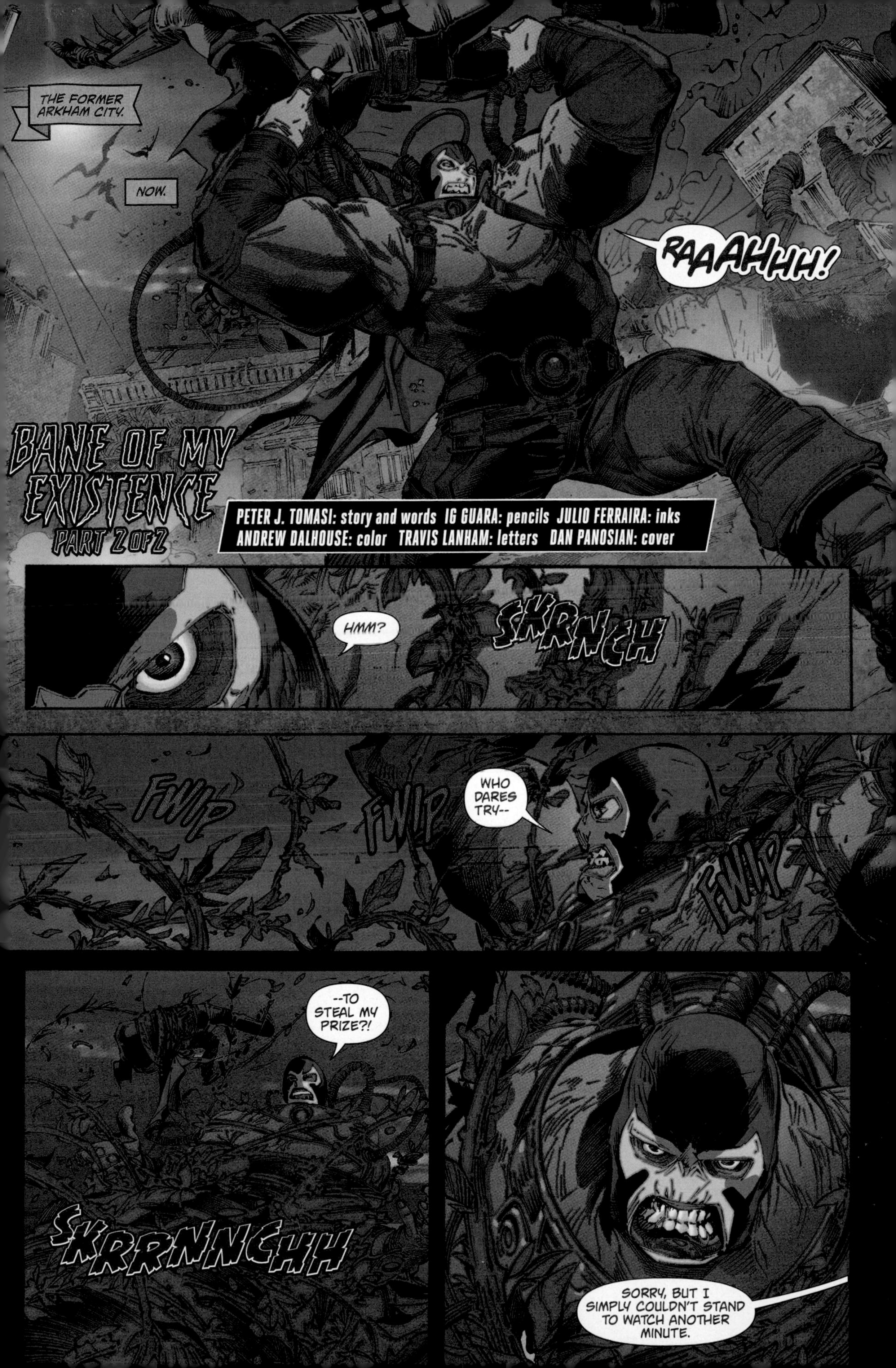
THE FORMER ARKHAM CITY.
NOW.
RAAAHHH!
BANE OF MY EXISTENCE PART 2 OF 2
PETER J. TOMASI: story and words IG GUARA: pencils JULIO FERRAIRA: inks
ANDREW DALHOUSE: color TRAVIS LANHAM: letters DAN PANOSIAN: cover
HMM?
SKRNCH
FWIP
FWIP
WHO DARES TRY--
FWIP
--TO STEAL MY PRIZE?!
SKRRNNCHH
SORRY, BUT I SIMPLY COULDN'T STAND TO WATCH ANOTHER MINUTE.

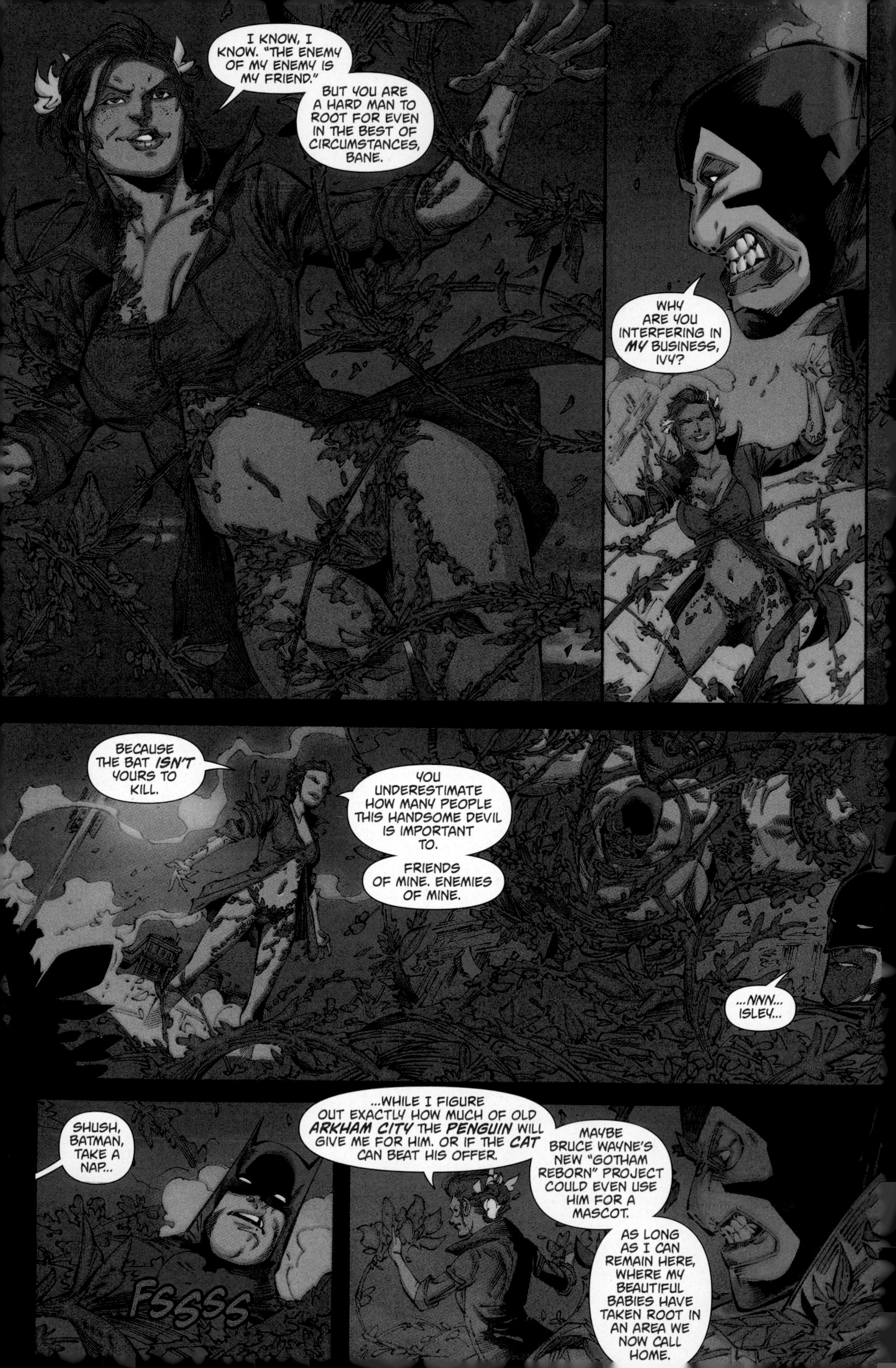
I KNOW, I KNOW. "THE ENEMY OF MY ENEMY IS MY FRIEND."
BUT YOU ARE A HARD MAN TO ROOT FOR EVEN IN THE BEST OF CIRCUMSTANCES, BANE.
WHY ARE YOU INTERFERING IN MY BUSINESS, IVY?
BECAUSE THE BAT ISN'T YOURS TO KILL.
YOU UNDERESTIMATE HOW MANY PEOPLE THIS HANDSOME DEVIL IS IMPORTANT TO.
FRIENDS OF MINE. ENEMIES OF MINE.
...NNN... ISLEY...
SHUSH, BATMAN, TAKE A NAP...
FSSSS
...WHILE I FIGURE OUT EXACTLY HOW MUCH OF OLD ARKHAM CITY THE PENGUIN WILL GIVE ME FOR HIM. OR IF THE CAT CAN BEAT HIS OFFER.
MAYBE BRUCE WAYNE'S NEW "GOTHAM REBORN" PROJECT COULD EVEN USE HIM FOR A MASCOT.
AS LONG AS I CAN REMAIN HERE, WHERE MY BEAUTIFUL BABIES HAVE TAKEN ROOT IN AN AREA WE NOW CALL HOME.

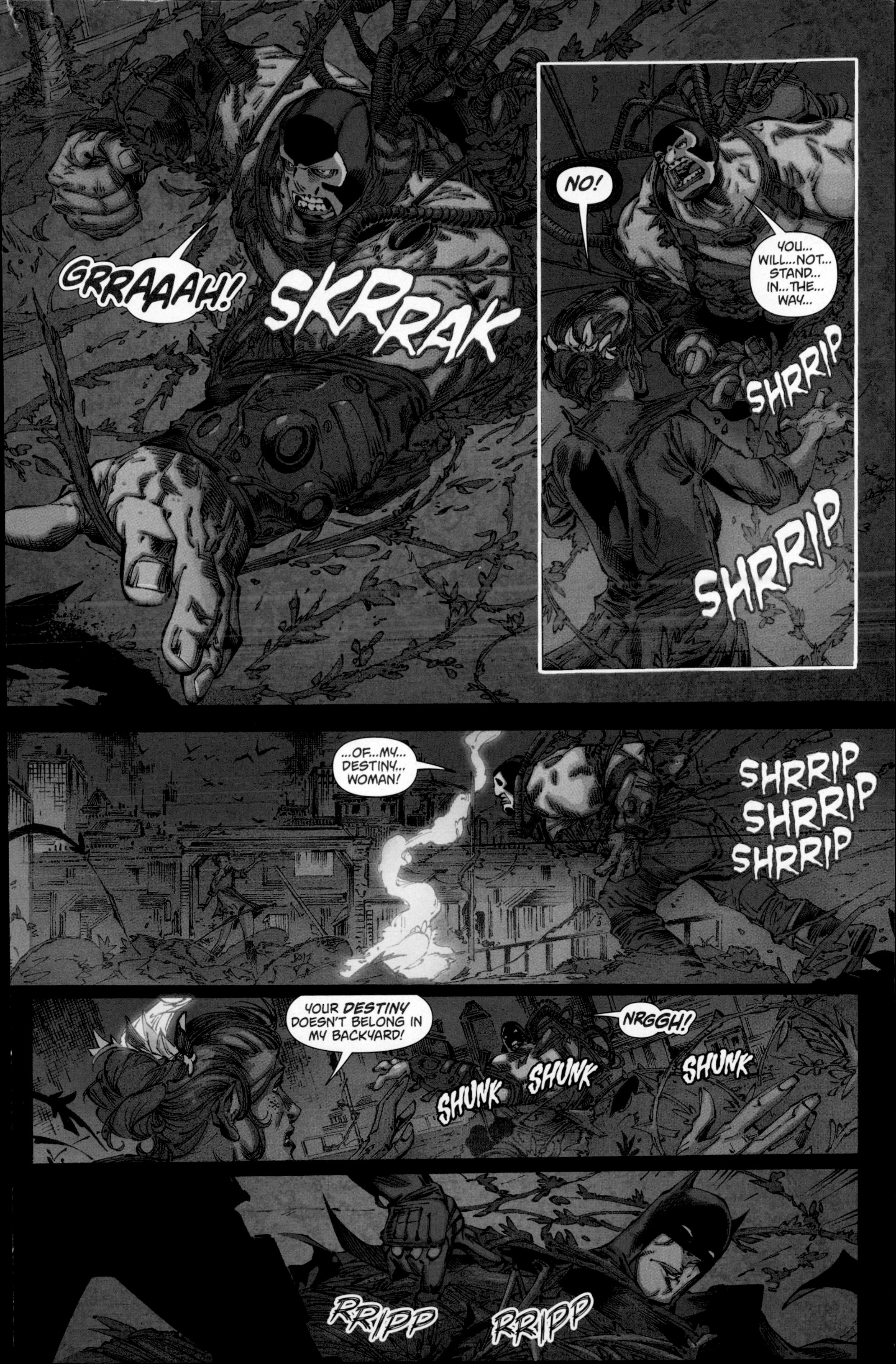
GRRAAAH!
SKRRAK
NO!
YOU... WILL...NOT... STAND... IN...THE... WAY...
SHRRIP
SHRRIP
...OF...MY... DESTINY... WOMAN!
SHRRIP
SHRRIP
SHRRIP
YOUR DESTINY DOESN'T BELONG IN MY BACKYARD!
NRGGH!
SHUNK
SHUNK
SHUNK
RRIPP
RRIPP

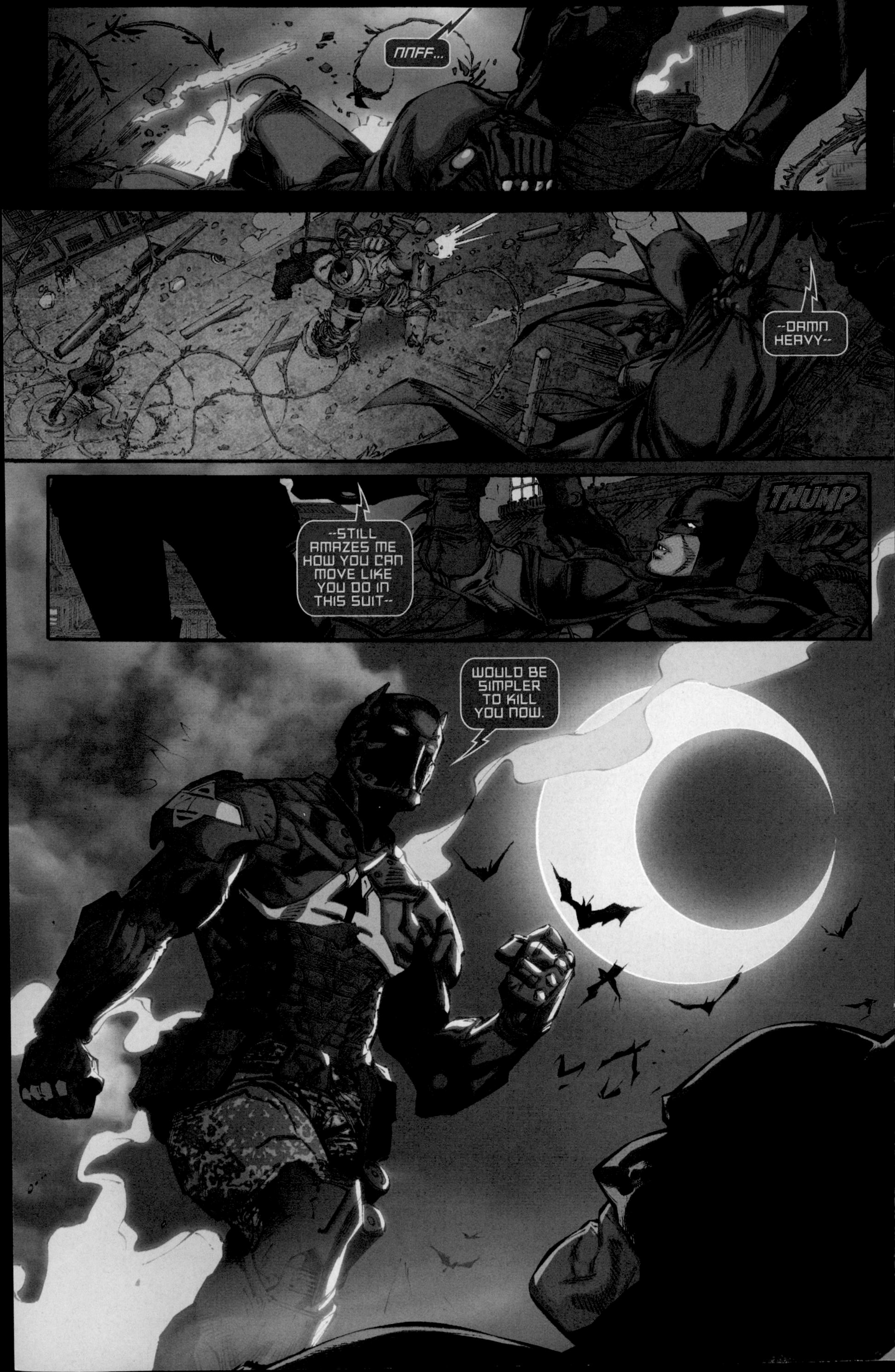
NNFF...
--DAMN HEAVY--
THUMP
--STILL AMAZES ME HOW YOU CAN MOVE LIKE YOU DO IN THIS SUIT--
WOULD BE SIMPLER TO KILL YOU NOW.

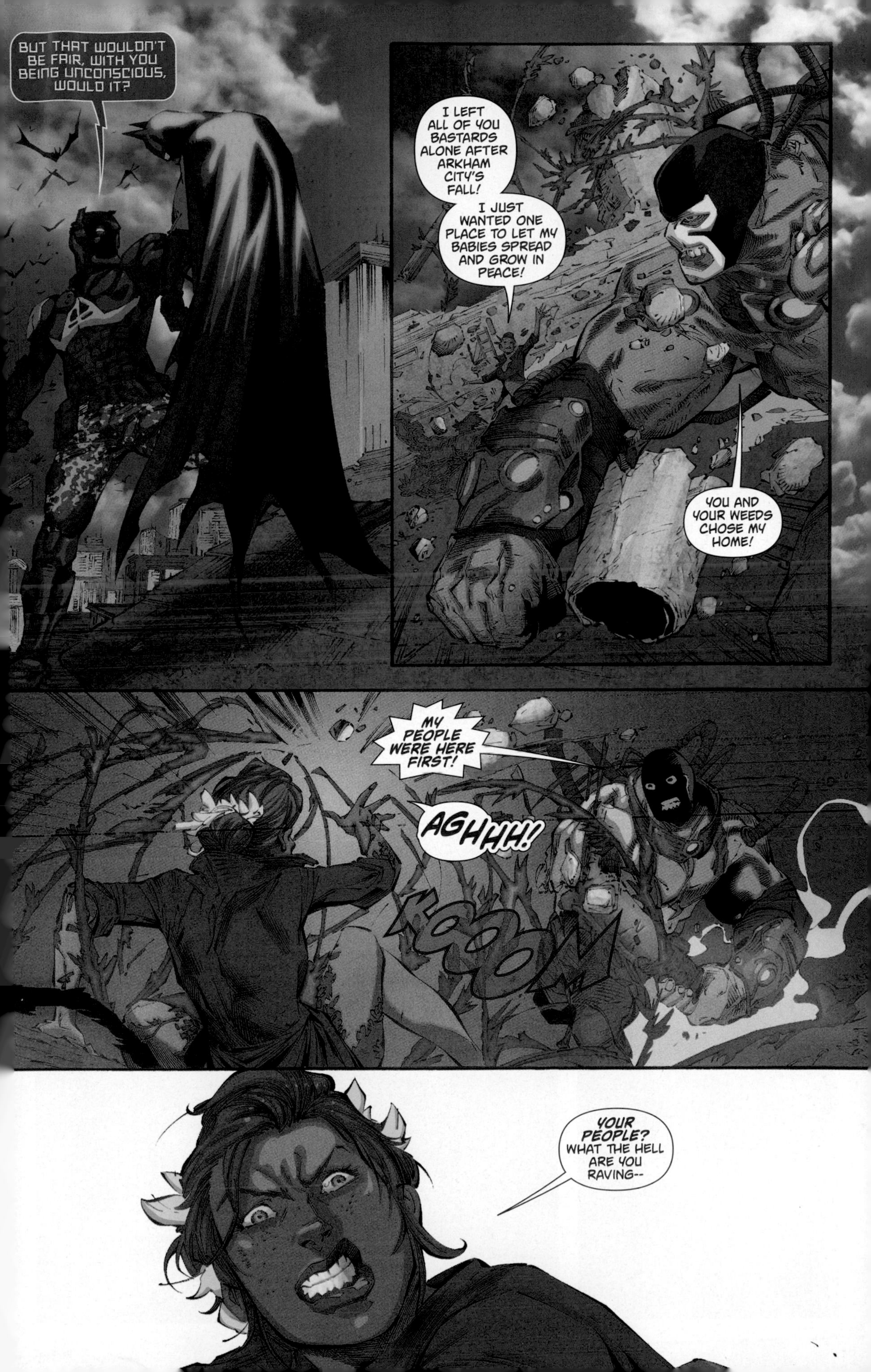
BUT THAT WOULDN'T BE FAIR, WITH YOU BEING UNCONSCIOUS, WOULD IT?
I LEFT ALL OF YOU BASTARDS ALONE AFTER ARKHAM CITY'S FALL!
I JUST WANTED ONE PLACE TO LET MY BABIES SPREAD AND GROW IN PEACE!
YOU AND YOUR WEEDS CHOSE MY HOME!
MY PEOPLE WERE HERE FIRST!
AGHHH!
KOOOOM
YOUR PEOPLE? WHAT THE HELL ARE YOU RAVING--

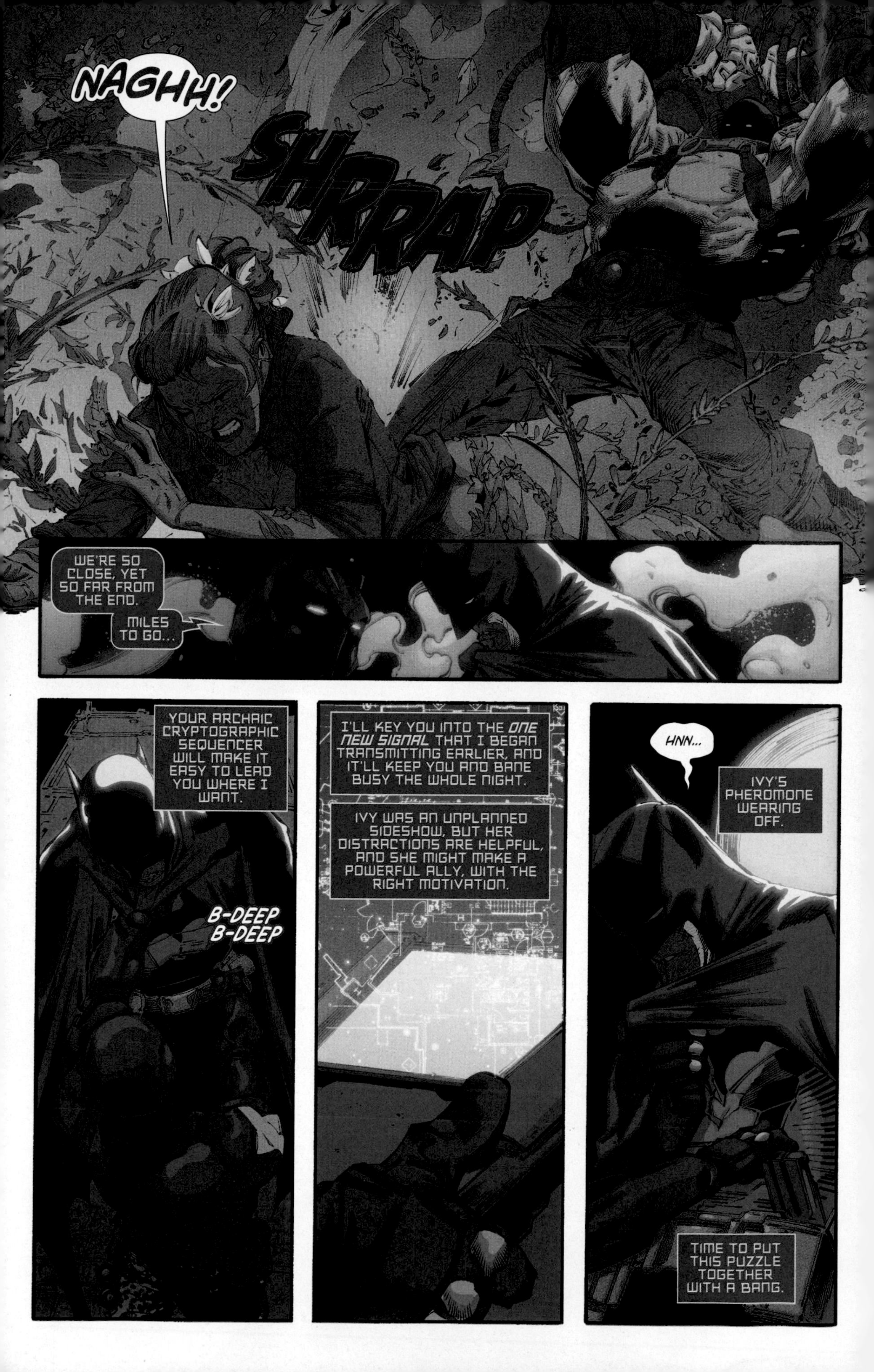
NAGHH!
SHRRAP
WE'RE SO CLOSE, YET SO FAR FROM THE END.
MILES TO GO...
YOUR ARCHAIC CRYPTOGRAPHIC SEQUENCER WILL MAKE IT EASY TO LEAD YOU WHERE I WANT.
B-DEEP B-DEEP
I'LL KEY YOU INTO THE *ONE NEW SIGNAL* THAT I BEGAN TRANSMITTING EARLIER, AND IT'LL KEEP YOU AND BANE BUSY THE WHOLE NIGHT.
IVY WAS AN UNPLANNED SIDESHOW, BUT HER DISTRACTIONS ARE HELPFUL, AND SHE MIGHT MAKE A POWERFUL ALLY, WITH THE RIGHT MOTIVATION.
HNN...
IVY'S PHEROMONE WEARING OFF.
TIME TO PUT THIS PUZZLE TOGETHER WITH A BANG.

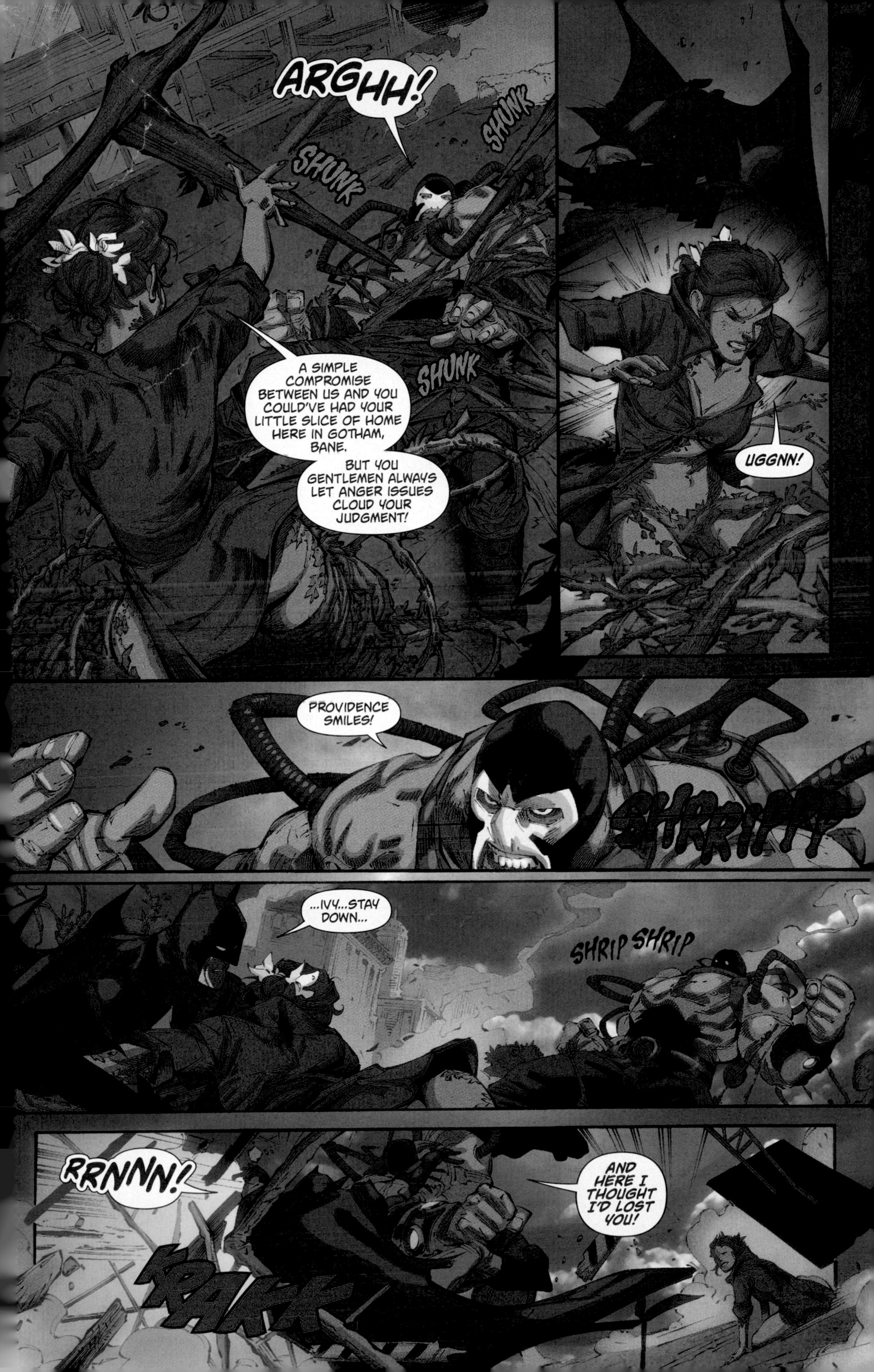
ARGHH!
SHUNK
SHUNK
A SIMPLE COMPROMISE BETWEEN US AND YOU COULD'VE HAD YOUR LITTLE SLICE OF HOME HERE IN GOTHAM, BANE.
BUT YOU GENTLEMEN ALWAYS LET ANGER ISSUES CLOUD YOUR JUDGMENT!
SHUNK
UGGNN!
PROVIDENCE SMILES!
SHRRIPPP
...IVY...STAY DOWN...
SHRIP SHRIP
RRNNN!
AND HERE I THOUGHT I'D LOST YOU!
KRAKK

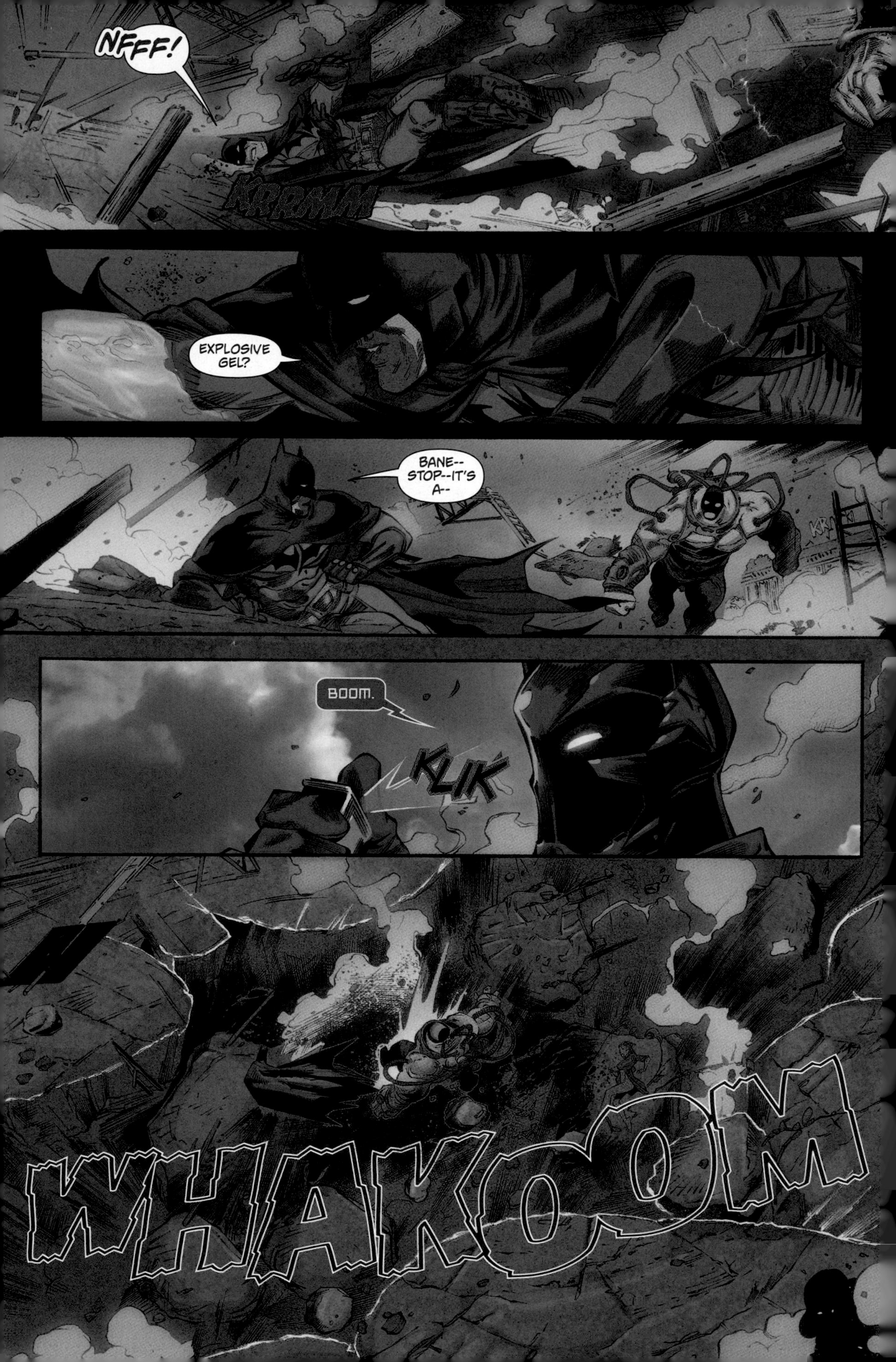
NFFF!
KRRMM
EXPLOSIVE GEL?
BANE-- STOP--IT'S A--
BOOM.
KLIK
WHAKOOM

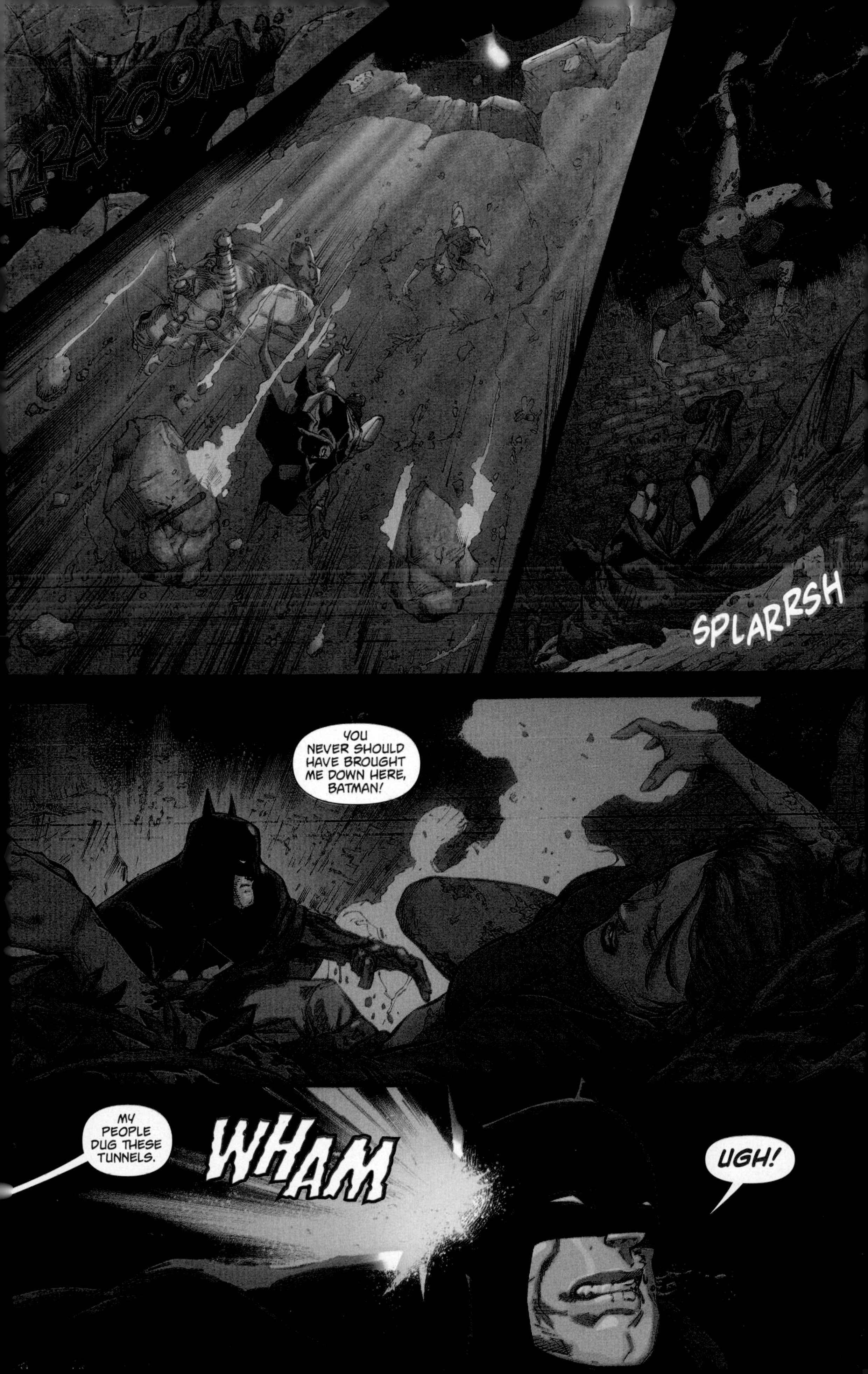
KRAKOOM
SPLARRSH
YOU NEVER SHOULD HAVE BROUGHT ME DOWN HERE, BATMAN!
MY PEOPLE DUG THESE TUNNELS.
WHAM
UGH!

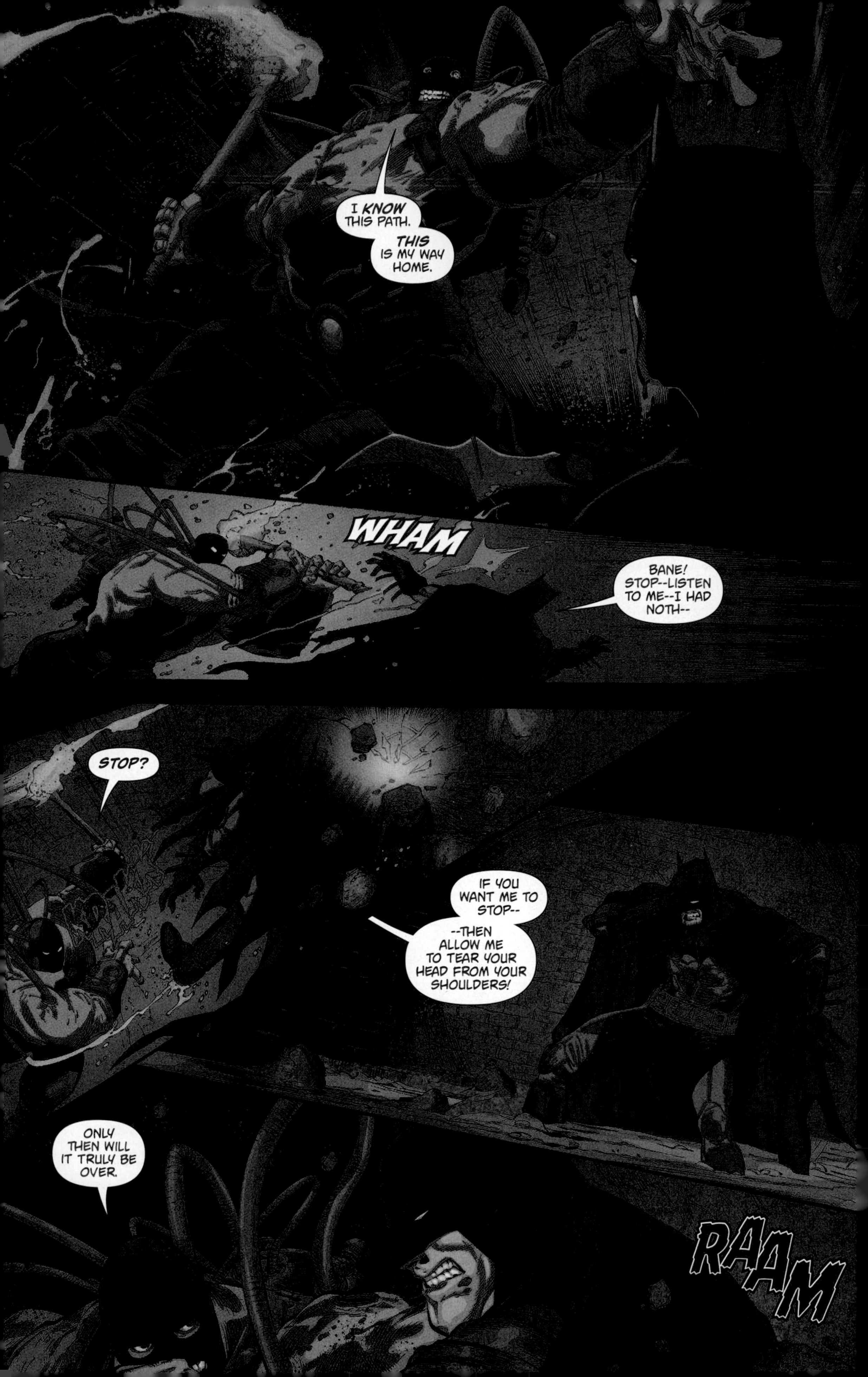
I KNOW THIS PATH.
THIS IS MY WAY HOME.
WHAM
BANE! STOP--LISTEN TO ME--I HAD NOTH--
STOP?
IF YOU WANT ME TO STOP--
--THEN ALLOW ME TO TEAR YOUR HEAD FROM YOUR SHOULDERS!
ONLY THEN WILL IT TRULY BE OVER.
RAAM

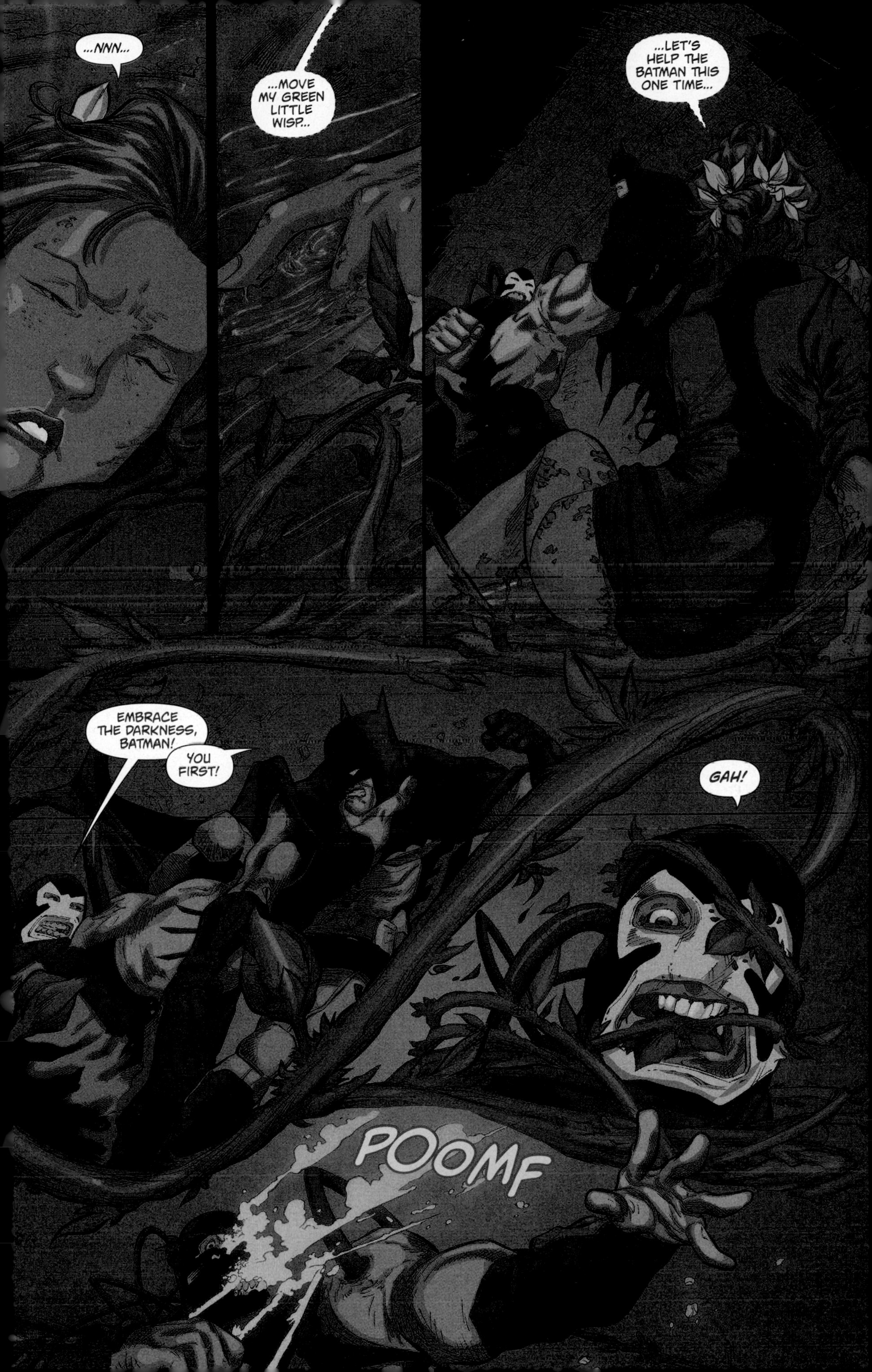
...NNN...
...MOVE MY GREEN LITTLE WISP...
...LET'S HELP THE BATMAN THIS ONE TIME...
EMBRACE THE DARKNESS, BATMAN!
YOU FIRST!
GAH!
POOMF

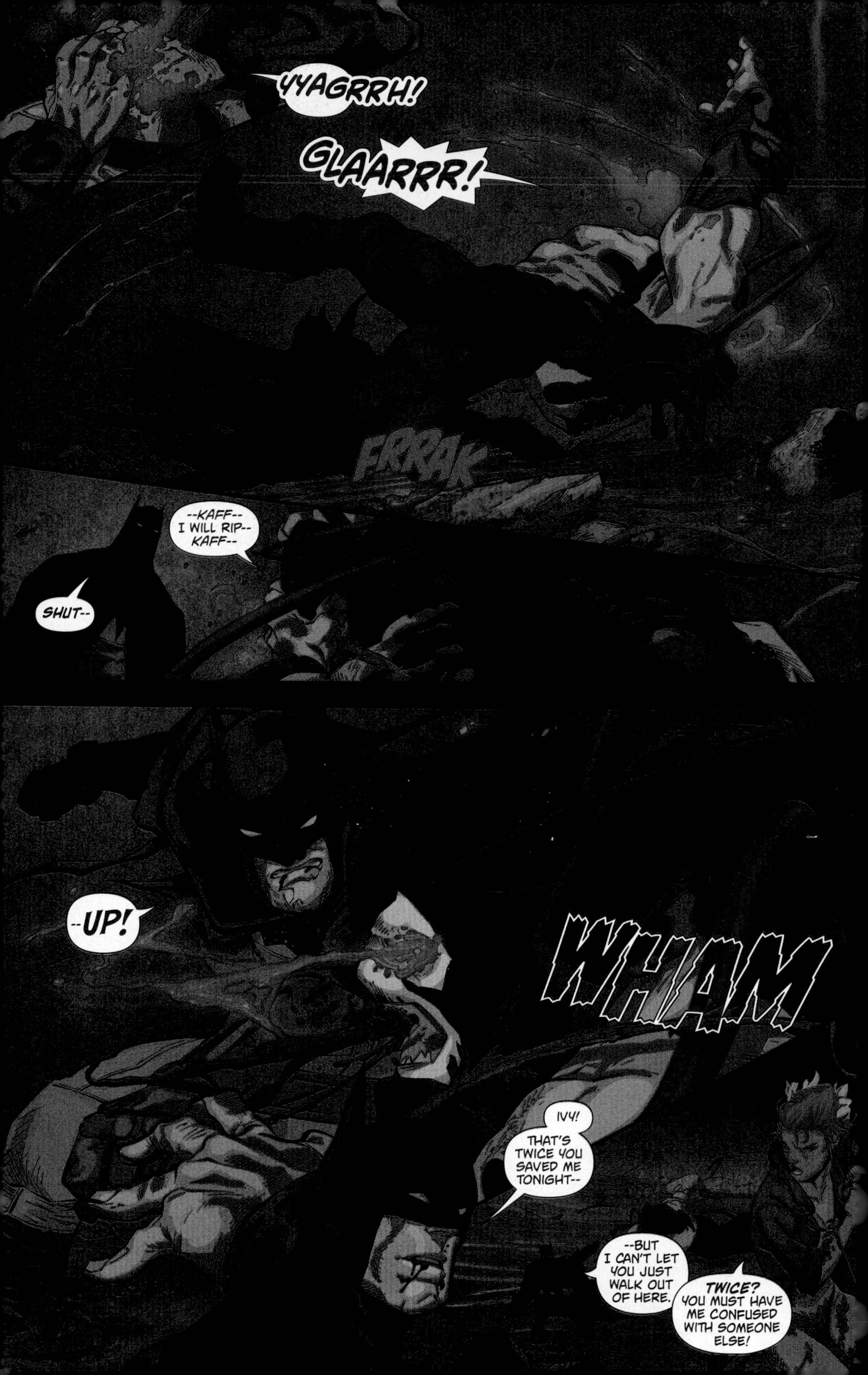
YYAGRRH!
GLAARRR!
FRRAK
--KAFF-- I WILL RIP-- KAFF--
SHUT--
--UP!
WHAM
IVY!
THAT'S TWICE YOU SAVED ME TONIGHT--
--BUT I CAN'T LET YOU JUST WALK OUT OF HERE.
TWICE? YOU MUST HAVE ME CONFUSED WITH SOMEONE ELSE!

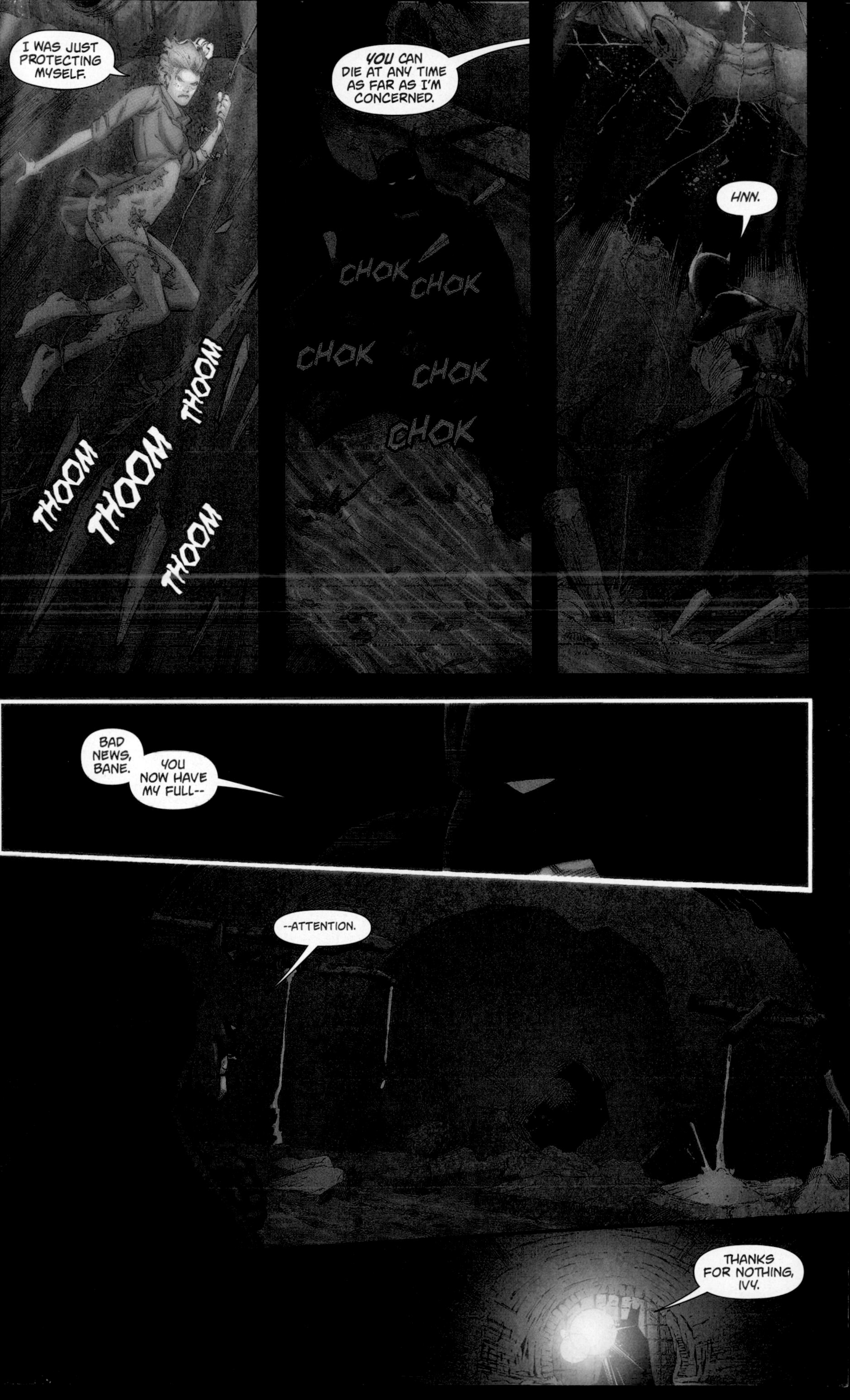
I WAS JUST PROTECTING MYSELF.
THOOM
THOOM
THOOM
THOOM
YOU CAN DIE AT ANY TIME AS FAR AS I'M CONCERNED.
CHOK CHOK
CHOK CHOK
CHOK
HNN.
BAD NEWS, BANE.
YOU NOW HAVE MY FULL--
--ATTENTION.
THANKS FOR NOTHING, IVY.

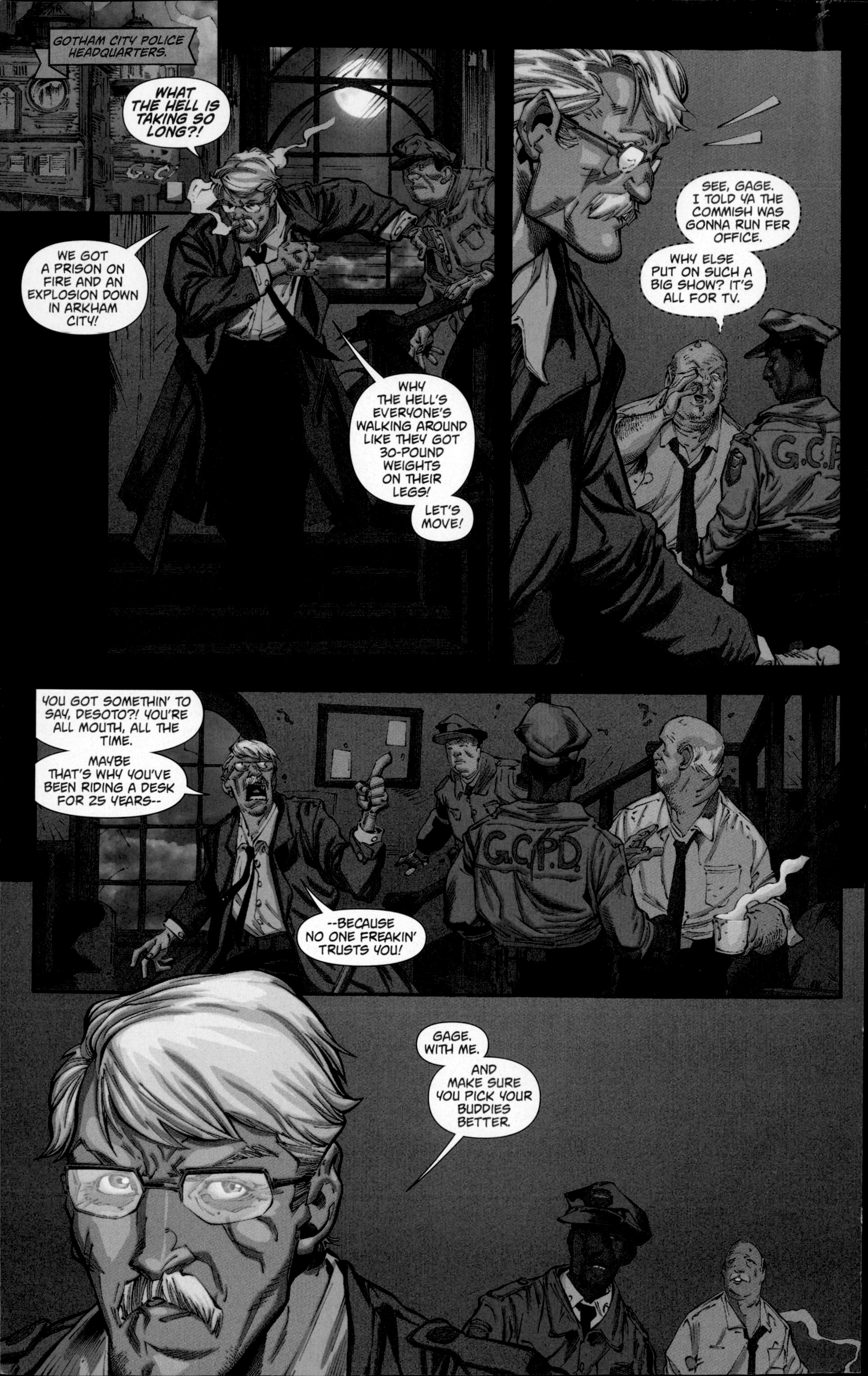
GOTHAM CITY POLICE HEADQUARTERS.
WHAT THE HELL IS TAKING SO LONG?!
WE GOT A PRISON ON FIRE AND AN EXPLOSION DOWN IN ARKHAM CITY!
WHY THE HELL'S EVERYONE'S WALKING AROUND LIKE THEY GOT 30-POUND WEIGHTS ON THEIR LEGS!
LET'S MOVE!
SEE, GAGE. I TOLD YA THE COMMISH WAS GONNA RUN FER OFFICE.
WHY ELSE PUT ON SUCH A BIG SHOW? IT'S ALL FOR TV.
YOU GOT SOMETHIN' TO SAY, DESOTO?! YOU'RE ALL MOUTH, ALL THE TIME.
MAYBE THAT'S WHY YOU'VE BEEN RIDING A DESK FOR 25 YEARS--
--BECAUSE NO ONE FREAKIN' TRUSTS YOU!
GAGE. WITH ME.
AND MAKE SURE YOU PICK YOUR BUDDIES BETTER.

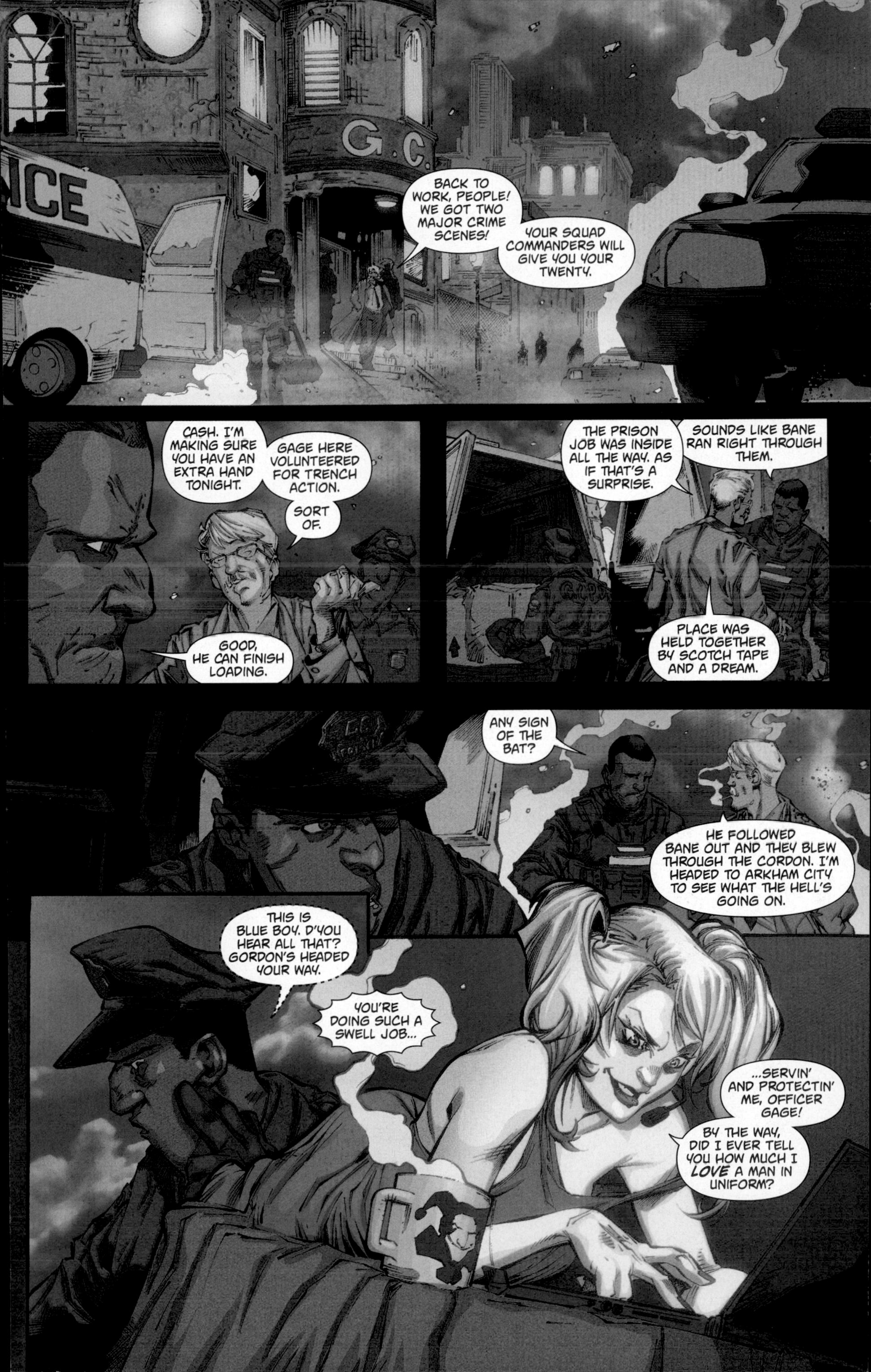
ICE
G.C.
BACK TO WORK, PEOPLE! WE GOT TWO MAJOR CRIME SCENES!
YOUR SQUAD COMMANDERS WILL GIVE YOU YOUR TWENTY.
CASH. I'M MAKING SURE YOU HAVE AN EXTRA HAND TONIGHT.
GAGE HERE VOLUNTEERED FOR TRENCH ACTION.
SORT OF.
GOOD, HE CAN FINISH LOADING.
THE PRISON JOB WAS INSIDE ALL THE WAY. AS IF THAT'S A SURPRISE.
SOUNDS LIKE BANE RAN RIGHT THROUGH THEM.
PLACE WAS HELD TOGETHER BY SCOTCH TAPE AND A DREAM.
ANY SIGN OF THE BAT?
HE FOLLOWED BANE OUT AND THEY BLEW THROUGH THE CORDON. I'M HEADED TO ARKHAM CITY TO SEE WHAT THE HELL'S GOING ON.
THIS IS BLUE BOY. D'YOU HEAR ALL THAT? GORDON'S HEADED YOUR WAY.
YOU'RE DOING SUCH A SWELL JOB...
...SERVIN' AND PROTECTIN' ME, OFFICER GAGE!
BY THE WAY, DID I EVER TELL YOU HOW MUCH I *LOVE* A MAN IN UNIFORM?

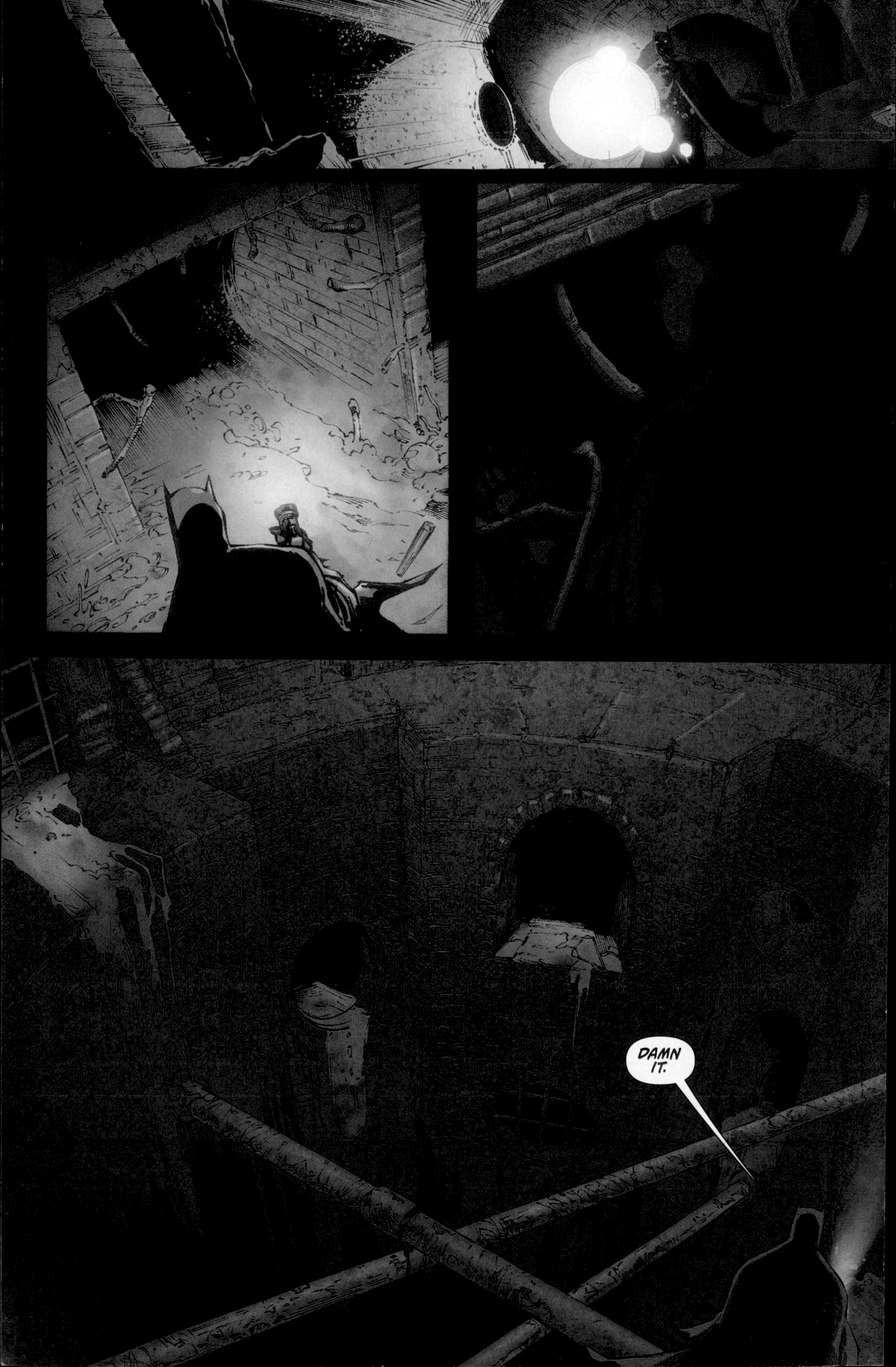
DAMN IT.

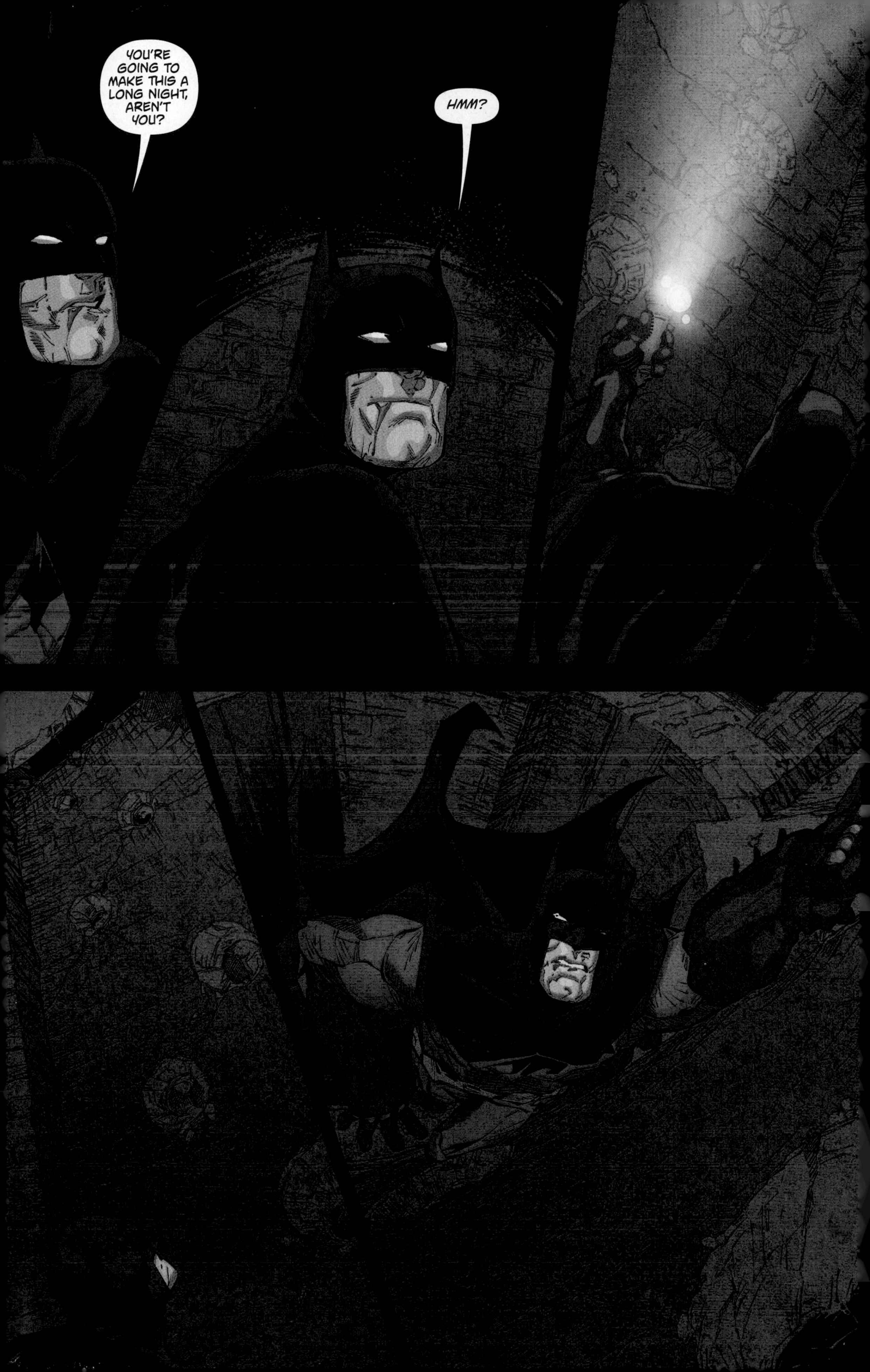
YOU'RE GOING TO MAKE THIS A LONG NIGHT, AREN'T YOU?
HMM?

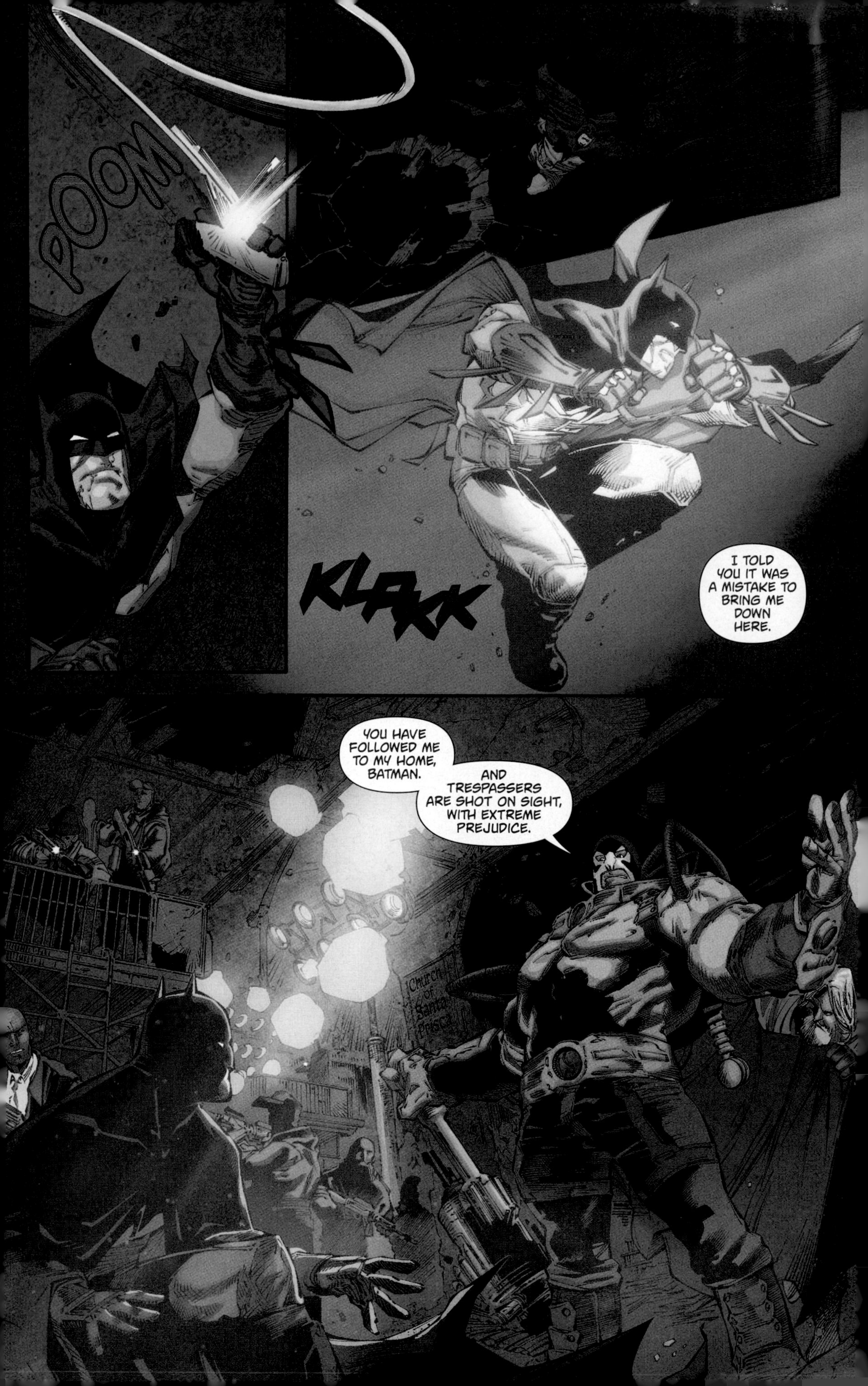
POOM
KLAKK
I TOLD YOU IT WAS A MISTAKE TO BRING ME DOWN HERE.
YOU HAVE FOLLOWED ME TO MY HOME, BATMAN.
AND TRESPASSERS ARE SHOT ON SIGHT, WITH EXTREME PREJUDICE.
Church of Santa Prisca

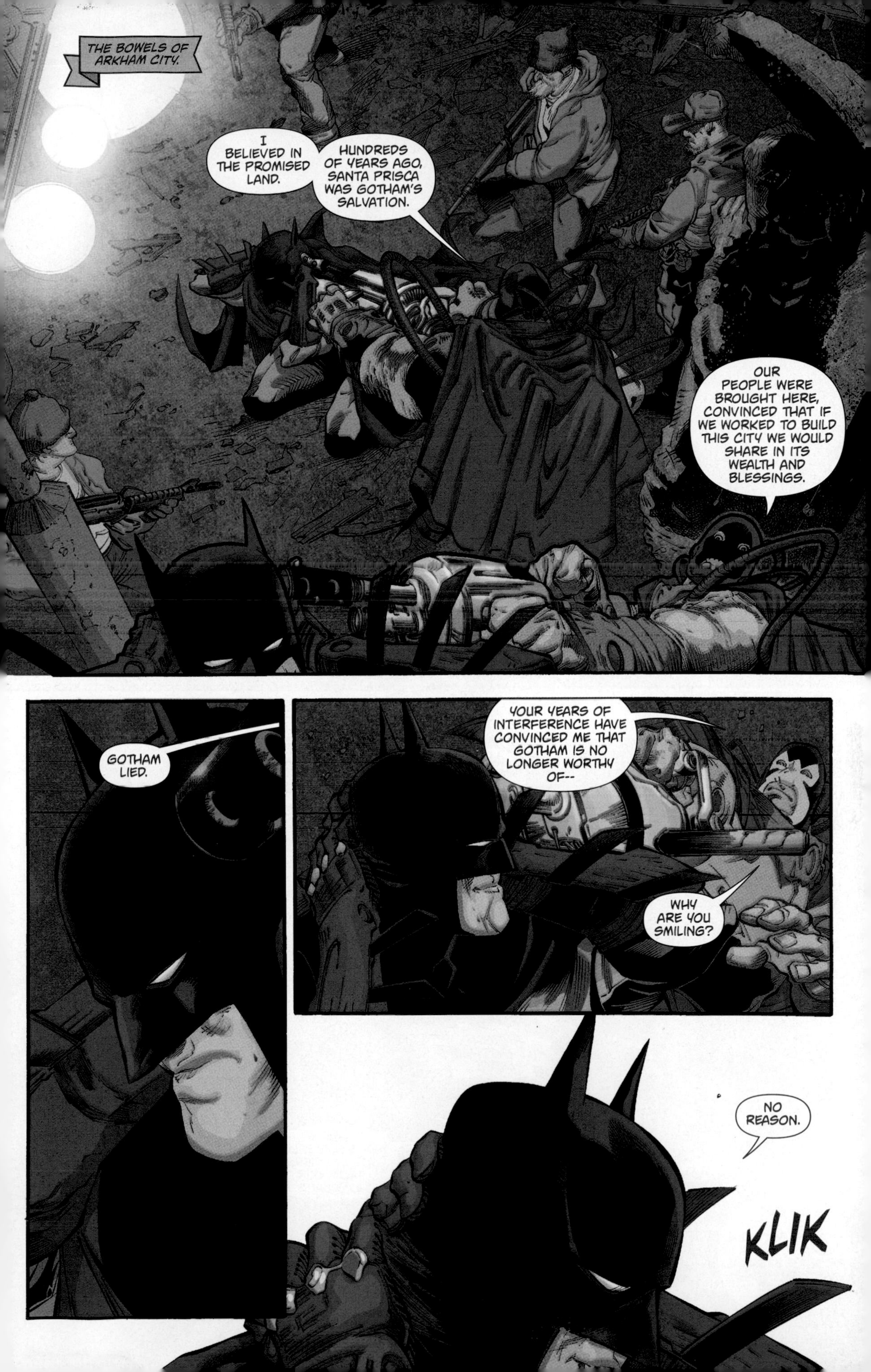
THE BOWELS OF ARKHAM CITY.
I BELIEVED IN THE PROMISED LAND.
HUNDREDS OF YEARS AGO, SANTA PRISCA WAS GOTHAM'S SALVATION.
OUR PEOPLE WERE BROUGHT HERE, CONVINCED THAT IF WE WORKED TO BUILD THIS CITY WE WOULD SHARE IN ITS WEALTH AND BLESSINGS.
GOTHAM LIED.
YOUR YEARS OF INTERFERENCE HAVE CONVINCED ME THAT GOTHAM IS NO LONGER WORTHY OF--
WHY ARE YOU SMILING?
NO REASON.
KLIK

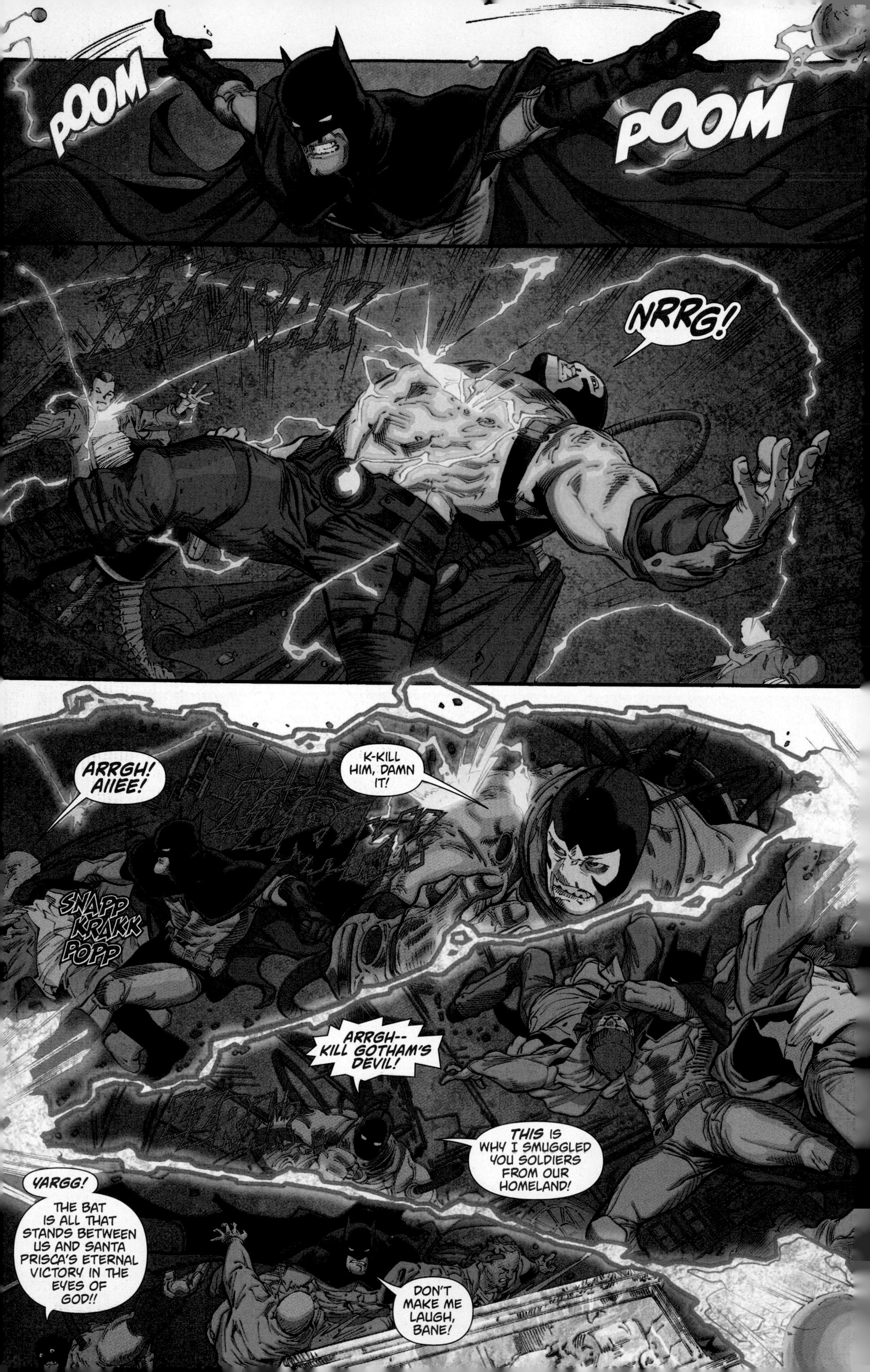

POOM
POOM
NRRG!
ARRGH! AIIEE!
K-KILL HIM, DAMN IT!
SNAPP KRAKK POPP
ARRGH-- KILL GOTHAM'S DEVIL!
THIS IS WHY I SMUGGLED YOU SOLDIERS FROM OUR HOMELAND!
YARGG!
THE BAT IS ALL THAT STANDS BETWEEN US AND SANTA PRISCA'S ETERNAL VICTORY IN THE EYES OF GOD!!
DON'T MAKE ME LAUGH, BANE!

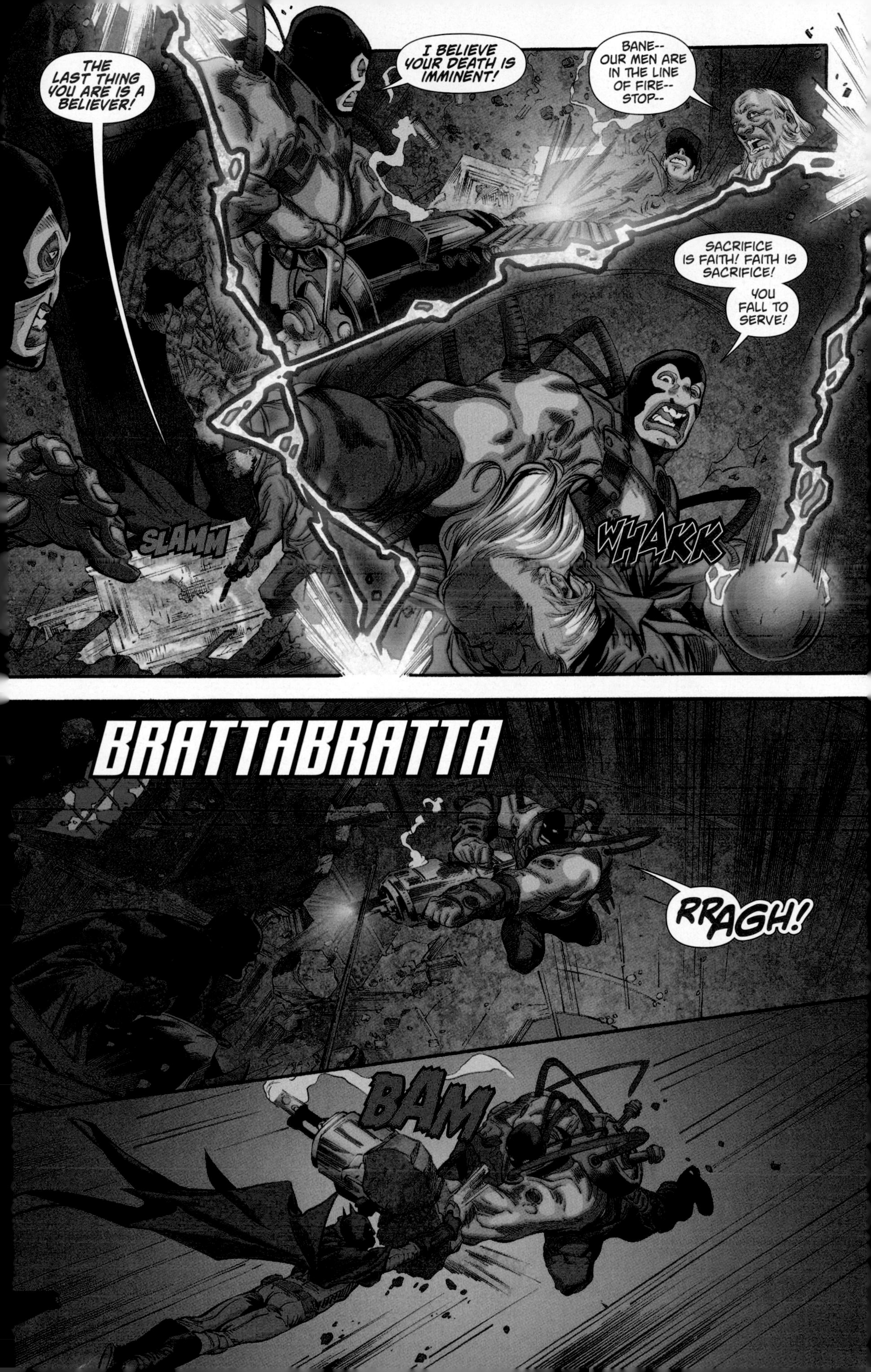
THE LAST THING YOU ARE IS A BELIEVER!
I BELIEVE YOUR DEATH IS IMMINENT!
BANE-- OUR MEN ARE IN THE LINE OF FIRE-- STOP--
SACRIFICE IS FAITH! FAITH IS SACRIFICE!
YOU FALL TO SERVE!
SLAMM
WHAKK
BRATTABRATTA
RRAGH!
BAM

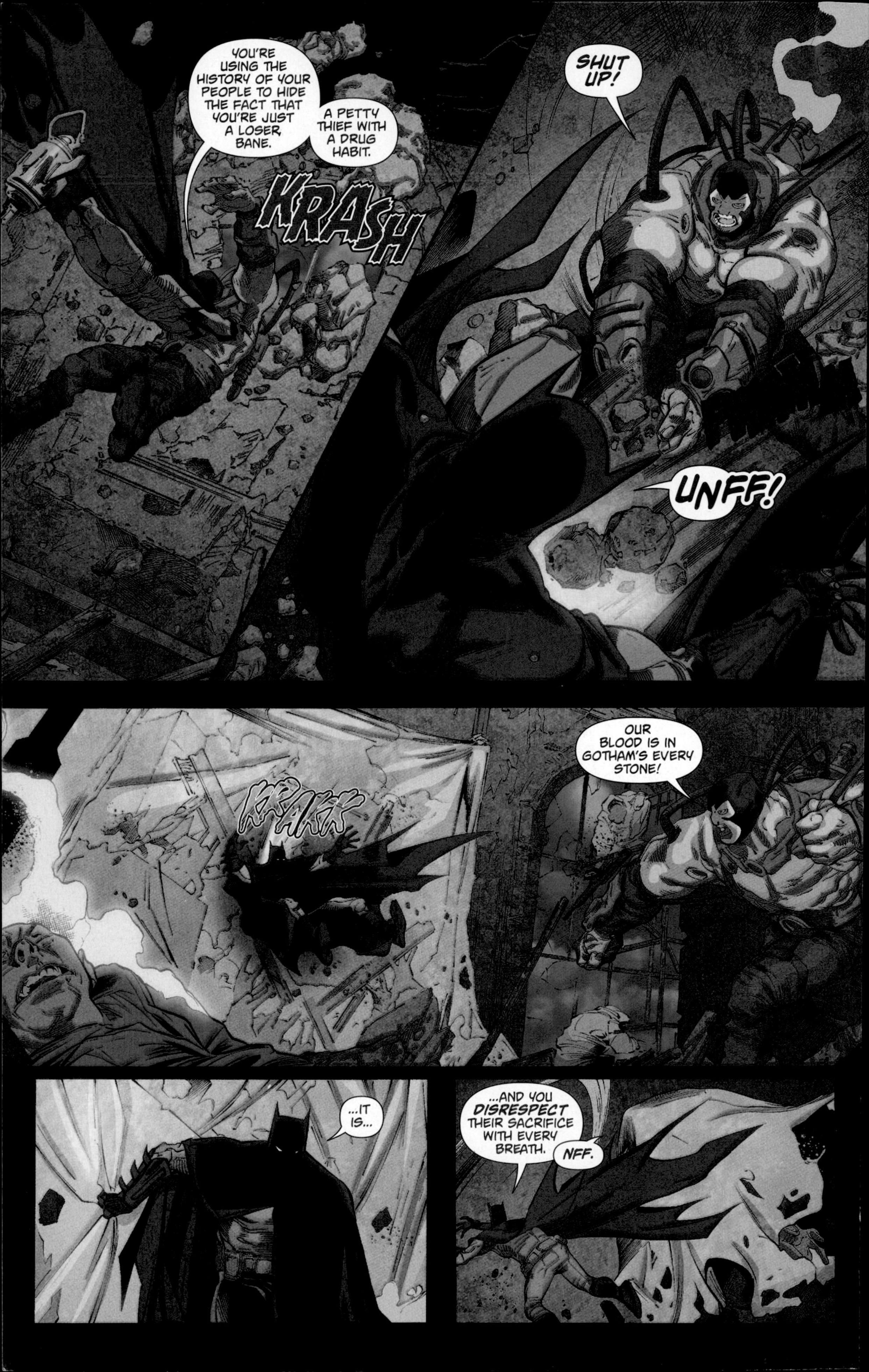
YOU'RE USING THE HISTORY OF YOUR PEOPLE TO HIDE THE FACT THAT YOU'RE JUST A LOSER, BANE.
A PETTY THIEF WITH A DRUG HABIT.
KRASH
SHUT UP!
UNFF!
KRAKK
OUR BLOOD IS IN GOTHAM'S EVERY STONE!
...IT IS...
...AND YOU DISRESPECT THEIR SACRIFICE WITH EVERY BREATH.
NFF.

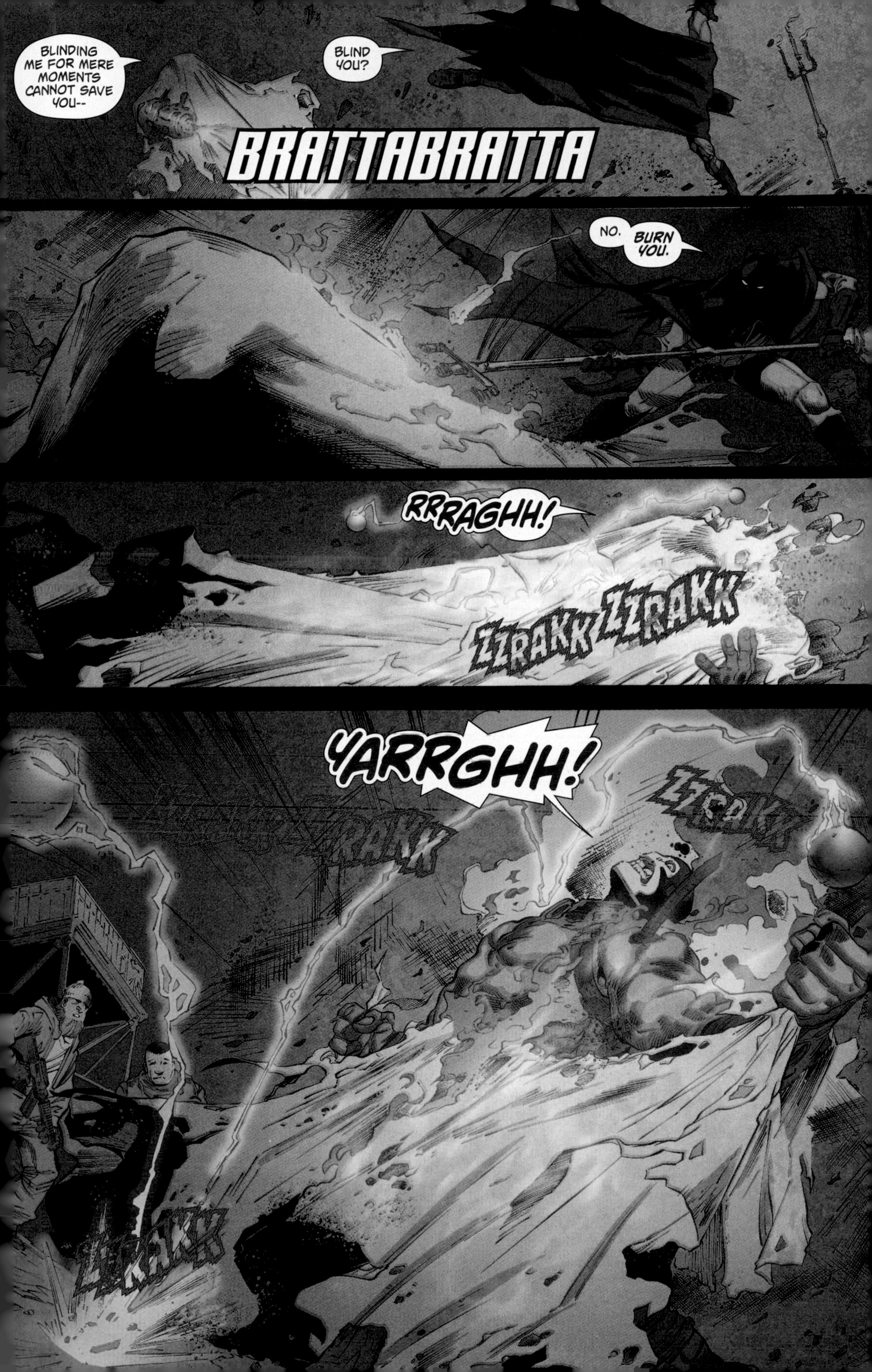
BLINDING ME FOR MERE MOMENTS CANNOT SAVE YOU--
BLIND YOU?
BRATTABRATTA
NO.
BURN YOU.
RRRAGHH!
ZZRAKK ZZRAKK
YARRGHH!
ZZRAKK
ZZRAKK

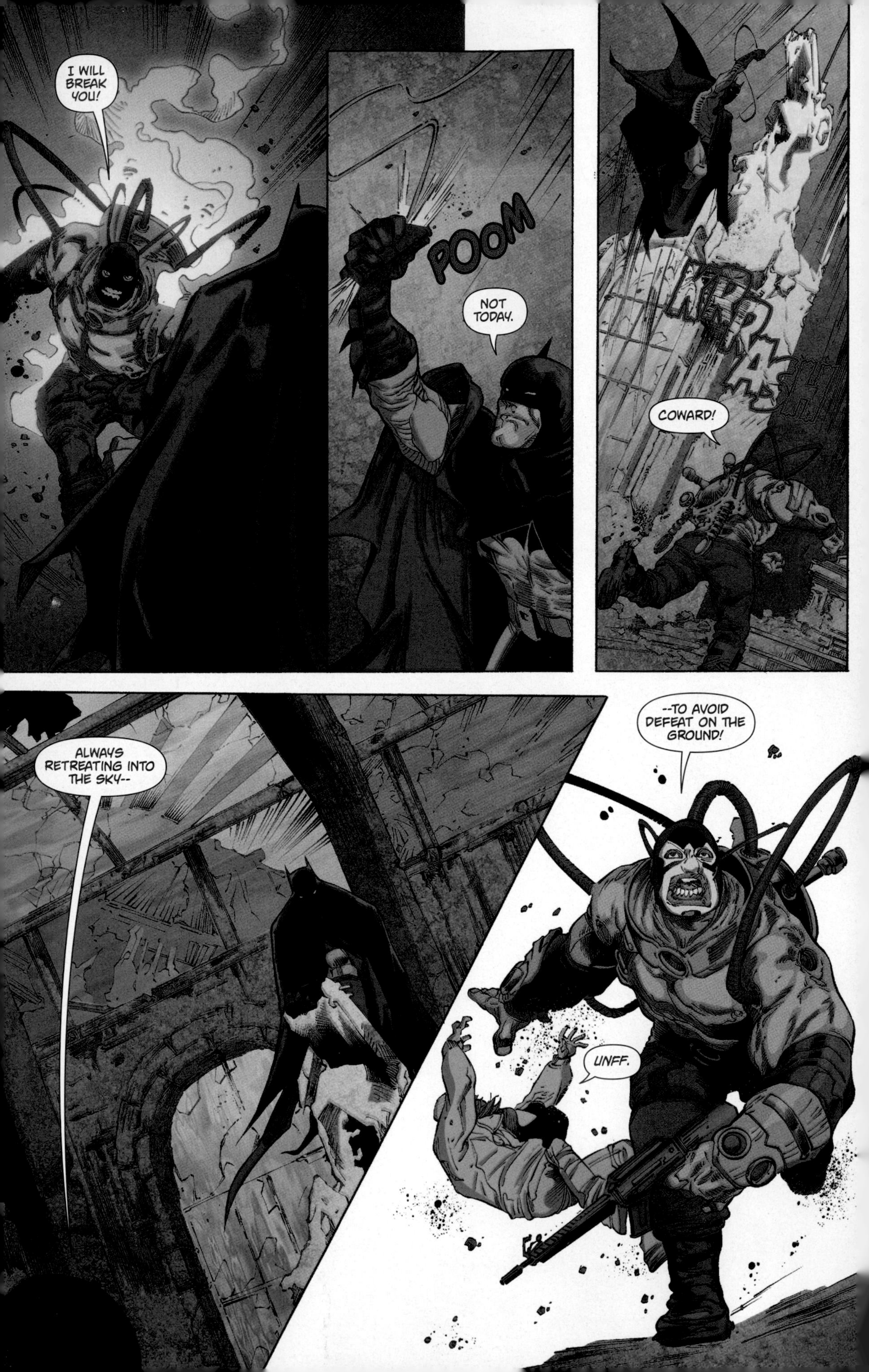
I WILL BREAK YOU!
POOM
NOT TODAY.
COWARD!
ALWAYS RETREATING INTO THE SKY--
--TO AVOID DEFEAT ON THE GROUND!
UNFF.

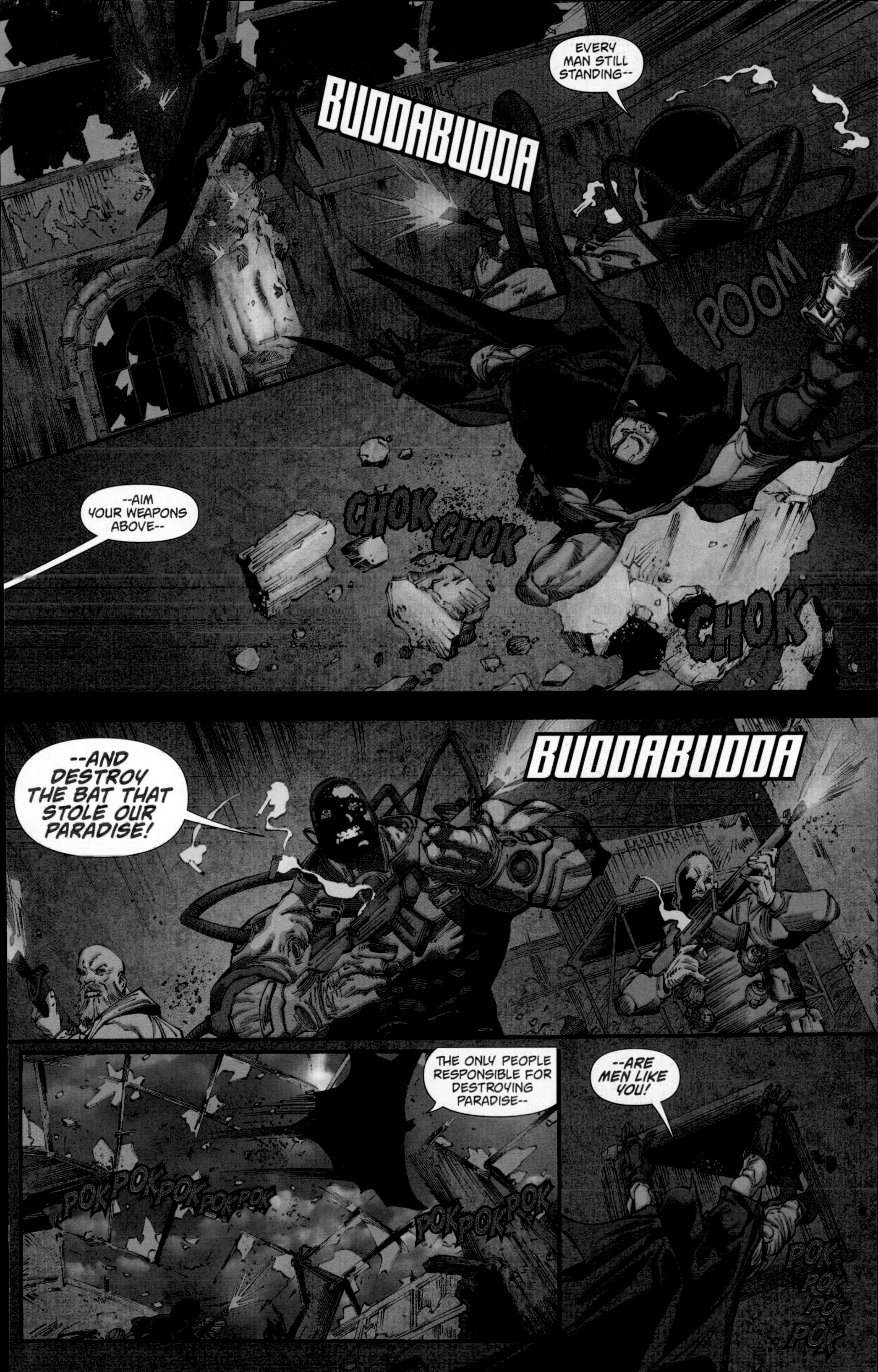
BUDDABUDDA
EVERY MAN STILL STANDING--
POOM
--AIM YOUR WEAPONS ABOVE--
CHOK CHOK
CHOK
BUDDABUDDA
--AND DESTROY THE BAT THAT STOLE OUR PARADISE!
THE ONLY PEOPLE RESPONSIBLE FOR DESTROYING PARADISE--
--ARE MEN LIKE YOU!
POKPOKPOKPOKPOK
POKPOKPOK
POK POK POK POK

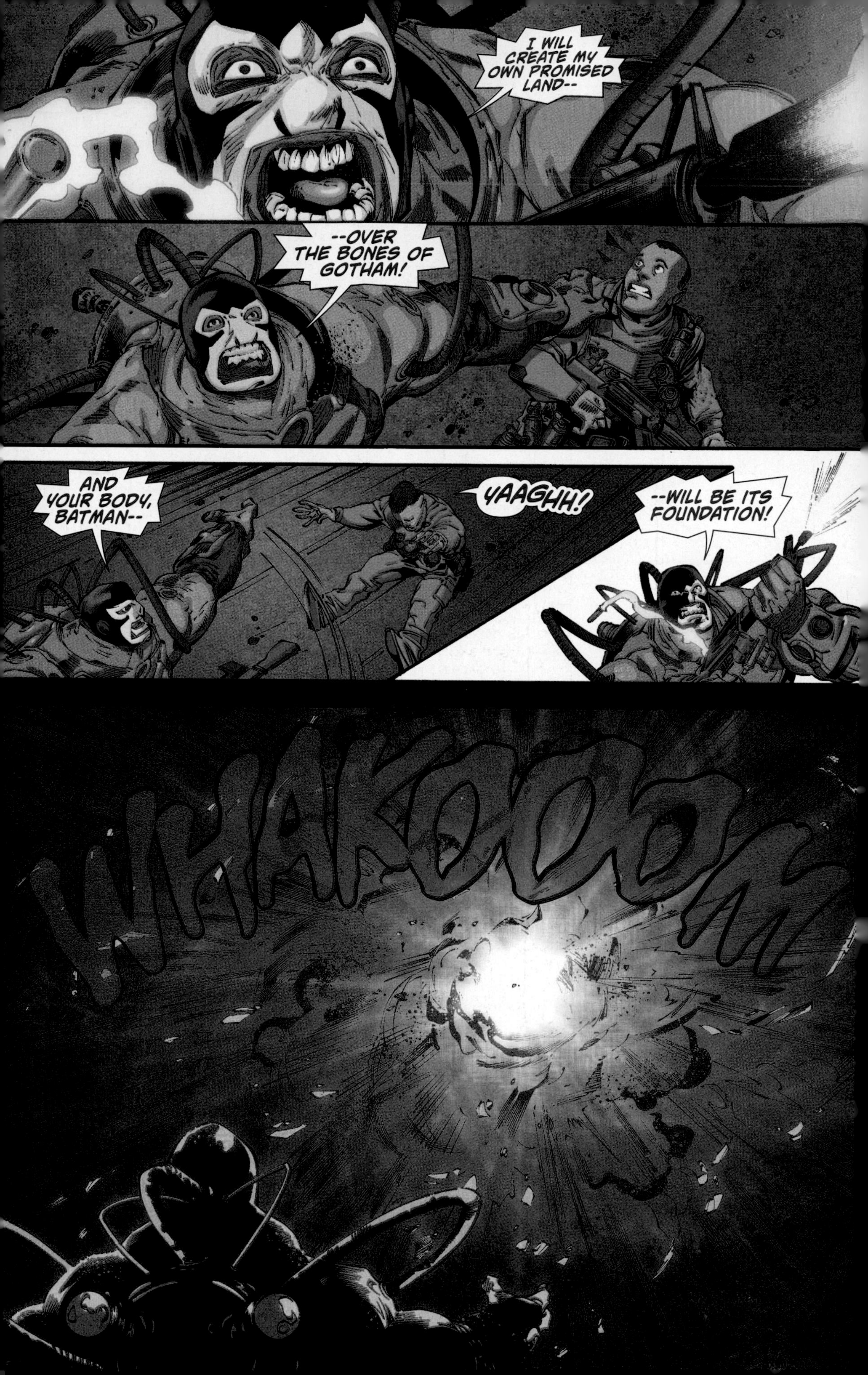
I WILL CREATE MY OWN PROMISED LAND--
--OVER THE BONES OF GOTHAM!
AND YOUR BODY, BATMAN--
YAAGHH!
--WILL BE ITS FOUNDATION!
WHAKOOOM

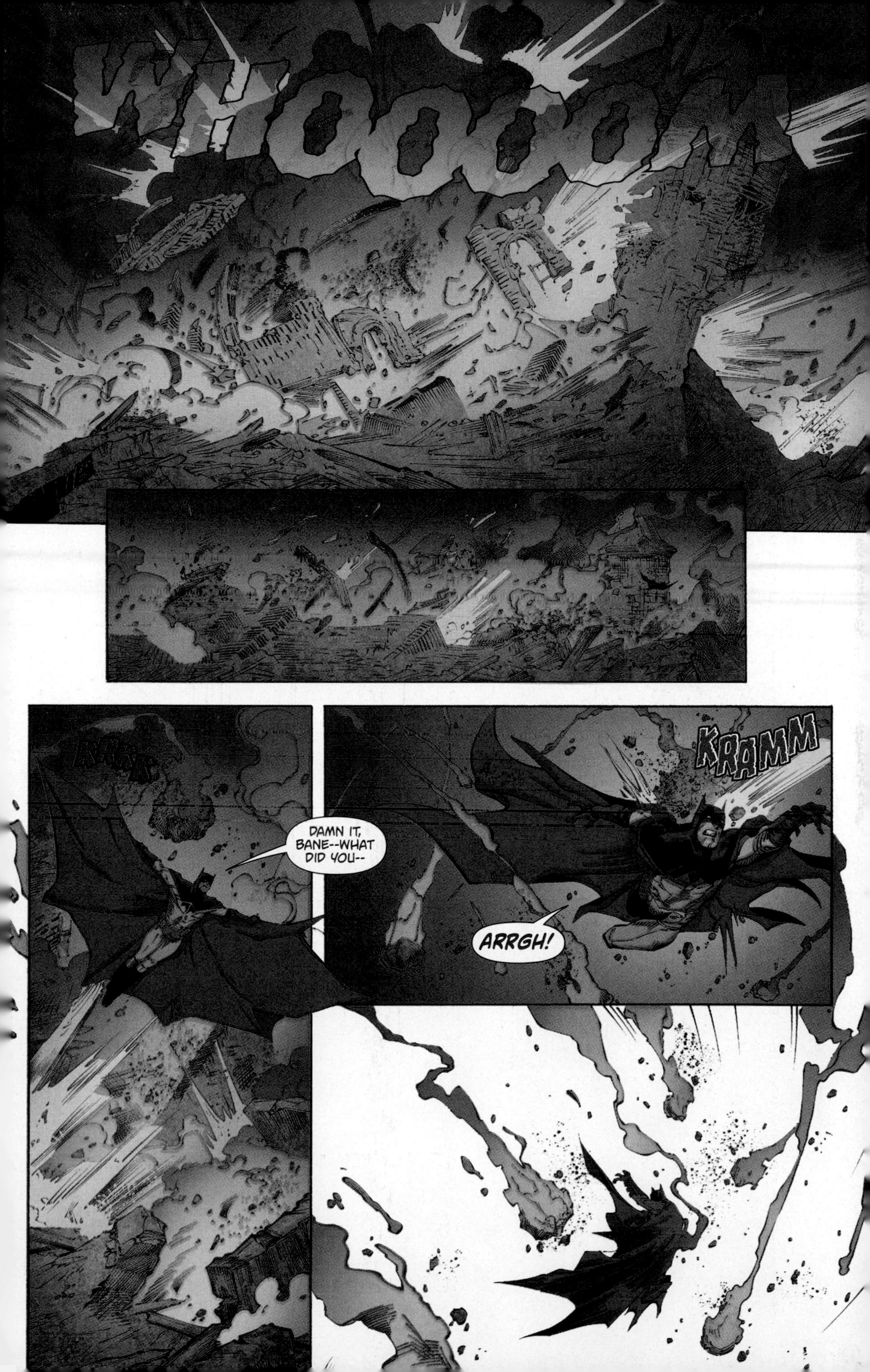
WHOOOOM
DAMN IT, BANE--WHAT DID YOU--
KRAMM
ARRGH!

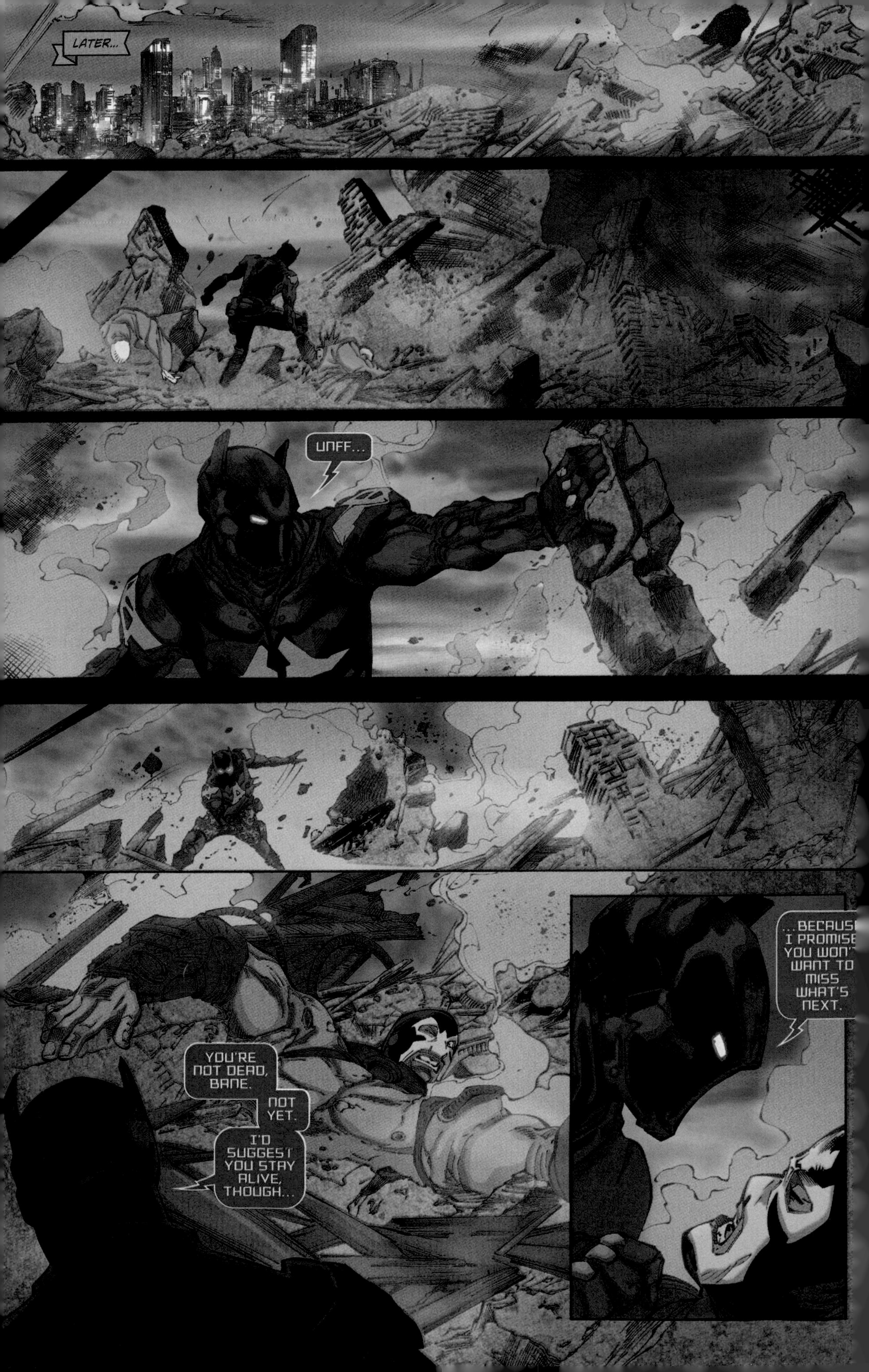
LATER...
UNFF...
YOU'RE NOT DEAD, BANE.
NOT YET.
I'D SUGGEST YOU STAY ALIVE, THOUGH...
...BECAUSE I PROMISE YOU WON'T WANT TO MISS WHAT'S NEXT.

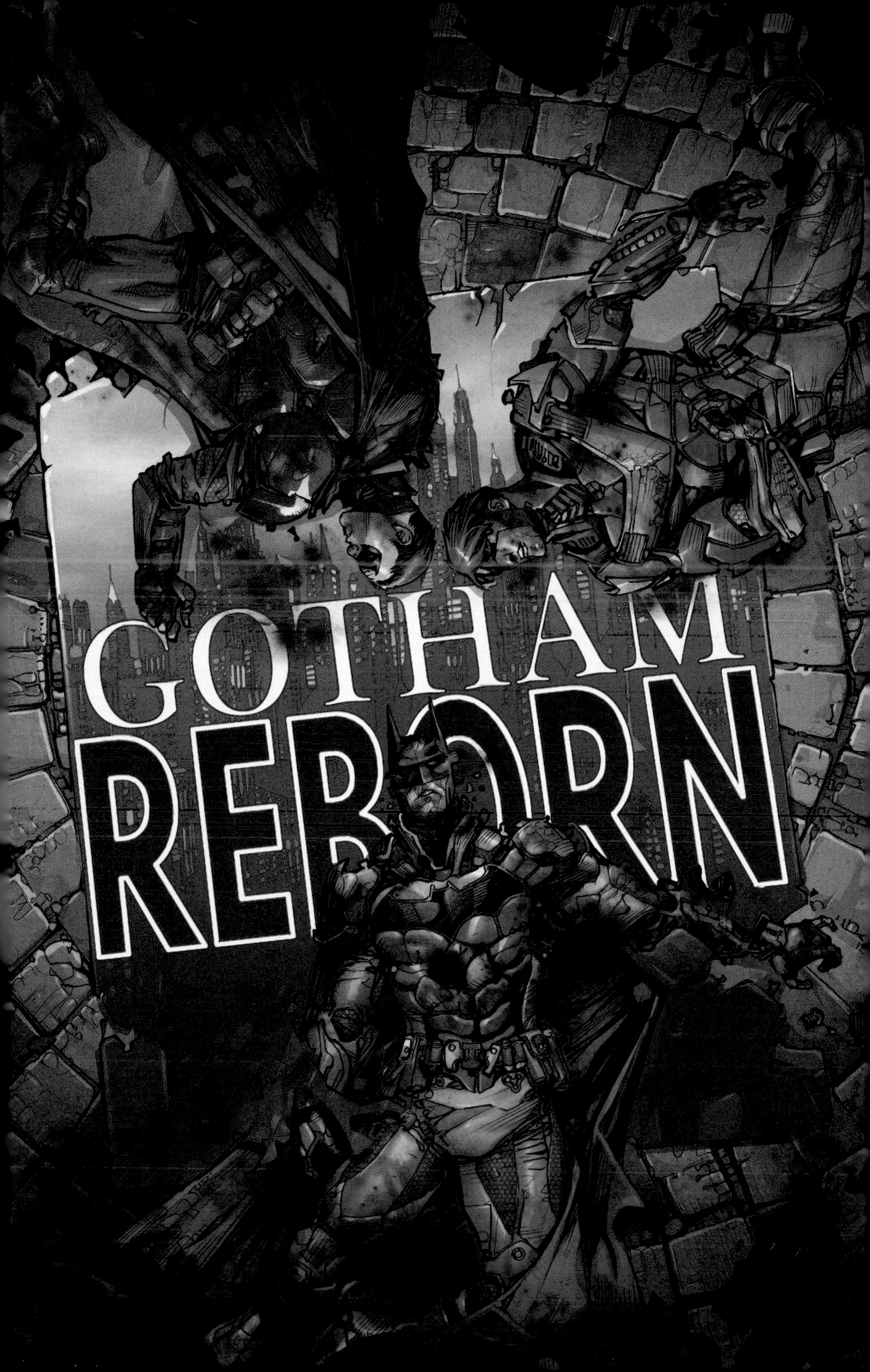
GOTHAM
REBORN

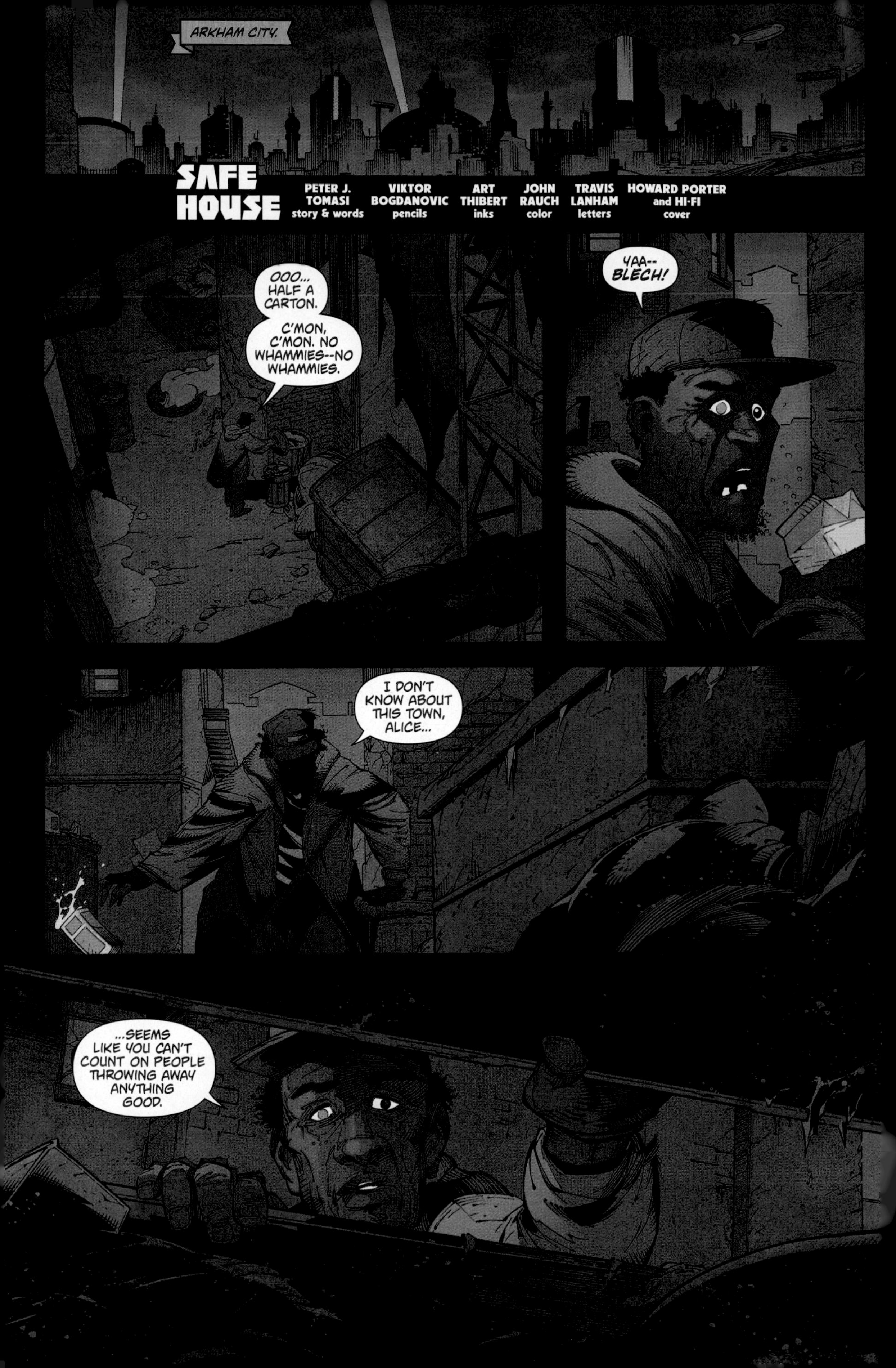
ARKHAM CITY.
SAFE HOUSE
PETER J. TOMASI story & words
VIKTOR BOGDANOVIC pencils
ART THIBERT inks
JOHN RAUCH color
TRAVIS LANHAM letters
HOWARD PORTER and HI-FI cover
OOO... HALF A CARTON.
C'MON, C'MON. NO WHAMMIES--NO WHAMMIES.
YAA-- BLECH!
I DON'T KNOW ABOUT THIS TOWN, ALICE...
...SEEMS LIKE YOU CAN'T COUNT ON PEOPLE THROWING AWAY ANYTHING GOOD.

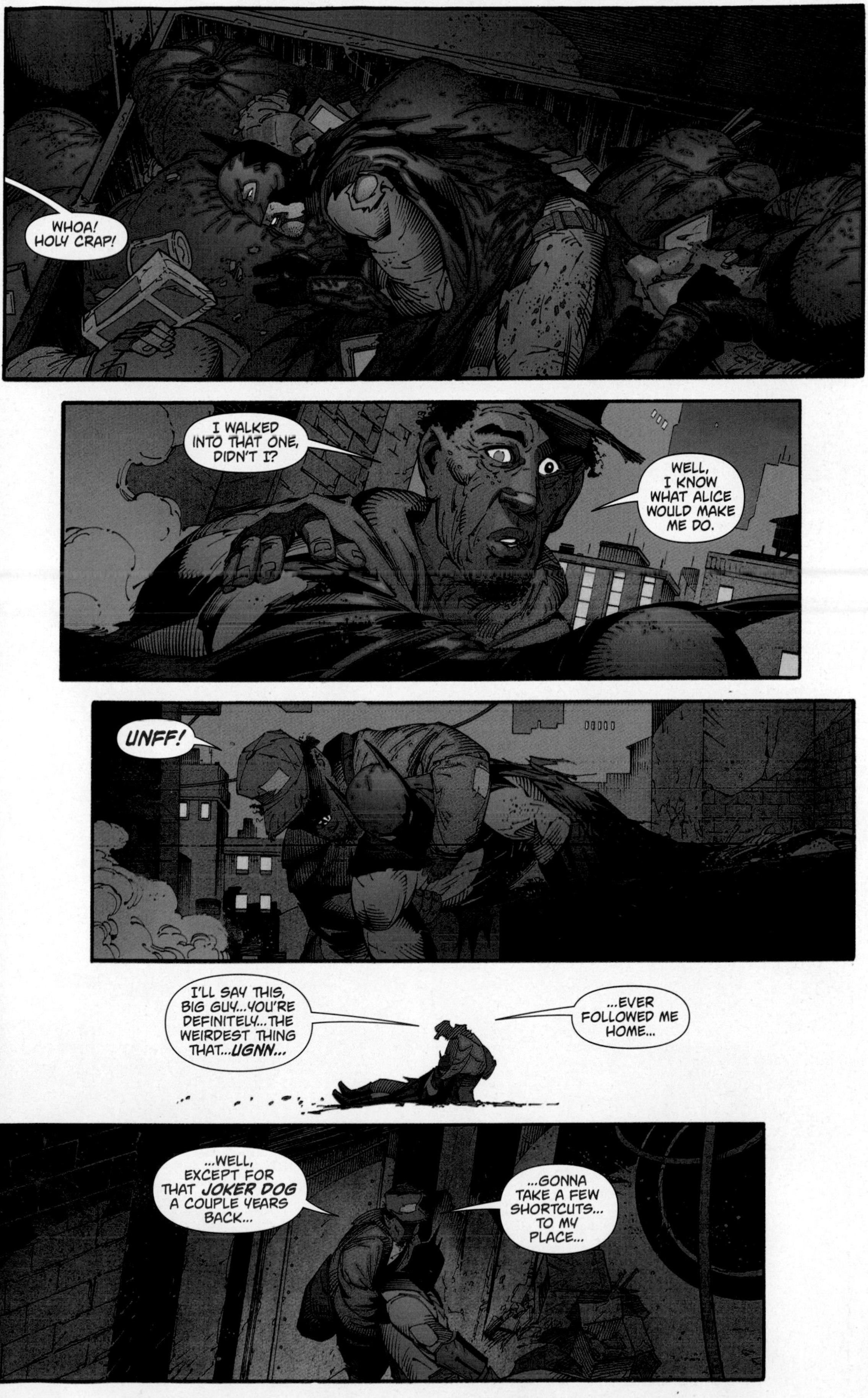
WHOA! HOLY CRAP!
I WALKED INTO THAT ONE, DIDN'T I?
WELL, I KNOW WHAT ALICE WOULD MAKE ME DO.
UNFF!
I'LL SAY THIS, BIG GUY...YOU'RE DEFINITELY...THE WEIRDEST THING THAT...UGNN...
...EVER FOLLOWED ME HOME...
...WELL, EXCEPT FOR THAT JOKER DOG A COUPLE YEARS BACK...
...GONNA TAKE A FEW SHORTCUTS... TO MY PLACE...

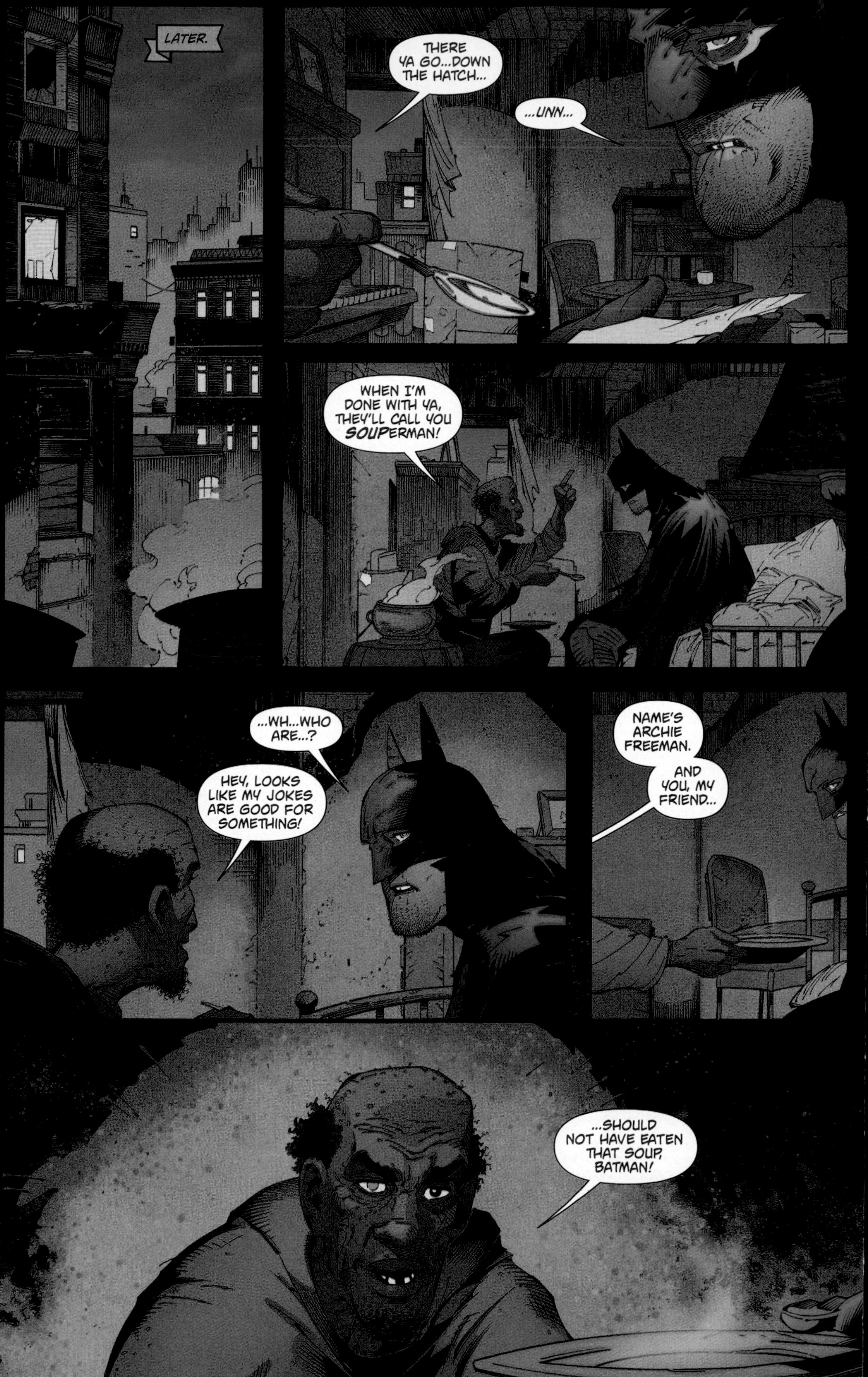
LATER.
THERE YA GO...DOWN THE HATCH...
...UNN...
WHEN I'M DONE WITH YA, THEY'LL CALL YOU SOUPERMAN!
...WH...WHO ARE...?
HEY, LOOKS LIKE MY JOKES ARE GOOD FOR SOMETHING!
NAME'S ARCHIE FREEMAN.
AND YOU, MY FRIEND...
...SHOULD NOT HAVE EATEN THAT SOUP, BATMAN!

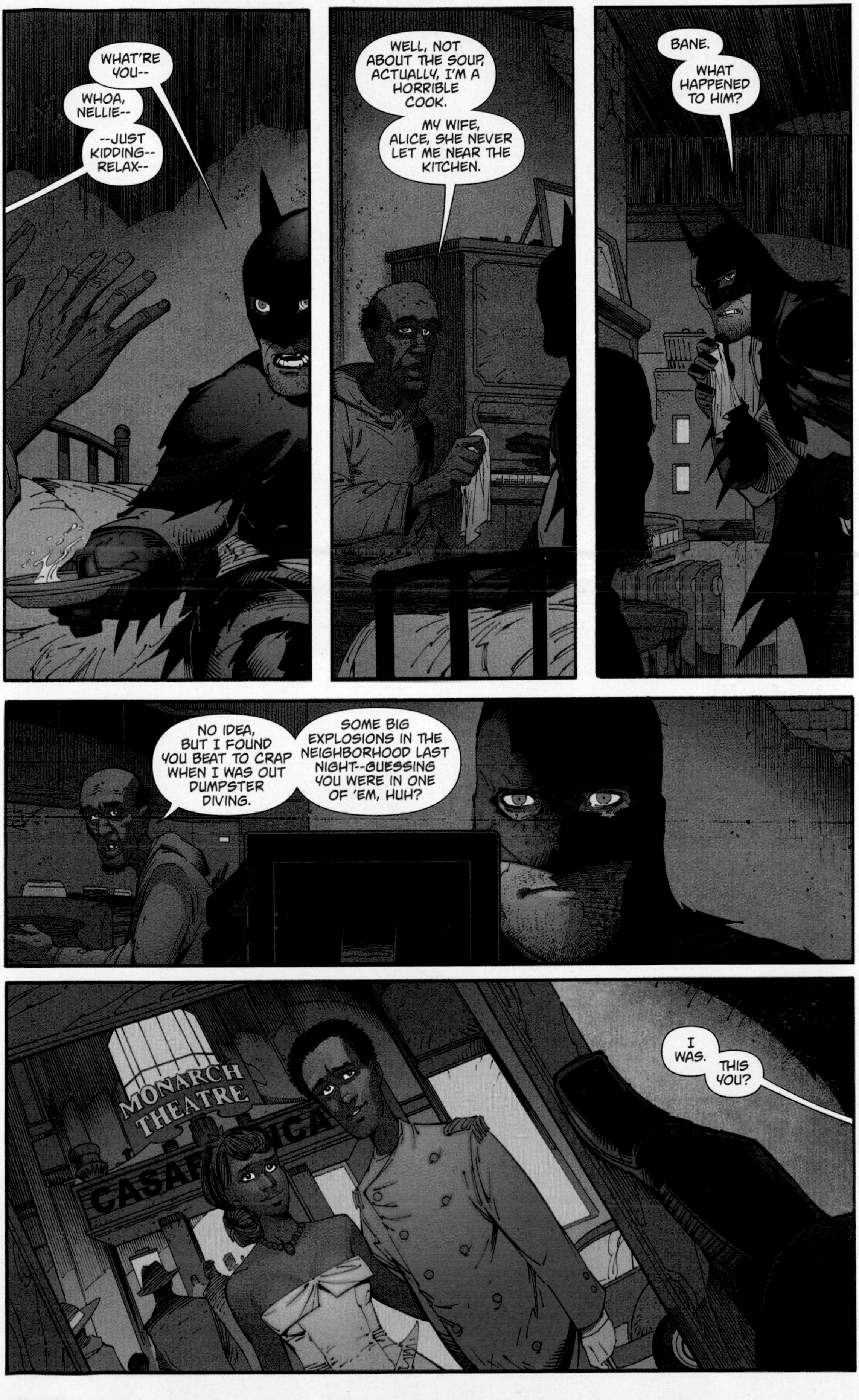
WHAT'RE YOU--
WHOA, NELLIE--
--JUST KIDDING--RELAX--
WELL, NOT ABOUT THE SOUP, ACTUALLY, I'M A HORRIBLE COOK.
MY WIFE, ALICE, SHE NEVER LET ME NEAR THE KITCHEN.
BANE.
WHAT HAPPENED TO HIM?
NO IDEA, BUT I FOUND YOU BEAT TO CRAP WHEN I WAS OUT DUMPSTER DIVING.
SOME BIG EXPLOSIONS IN THE NEIGHBORHOOD LAST NIGHT--GUESSING YOU WERE IN ONE OF 'EM, HUH?
I WAS.
THIS YOU?
MONARCH THEATRE

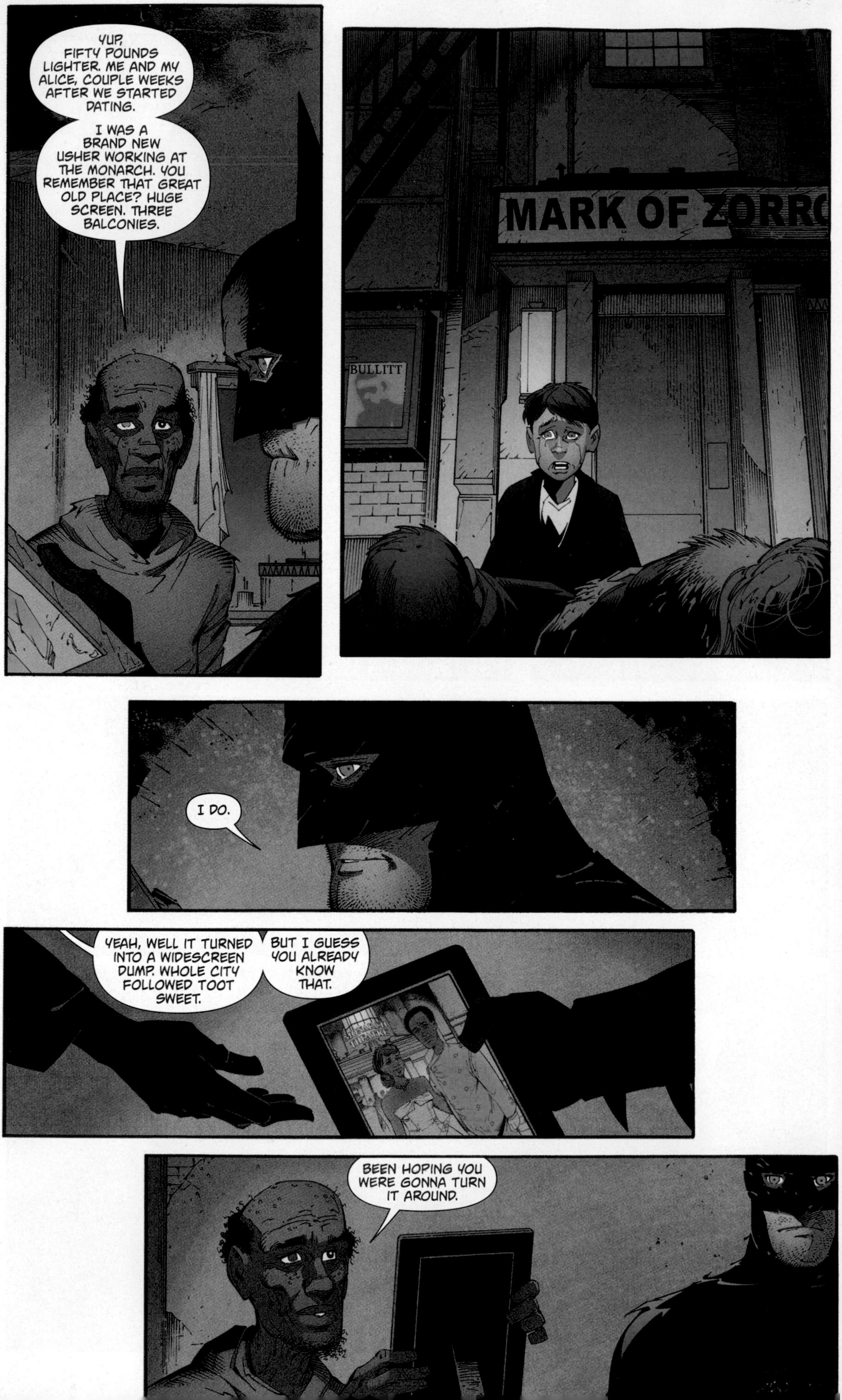
YUP, FIFTY POUNDS LIGHTER. ME AND MY ALICE, COUPLE WEEKS AFTER WE STARTED DATING.
I WAS A BRAND NEW USHER WORKING AT THE MONARCH. YOU REMEMBER THAT GREAT OLD PLACE? HUGE SCREEN. THREE BALCONIES.
MARK OF ZORRO
BULLITT
I DO.
YEAH, WELL IT TURNED INTO A WIDESCREEN DUMP. WHOLE CITY FOLLOWED TOOT SWEET.
BUT I GUESS YOU ALREADY KNOW THAT.
BEEN HOPING YOU WERE GONNA TURN IT AROUND.

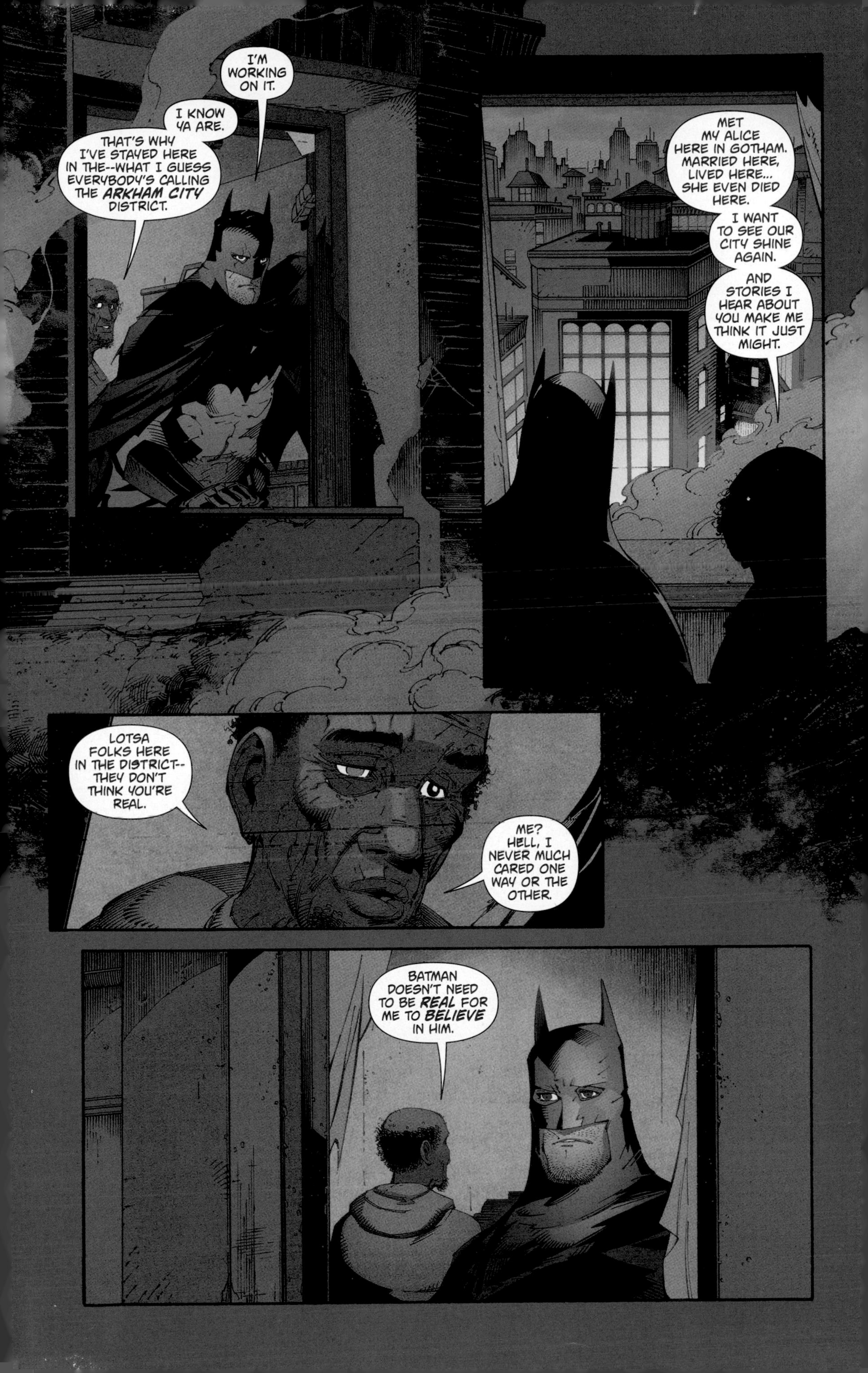
I'M WORKING ON IT.
I KNOW YA ARE.
THAT'S WHY I'VE STAYED HERE IN THE--WHAT I GUESS EVERYBODY'S CALLING THE ARKHAM CITY DISTRICT.
MET MY ALICE HERE IN GOTHAM. MARRIED HERE, LIVED HERE... SHE EVEN DIED HERE.
I WANT TO SEE OUR CITY SHINE AGAIN.
AND STORIES I HEAR ABOUT YOU MAKE ME THINK IT JUST MIGHT.
LOTSA FOLKS HERE IN THE DISTRICT--THEY DON'T THINK YOU'RE REAL.
ME? HELL, I NEVER MUCH CARED ONE WAY OR THE OTHER.
BATMAN DOESN'T NEED TO BE REAL FOR ME TO BELIEVE IN HIM.

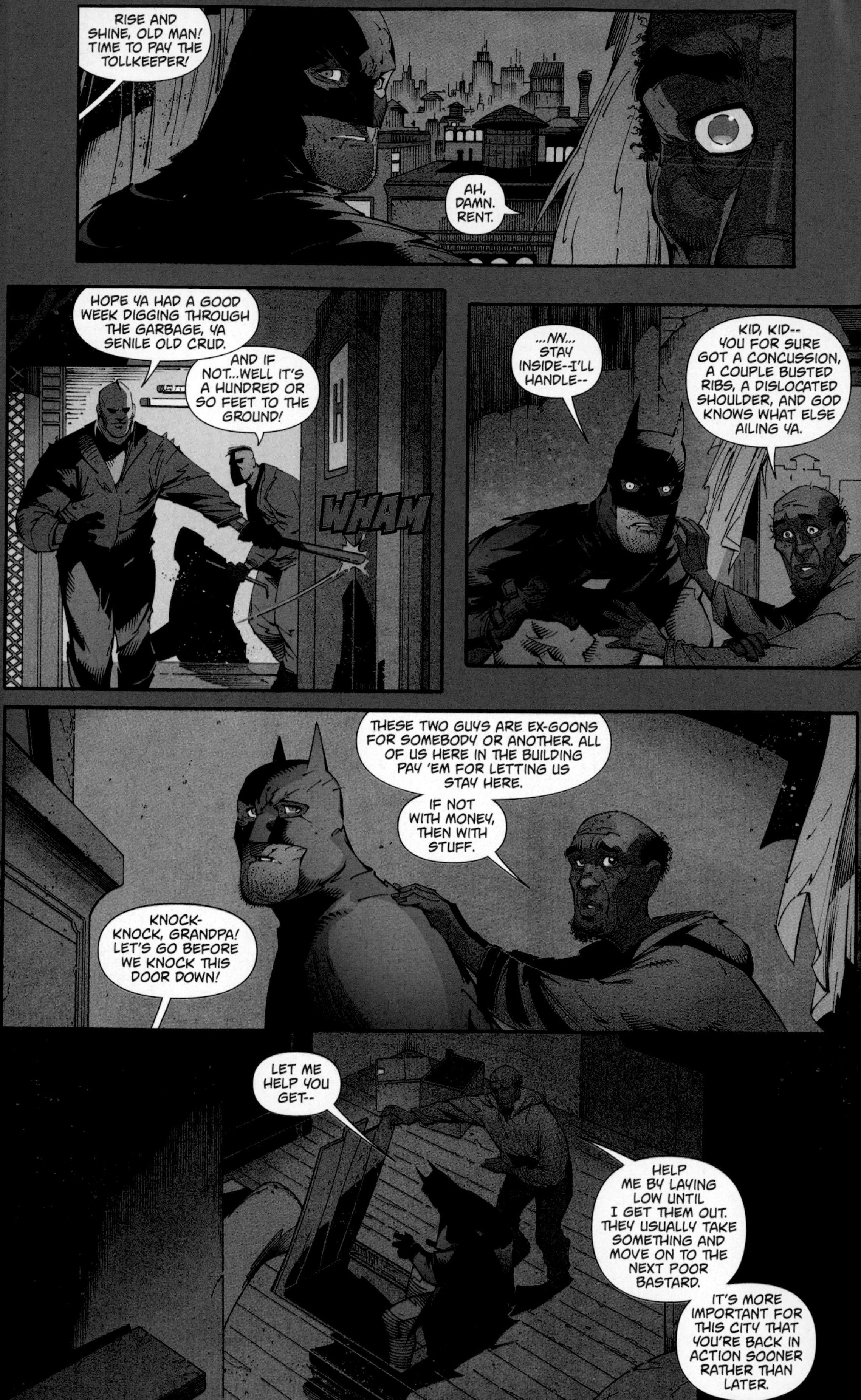
RISE AND SHINE, OLD MAN! TIME TO PAY THE TOLLKEEPER!
AH, DAMN. RENT.
HOPE YA HAD A GOOD WEEK DIGGING THROUGH THE GARBAGE, YA SENILE OLD CRUD.
AND IF NOT...WELL IT'S A HUNDRED OR SO FEET TO THE GROUND!
WHAM
...NN... STAY INSIDE--I'LL HANDLE--
KID, KID-- YOU FOR SURE GOT A CONCUSSION, A COUPLE BUSTED RIBS, A DISLOCATED SHOULDER, AND GOD KNOWS WHAT ELSE AILING YA.
THESE TWO GUYS ARE EX-GOONS FOR SOMEBODY OR ANOTHER. ALL OF US HERE IN THE BUILDING PAY 'EM FOR LETTING US STAY HERE.
IF NOT WITH MONEY, THEN WITH STUFF.
KNOCK-KNOCK, GRANDPA! LET'S GO BEFORE WE KNOCK THIS DOOR DOWN!
LET ME HELP YOU GET--
HELP ME BY LAYING LOW UNTIL I GET THEM OUT. THEY USUALLY TAKE SOMETHING AND MOVE ON TO THE NEXT POOR BASTARD.
IT'S MORE IMPORTANT FOR THIS CITY THAT YOU'RE BACK IN ACTION SOONER RATHER THAN LATER.

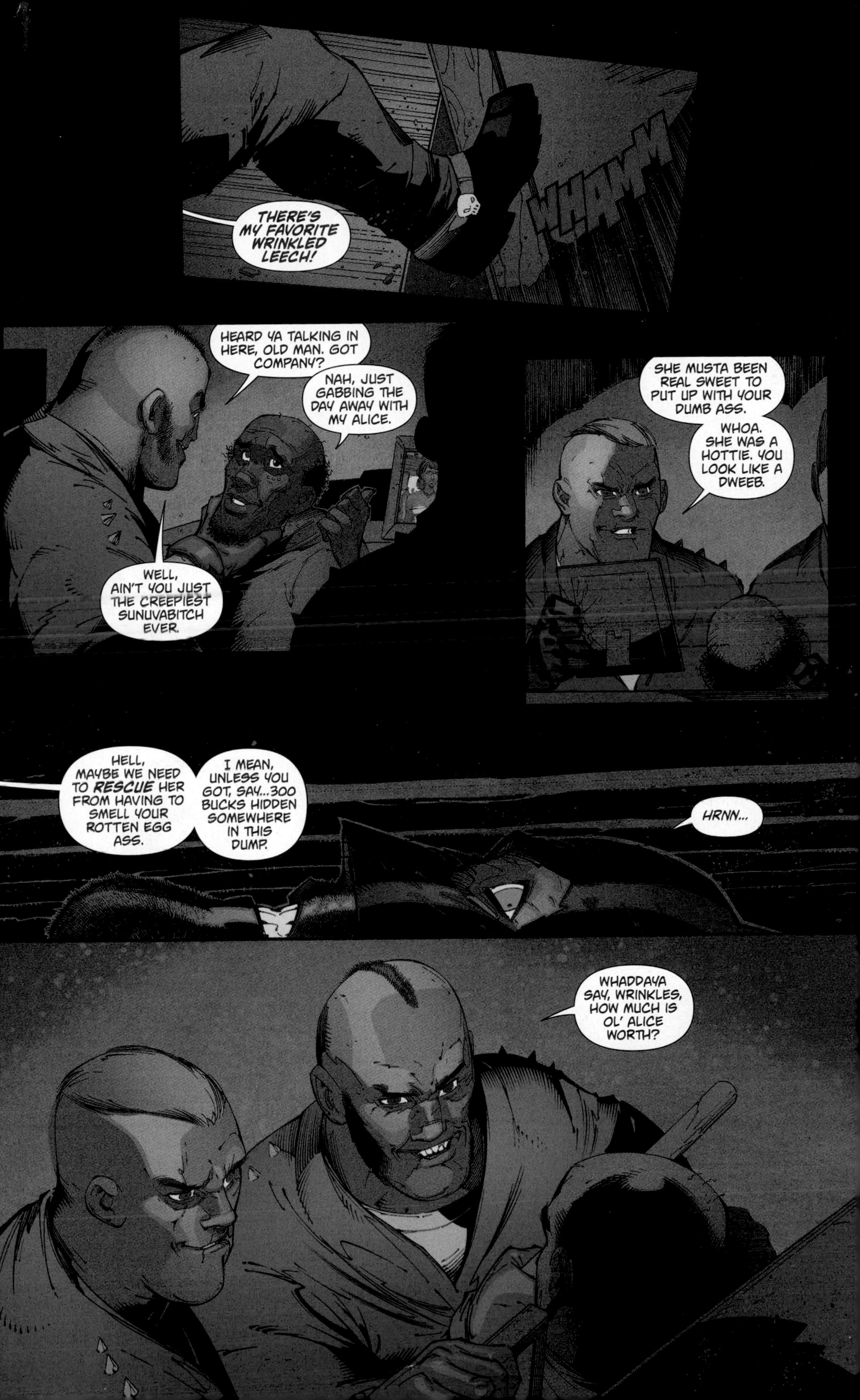
THERE'S MY FAVORITE WRINKLED LEECH!
WHAMM
HEARD YA TALKING IN HERE, OLD MAN. GOT COMPANY?
NAH, JUST GABBING THE DAY AWAY WITH MY ALICE.
WELL, AIN'T YOU JUST THE CREEPIEST SUNUVABITCH EVER.
SHE MUSTA BEEN REAL SWEET TO PUT UP WITH YOUR DUMB ASS.
WHOA. SHE WAS A HOTTIE. YOU LOOK LIKE A DWEEB.
HELL, MAYBE WE NEED TO RESCUE HER FROM HAVING TO SMELL YOUR ROTTEN EGG ASS.
I MEAN, UNLESS YOU GOT, SAY...300 BUCKS HIDDEN SOMEWHERE IN THIS DUMP.
HRNN...
WHADDAYA SAY, WRINKLES, HOW MUCH IS OL' ALICE WORTH?

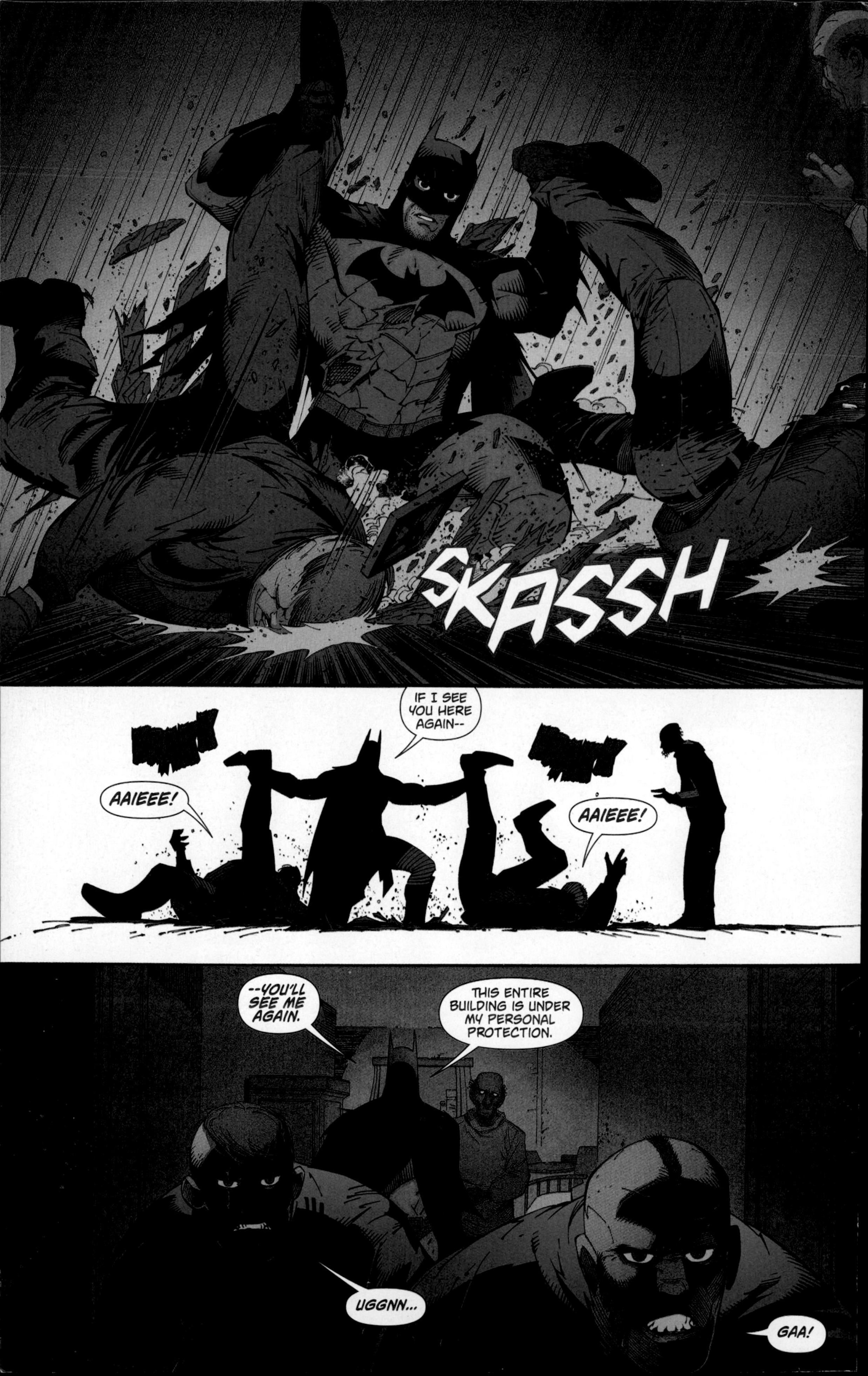
SKASSH
IF I SEE YOU HERE AGAIN--
AAIEEE!
AAIEEE!
--YOU'LL SEE ME AGAIN.
THIS ENTIRE BUILDING IS UNDER MY PERSONAL PROTECTION.
UGGNN...
GAA!

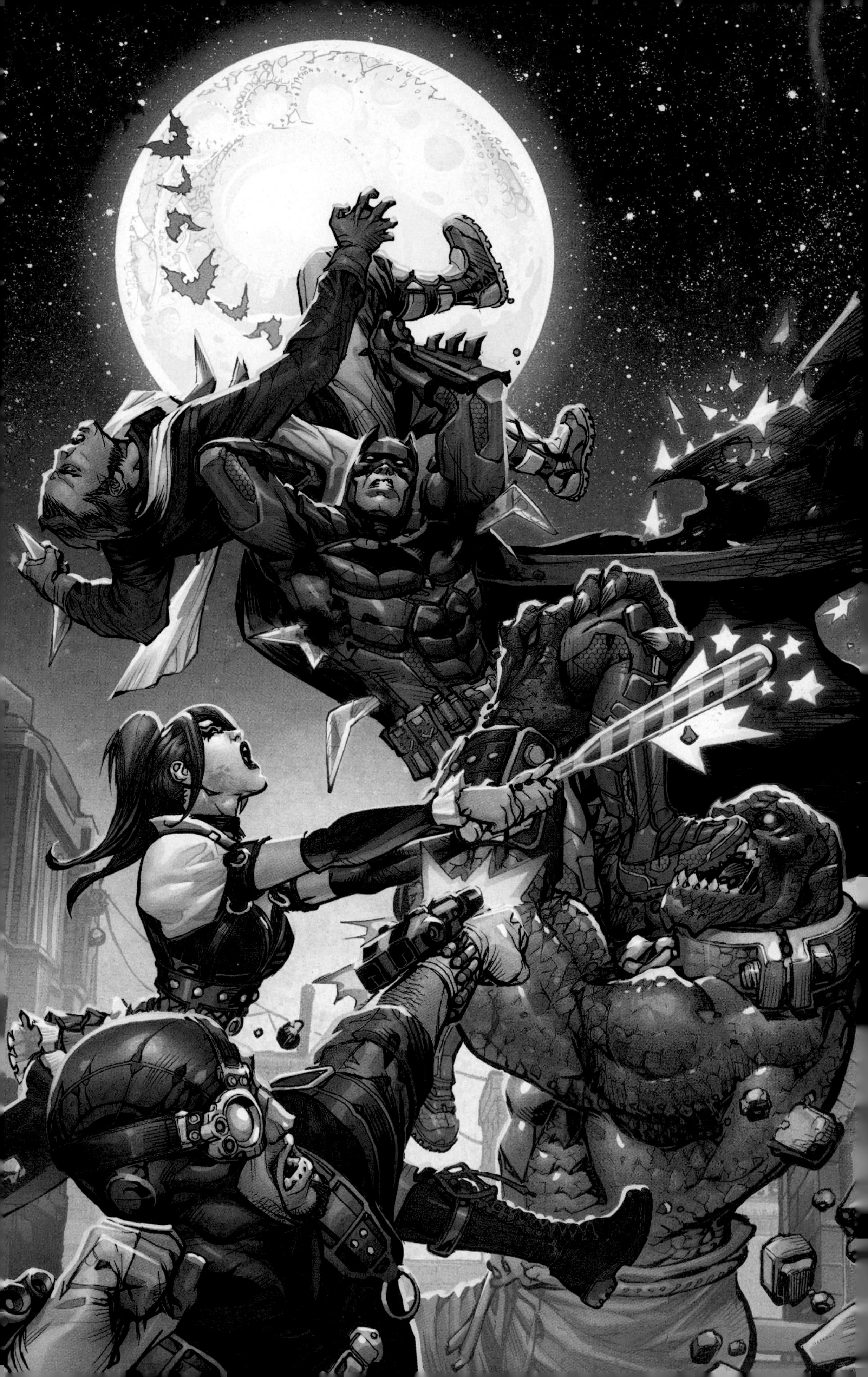

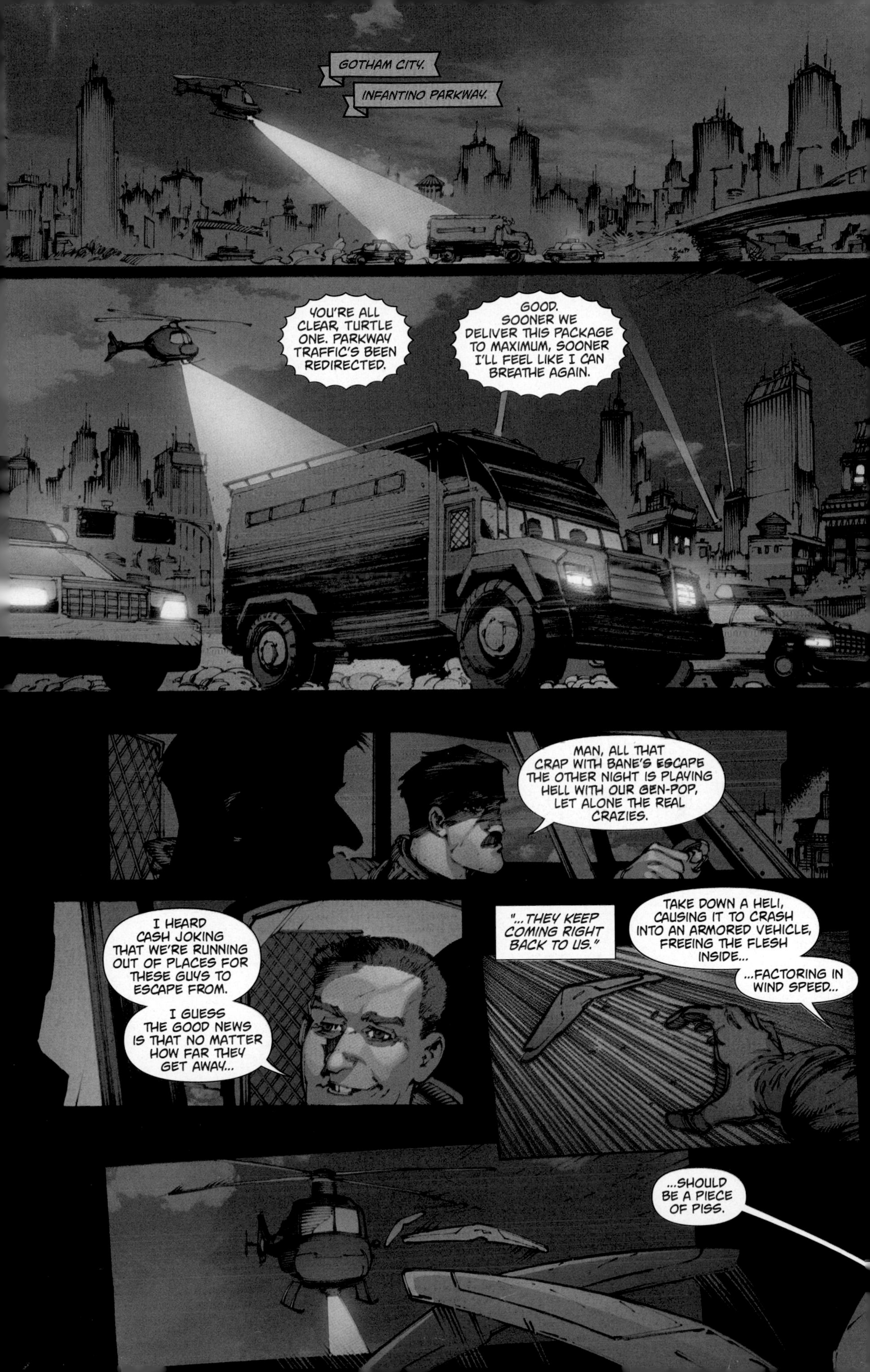

GOTHAM CITY.
INFANTINO PARKWAY.
YOU'RE ALL CLEAR, TURTLE ONE. PARKWAY TRAFFIC'S BEEN REDIRECTED.
GOOD. SOONER WE DELIVER THIS PACKAGE TO MAXIMUM, SOONER I'LL FEEL LIKE I CAN BREATHE AGAIN.
MAN, ALL THAT CRAP WITH BANE'S ESCAPE THE OTHER NIGHT IS PLAYING HELL WITH OUR GEN-POP, LET ALONE THE REAL CRAZIES.
I HEARD CASH JOKING THAT WE'RE RUNNING OUT OF PLACES FOR THESE GUYS TO ESCAPE FROM.
I GUESS THE GOOD NEWS IS THAT NO MATTER HOW FAR THEY GET AWAY...
"...THEY KEEP COMING RIGHT BACK TO US."
TAKE DOWN A HELI, CAUSING IT TO CRASH INTO AN ARMORED VEHICLE, FREEING THE FLESH INSIDE...
...FACTORING IN WIND SPEED...
...SHOULD BE A PIECE OF PISS.

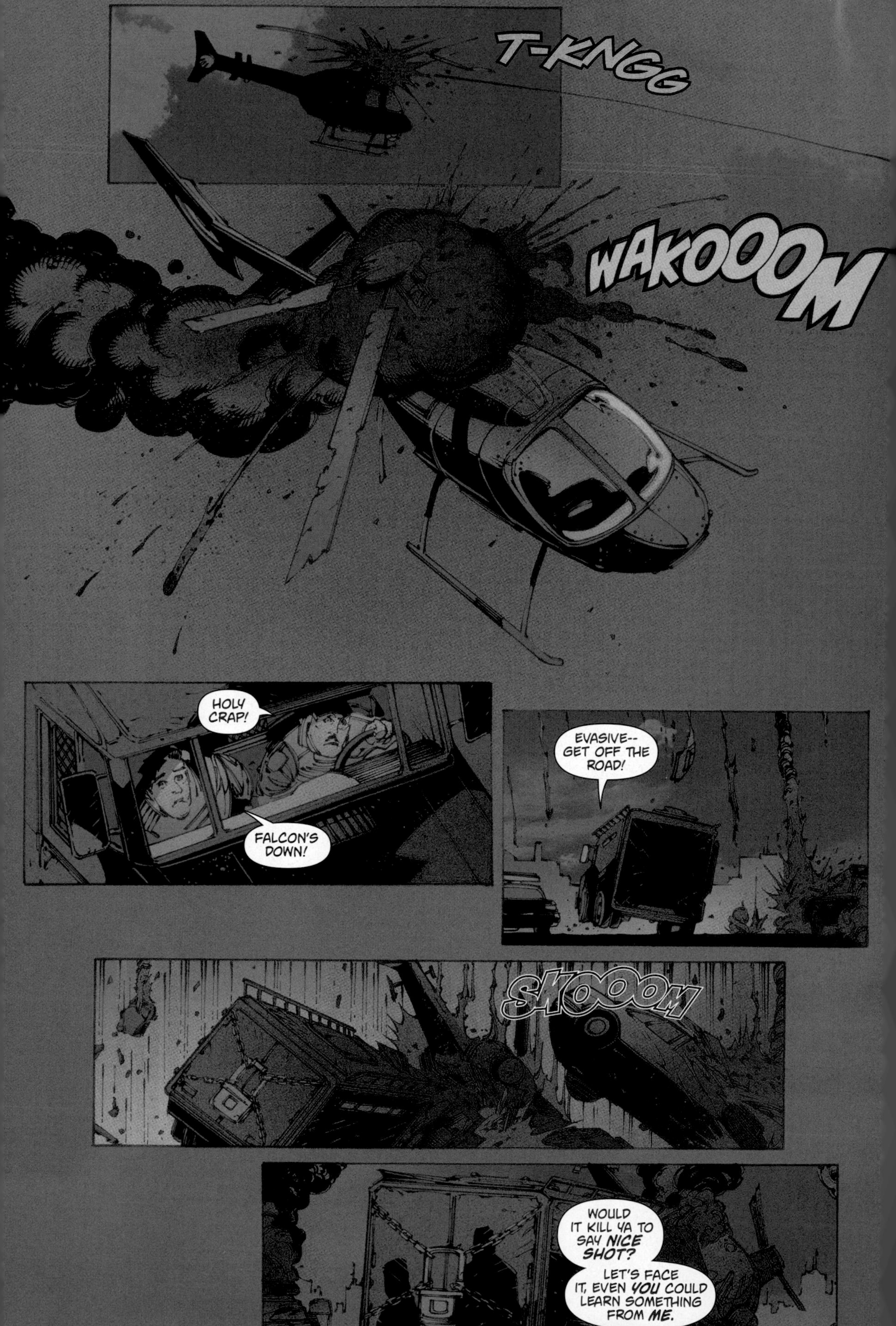
T-KNGG
WAKOOOM
HOLY CRAP!
FALCON'S DOWN!
EVASIVE-- GET OFF THE ROAD!
SKOOOM
WOULD IT KILL YA TO SAY NICE SHOT?
LET'S FACE IT, EVEN YOU COULD LEARN SOMETHING FROM ME.

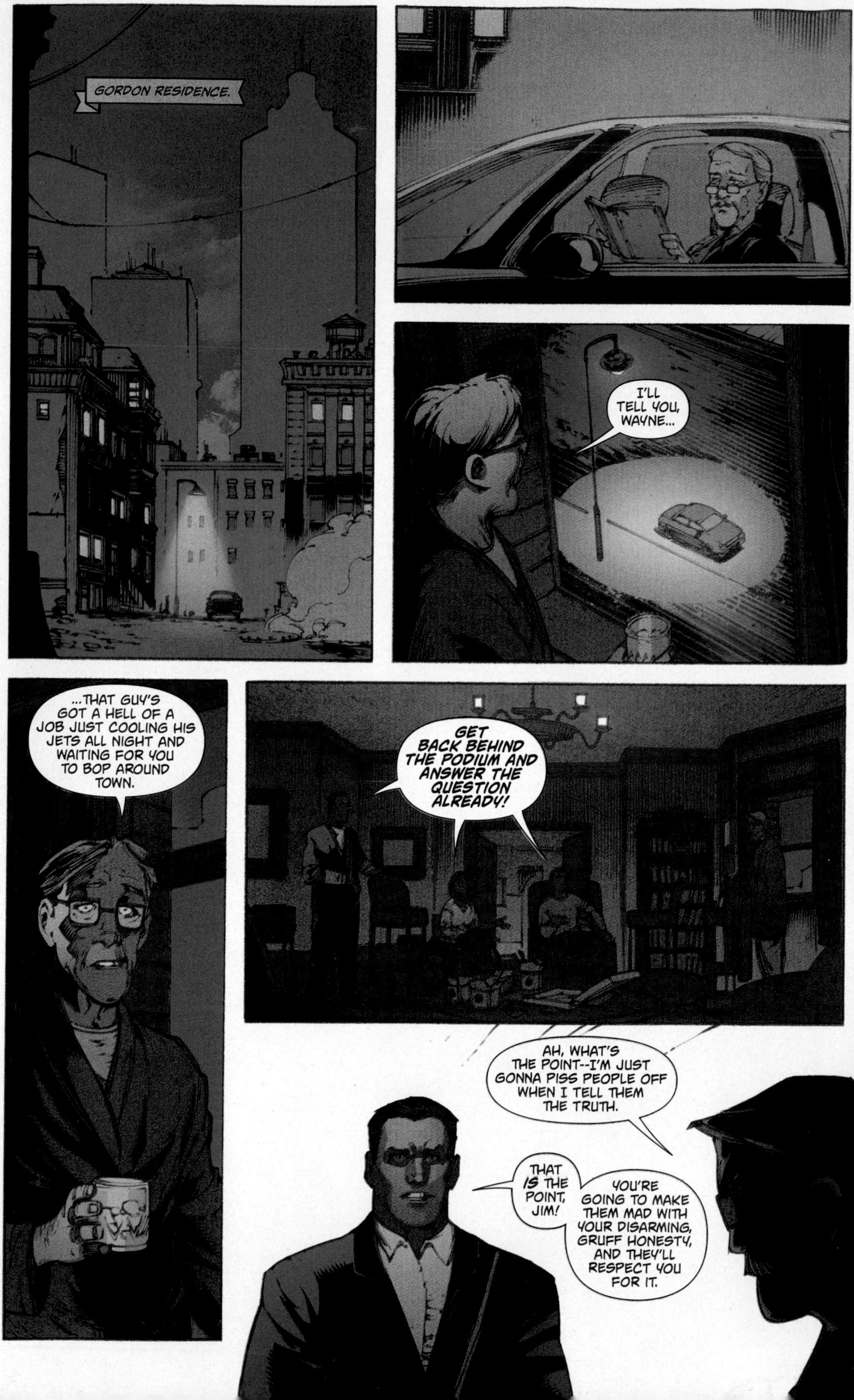
GORDON RESIDENCE.
I'LL TELL YOU, WAYNE...
...THAT GUY'S GOT A HELL OF A JOB JUST COOLING HIS JETS ALL NIGHT AND WAITING FOR YOU TO BOP AROUND TOWN.
GET BACK BEHIND THE PODIUM AND ANSWER THE QUESTION ALREADY!
AH, WHAT'S THE POINT--I'M JUST GONNA PISS PEOPLE OFF WHEN I TELL THEM THE TRUTH.
THAT IS THE POINT, JIM!
YOU'RE GOING TO MAKE THEM MAD WITH YOUR DISARMING, GRUFF HONESTY, AND THEY'LL RESPECT YOU FOR IT.

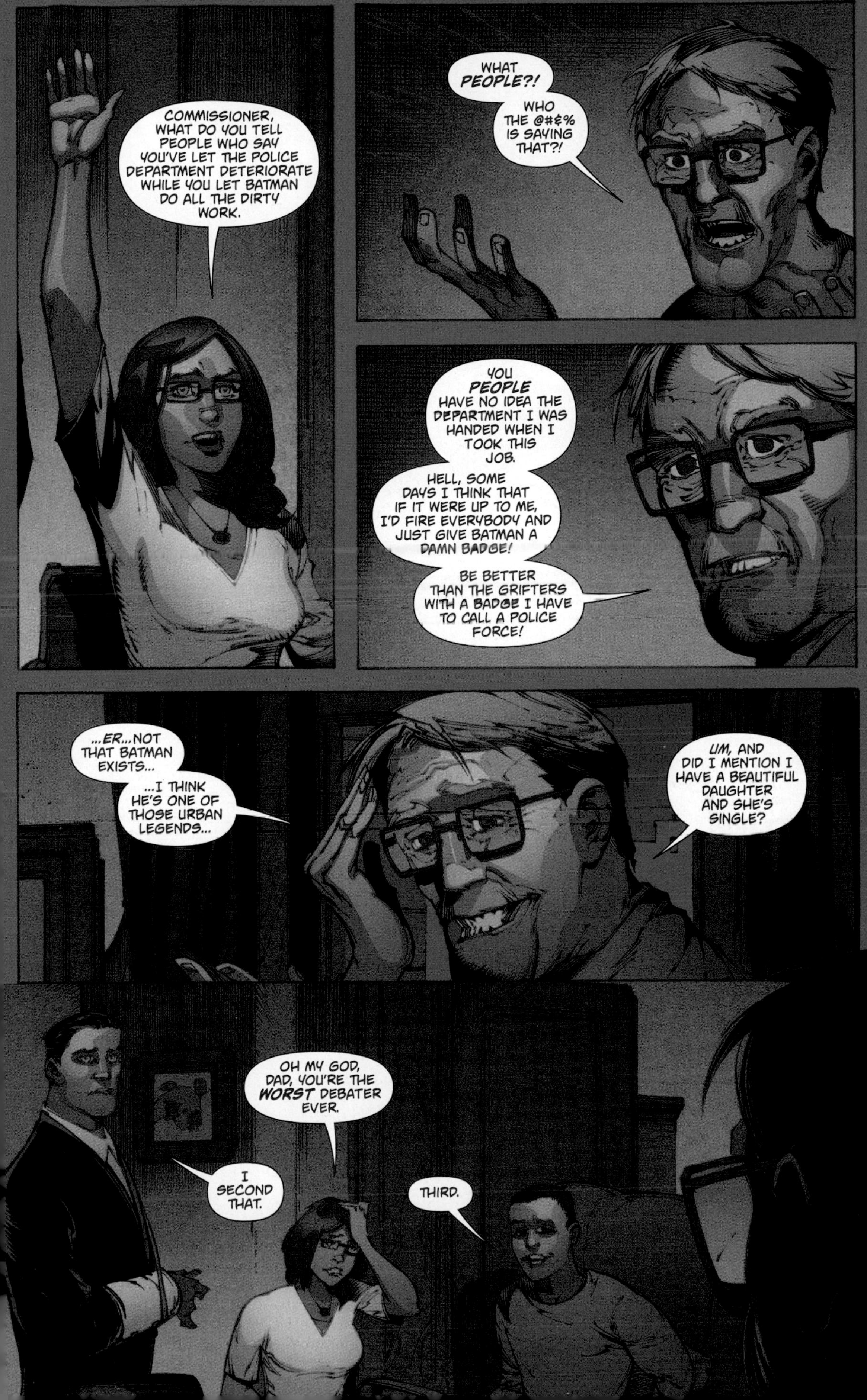
COMMISSIONER, WHAT DO YOU TELL PEOPLE WHO SAY YOU'VE LET THE POLICE DEPARTMENT DETERIORATE WHILE YOU LET BATMAN DO ALL THE DIRTY WORK.
WHAT PEOPLE?!
WHO THE @#&% IS SAYING THAT?!
YOU PEOPLE HAVE NO IDEA THE DEPARTMENT I WAS HANDED WHEN I TOOK THIS JOB.
HELL, SOME DAYS I THINK THAT IF IT WERE UP TO ME, I'D FIRE EVERYBODY AND JUST GIVE BATMAN A DAMN BADGE!
BE BETTER THAN THE GRIFTERS WITH A BADGE I HAVE TO CALL A POLICE FORCE!
...ER...NOT THAT BATMAN EXISTS...
...I THINK HE'S ONE OF THOSE URBAN LEGENDS...
UM, AND DID I MENTION I HAVE A BEAUTIFUL DAUGHTER AND SHE'S SINGLE?
OH MY GOD, DAD, YOU'RE THE WORST DEBATER EVER.
I SECOND THAT.
THIRD.

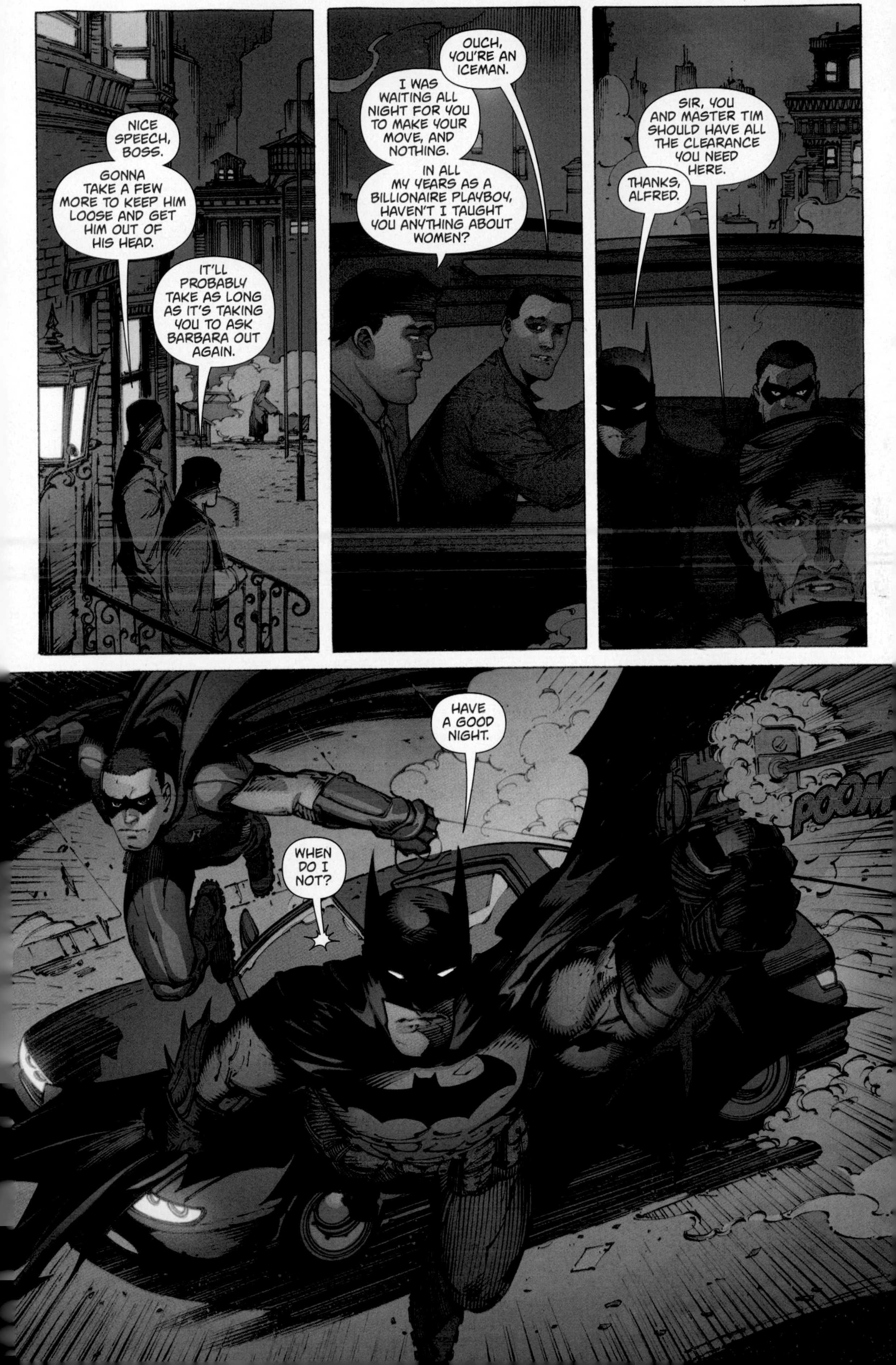
NICE SPEECH, BOSS.
GONNA TAKE A FEW MORE TO KEEP HIM LOOSE AND GET HIM OUT OF HIS HEAD.
IT'LL PROBABLY TAKE AS LONG AS IT'S TAKING YOU TO ASK BARBARA OUT AGAIN.
I WAS WAITING ALL NIGHT FOR YOU TO MAKE YOUR MOVE, AND NOTHING.
OUCH, YOU'RE AN ICEMAN.
IN ALL MY YEARS AS A BILLIONAIRE PLAYBOY, HAVEN'T I TAUGHT YOU ANYTHING ABOUT WOMEN?
SIR, YOU AND MASTER TIM SHOULD HAVE ALL THE CLEARANCE YOU NEED HERE.
THANKS, ALFRED.
HAVE A GOOD NIGHT.
WHEN DO I NOT?
POOM

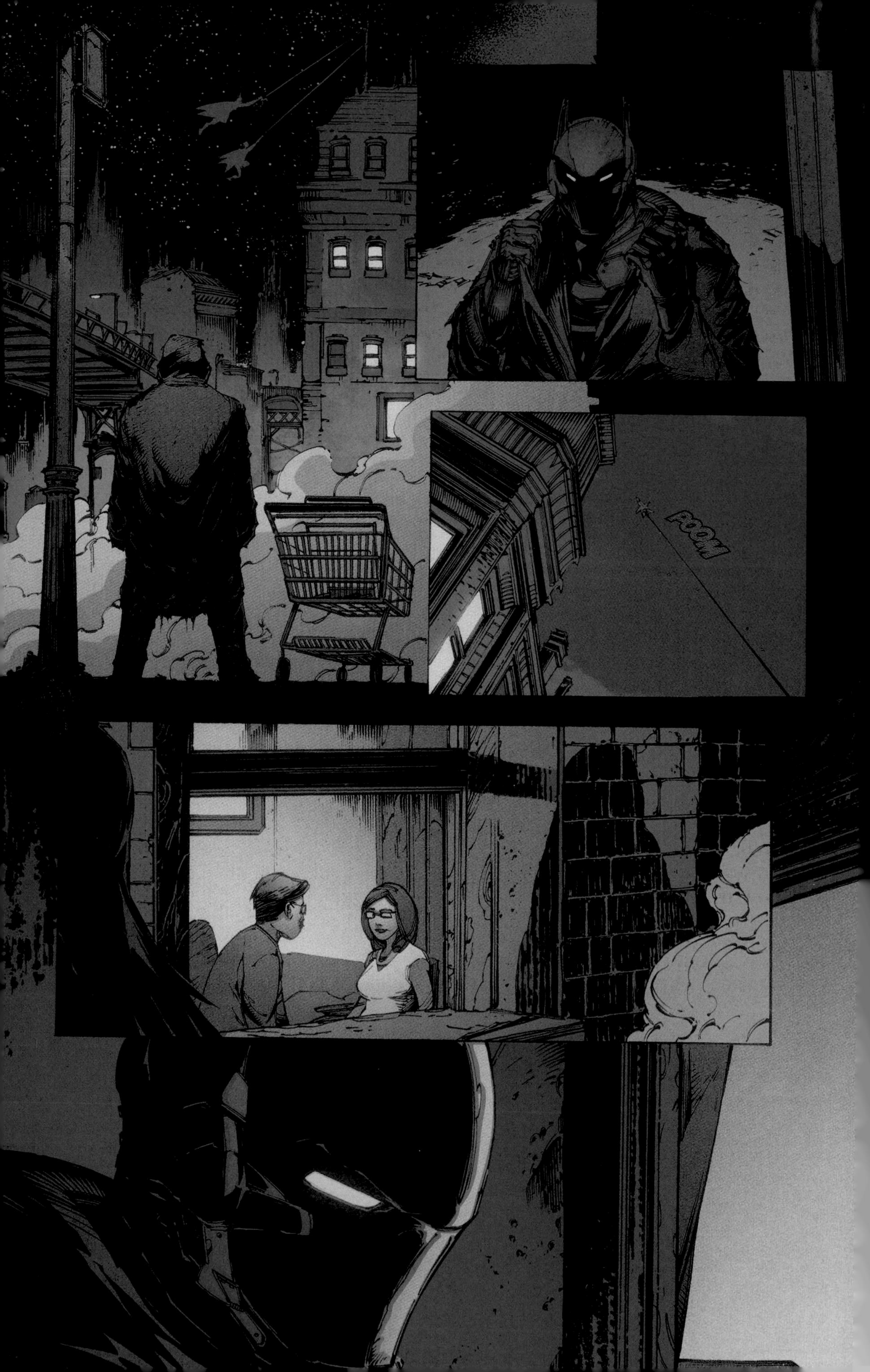
POOM

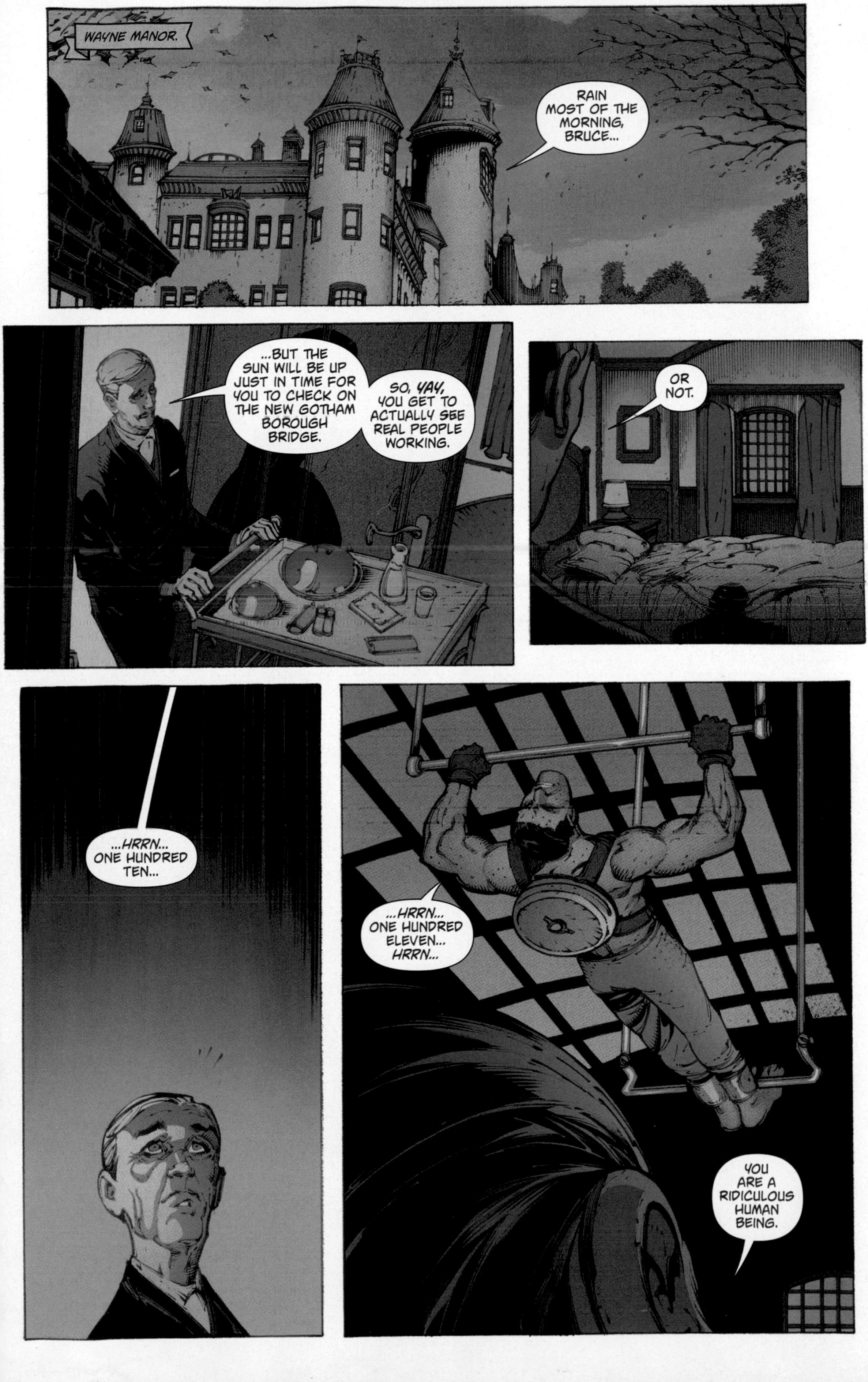
WAYNE MANOR.
RAIN MOST OF THE MORNING, BRUCE...
...BUT THE SUN WILL BE UP JUST IN TIME FOR YOU TO CHECK ON THE NEW GOTHAM BOROUGH BRIDGE.
SO, YAY, YOU GET TO ACTUALLY SEE REAL PEOPLE WORKING.
OR NOT.
...HRRN... ONE HUNDRED TEN...
...HRRN... ONE HUNDRED ELEVEN... HRRN...
YOU ARE A RIDICULOUS HUMAN BEING.

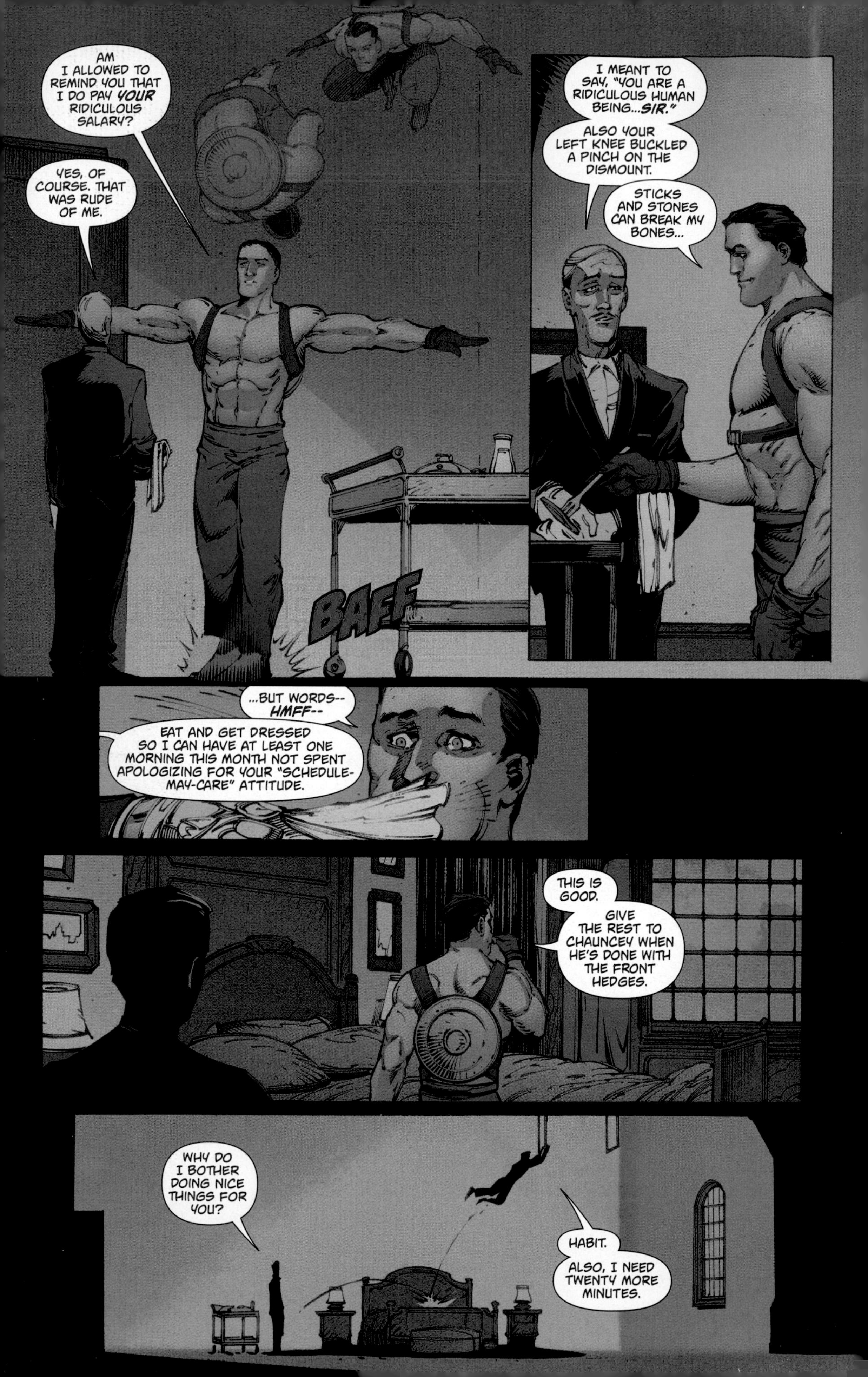

AM I ALLOWED TO REMIND YOU THAT I DO PAY YOUR RIDICULOUS SALARY?
YES, OF COURSE. THAT WAS RUDE OF ME.
BAFF
I MEANT TO SAY, "YOU ARE A RIDICULOUS HUMAN BEING...SIR."
ALSO YOUR LEFT KNEE BUCKLED A PINCH ON THE DISMOUNT.
STICKS AND STONES CAN BREAK MY BONES...
...BUT WORDS-- HMFF--
EAT AND GET DRESSED SO I CAN HAVE AT LEAST ONE MORNING THIS MONTH NOT SPENT APOLOGIZING FOR YOUR "SCHEDULE-MAY-CARE" ATTITUDE.
THIS IS GOOD.
GIVE THE REST TO CHAUNCEY WHEN HE'S DONE WITH THE FRONT HEDGES.
WHY DO I BOTHER DOING NICE THINGS FOR YOU?
HABIT.
ALSO, I NEED TWENTY MORE MINUTES.

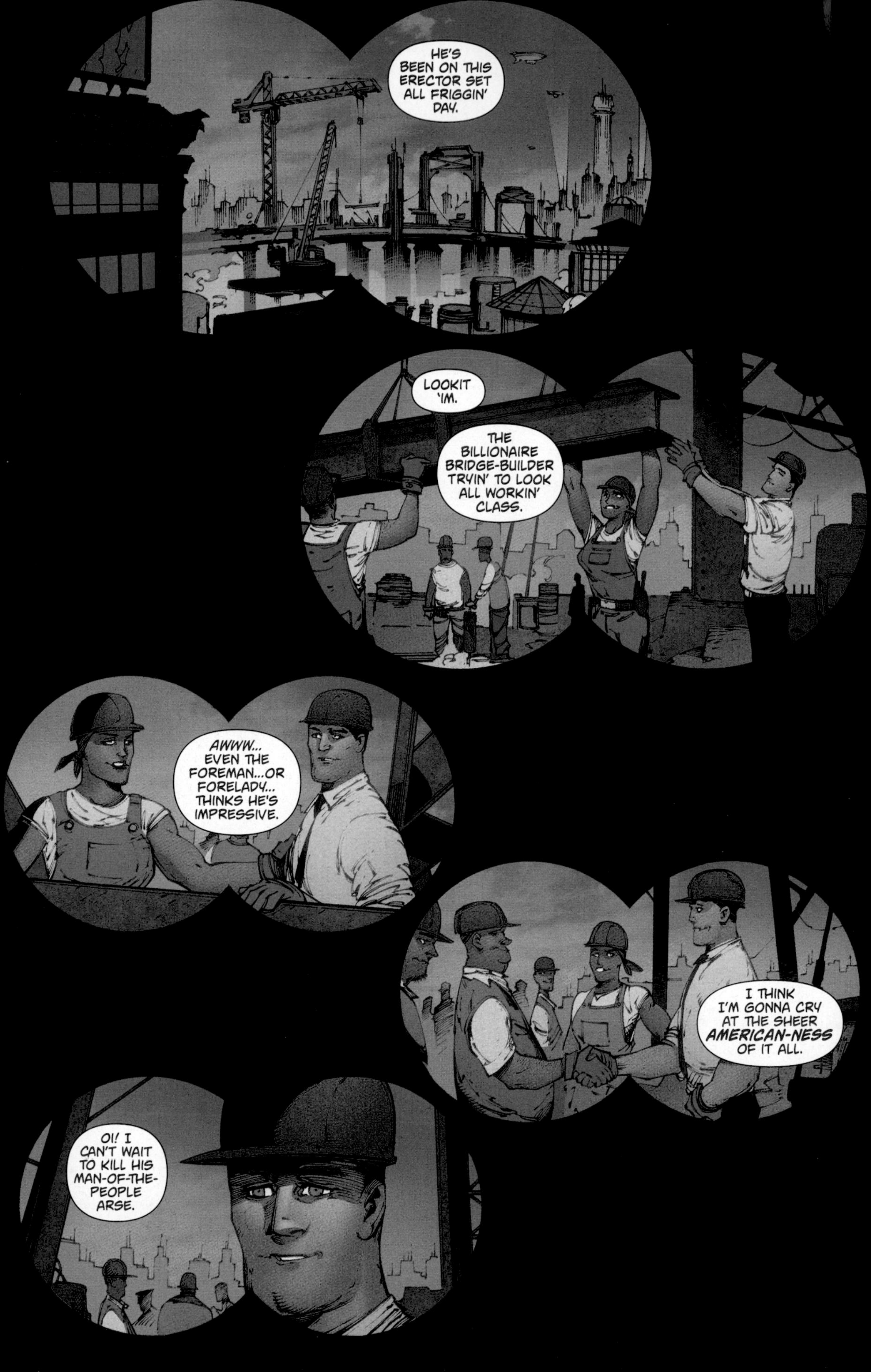
HE'S BEEN ON THIS ERECTOR SET ALL FRIGGIN' DAY.
LOOKIT 'IM.
THE BILLIONAIRE BRIDGE-BUILDER TRYIN' TO LOOK ALL WORKIN' CLASS.
AWWW... EVEN THE FOREMAN...OR FORELADY... THINKS HE'S IMPRESSIVE.
I THINK I'M GONNA CRY AT THE SHEER AMERICAN-NESS OF IT ALL.
OI! I CAN'T WAIT TO KILL HIS MAN-OF-THE-PEOPLE ARSE.

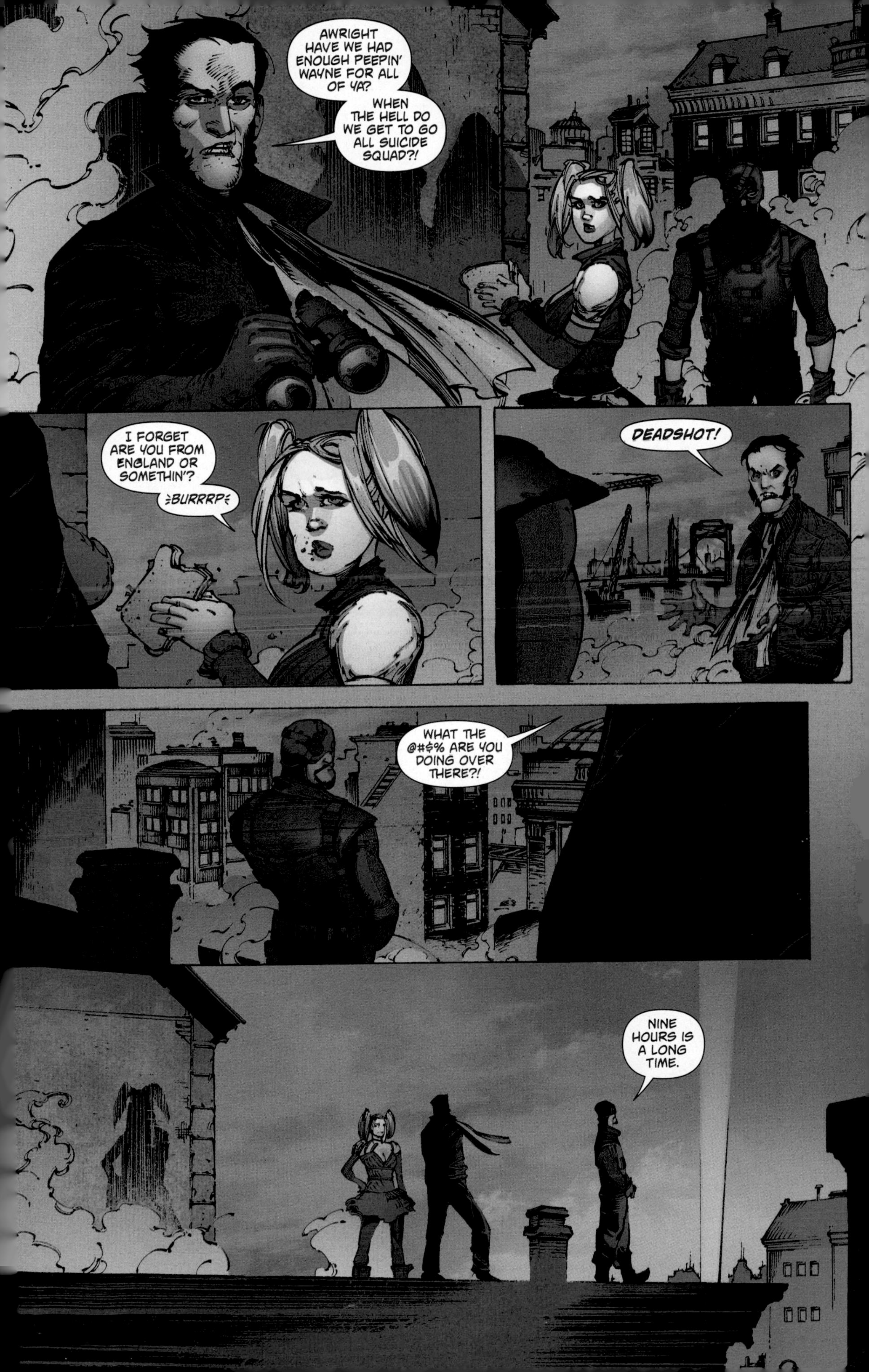
AWRIGHT HAVE WE HAD ENOUGH PEEPIN' WAYNE FOR ALL OF YA?
WHEN THE HELL DO WE GET TO GO ALL SUICIDE SQUAD?!
I FORGET ARE YOU FROM ENGLAND OR SOMETHIN'?
BURRRP
DEADSHOT!
WHAT THE @#$% ARE YOU DOING OVER THERE?!
NINE HOURS IS A LONG TIME.

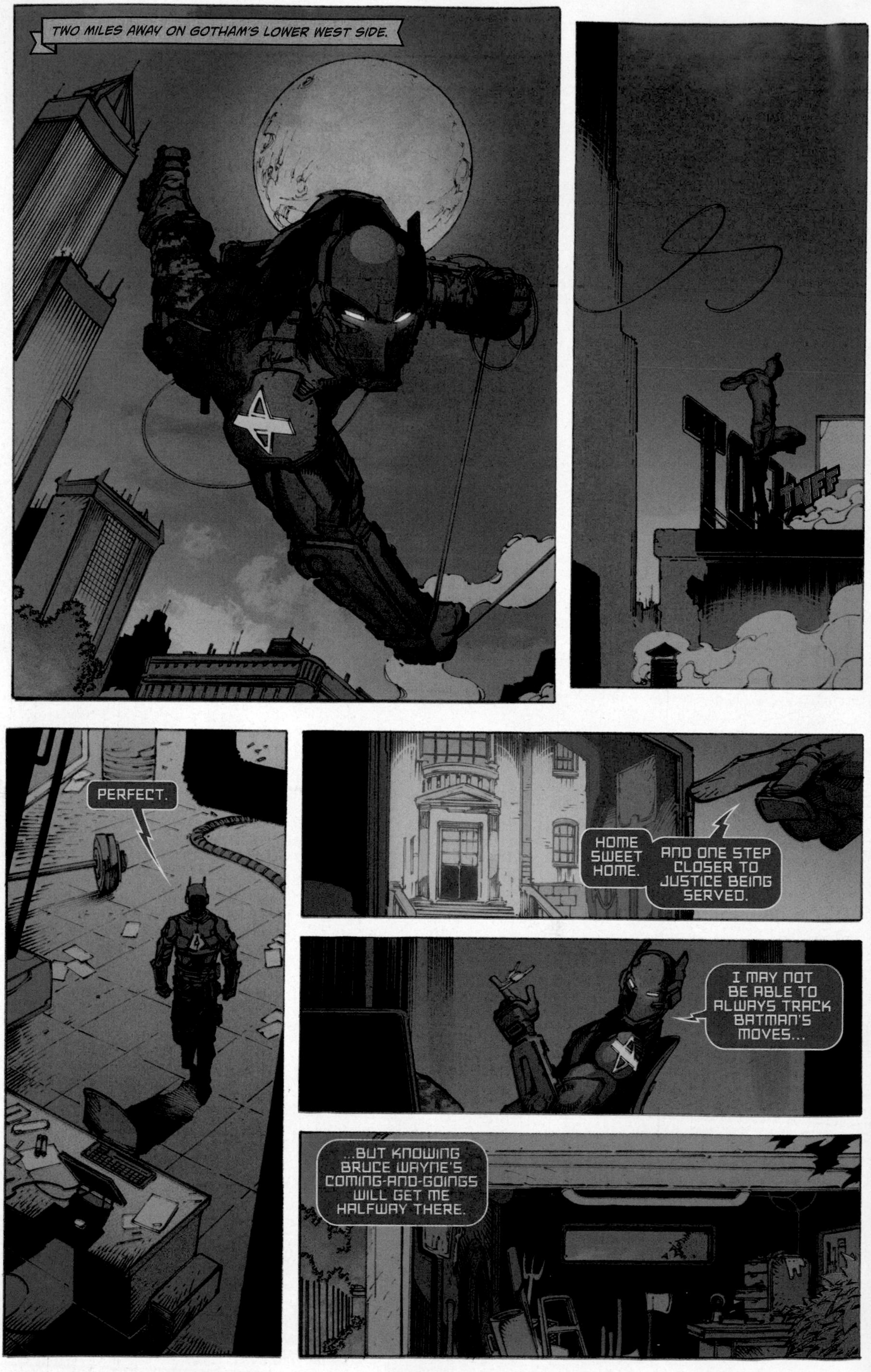
TWO MILES AWAY ON GOTHAM'S LOWER WEST SIDE.
TNFF
PERFECT.
HOME SWEET HOME.
AND ONE STEP CLOSER TO JUSTICE BEING SERVED.
I MAY NOT BE ABLE TO ALWAYS TRACK BATMAN'S MOVES...
...BUT KNOWING BRUCE WAYNE'S COMING-AND-GOINGS WILL GET ME HALFWAY THERE.

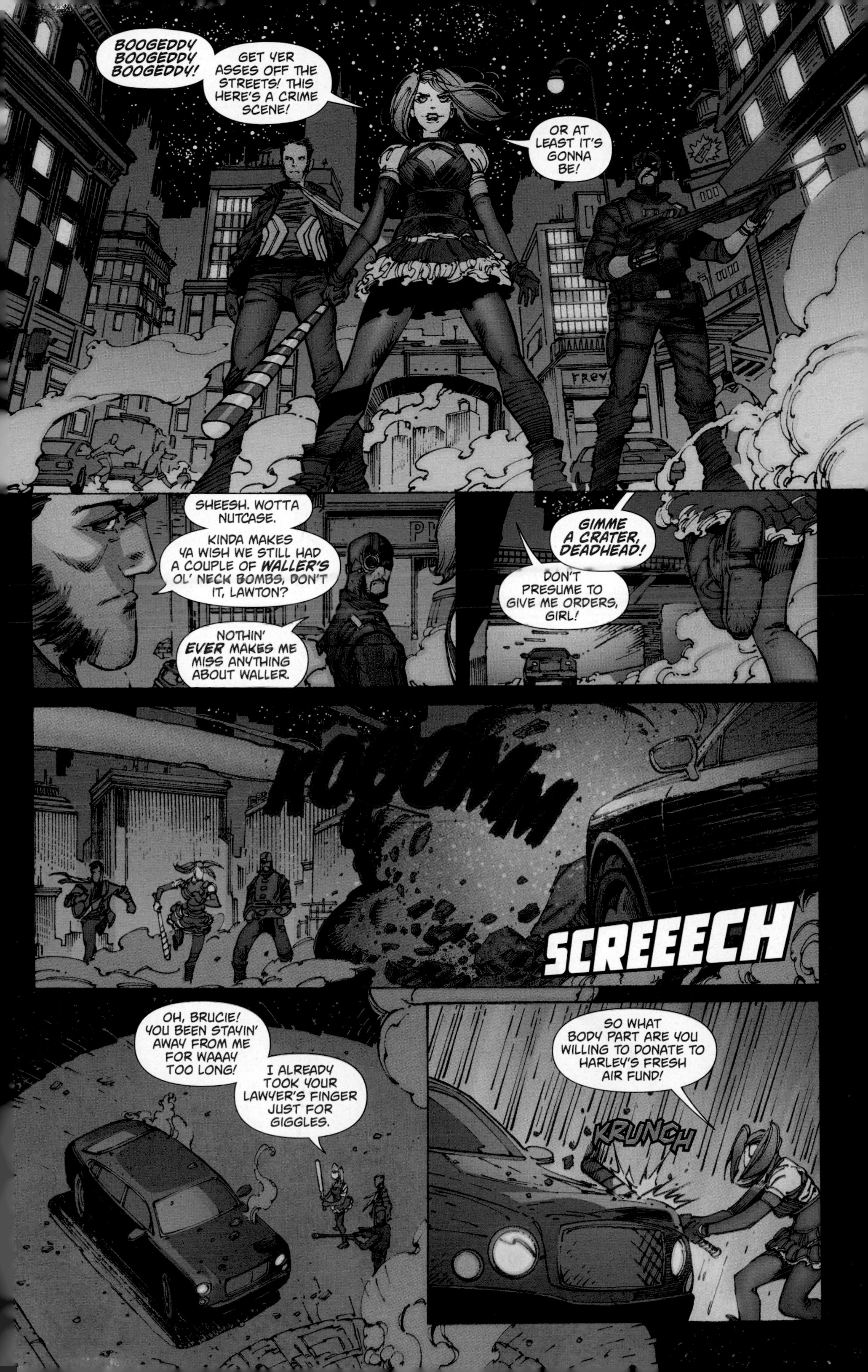
BOOGEDDY BOOGEDDY BOOGEDDY!
GET YER ASSES OFF THE STREETS! THIS HERE'S A CRIME SCENE!
OR AT LEAST IT'S GONNA BE!
SHEESH. WOTTA NUTCASE.
KINDA MAKES YA WISH WE STILL HAD A COUPLE OF WALLER'S OL' NECK BOMBS, DON'T IT, LAWTON?
NOTHIN' EVER MAKES ME MISS ANYTHING ABOUT WALLER.
GIMME A CRATER, DEADHEAD!
DON'T PRESUME TO GIVE ME ORDERS, GIRL!
SCREEECH
OH, BRUCIE! YOU BEEN STAYIN' AWAY FROM ME FOR WAAAY TOO LONG!
I ALREADY TOOK YOUR LAWYER'S FINGER JUST FOR GIGGLES.
SO WHAT BODY PART ARE YOU WILLING TO DONATE TO HARLEY'S FRESH AIR FUND!
KRUNCH

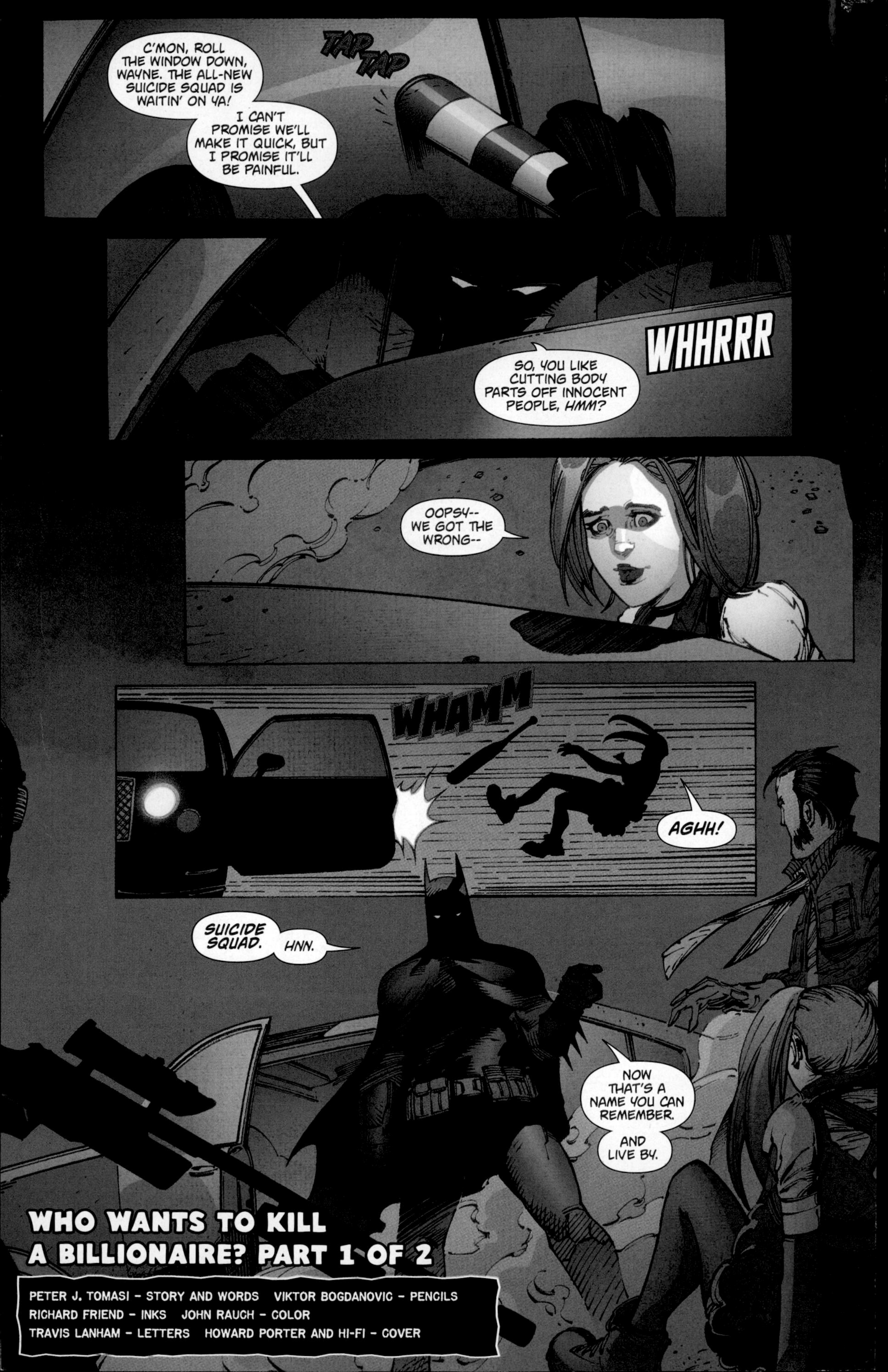
TAP TAP
C'MON, ROLL THE WINDOW DOWN, WAYNE. THE ALL-NEW SUICIDE SQUAD IS WAITIN' ON YA!
I CAN'T PROMISE WE'LL MAKE IT QUICK, BUT I PROMISE IT'LL BE PAINFUL.
WHHRRR
SO, YOU LIKE CUTTING BODY PARTS OFF INNOCENT PEOPLE, HMM?
OOPSY-- WE GOT THE WRONG--
WHAMM
AGHH!
SUICIDE SQUAD.
HNN.
NOW THAT'S A NAME YOU CAN REMEMBER.
AND LIVE BY.

WHO WANTS TO KILL A BILLIONAIRE? PART 1 OF 2

PETER J. TOMASI – STORY AND WORDS VIKTOR BOGDANOVIC – PENCILS
RICHARD FRIEND – INKS JOHN RAUCH – COLOR
TRAVIS LANHAM – LETTERS HOWARD PORTER AND HI-FI – COVER

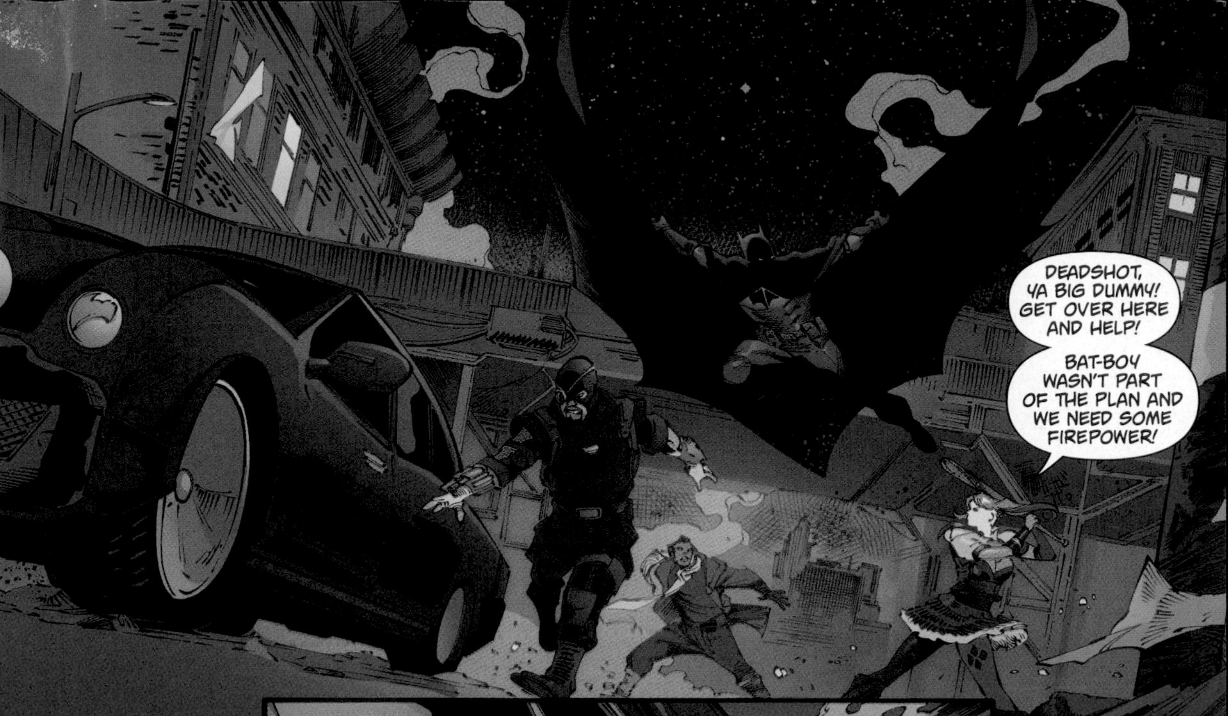
DEADSHOT, YA BIG DUMMY! GET OVER HERE AND HELP!
BAT-BOY WASN'T PART OF THE PLAN AND WE NEED SOME FIREPOWER!

WHO WANTS TO KILL A BILLIONAIRE? PART 2 OF 2

PETER J. TOMASI: STORY & WORDS
IG GUARA: PENCILS
JULIO FERREIRA: INKS

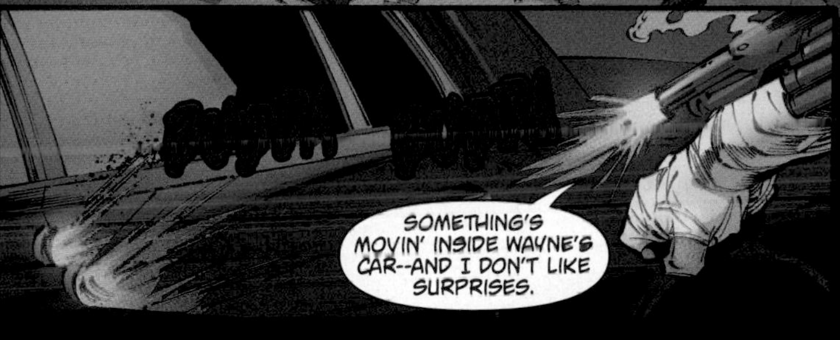
SOMETHING'S MOVIN' INSIDE WAYNE'S CAR--AND I DON'T LIKE SURPRISES.

ANDREW DALHOUSE: COLOR
TRAVIS LANHAM: LETTERS
HOWARD PORTER & HI-FI: COVER

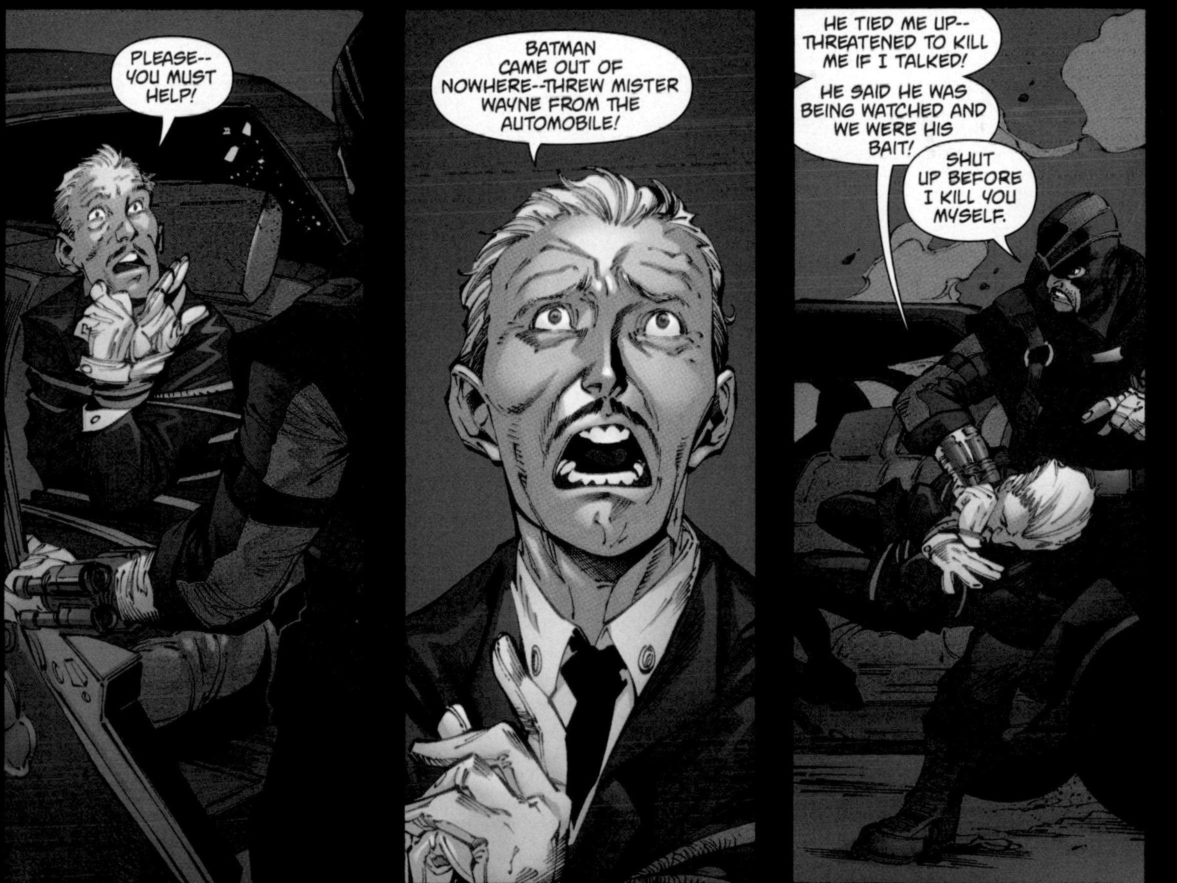
PLEASE-- YOU MUST HELP!
BATMAN CAME OUT OF NOWHERE--THREW MISTER WAYNE FROM THE AUTOMOBILE!
HE TIED ME UP-- THREATENED TO KILL ME IF I TALKED!
HE SAID HE WAS BEING WATCHED AND WE WERE HIS BAIT!
SHUT UP BEFORE I KILL YOU MYSELF.

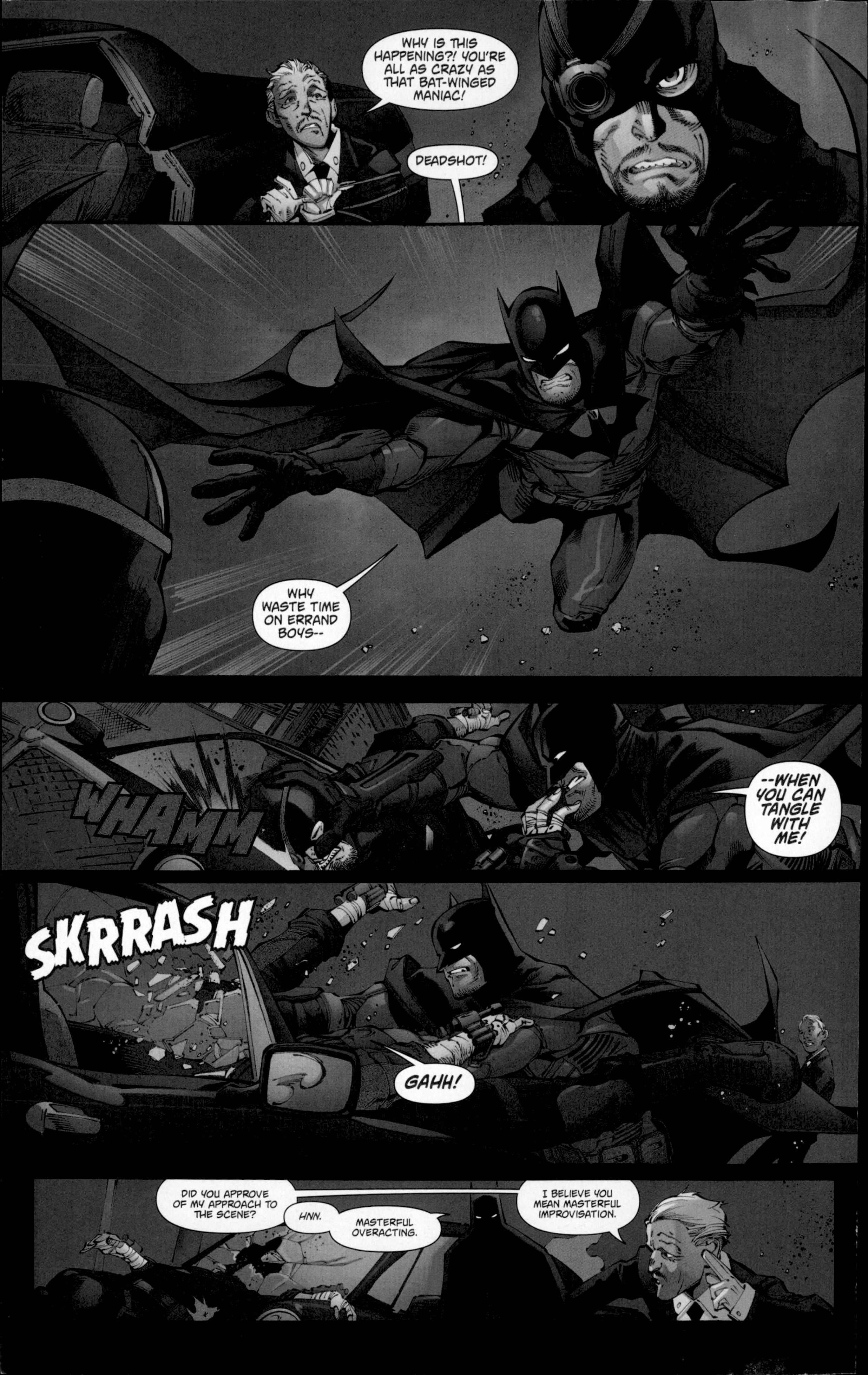
WHY IS THIS HAPPENING?! YOU'RE ALL AS CRAZY AS THAT BAT-WINGED MANIAC!
DEADSHOT!
WHY WASTE TIME ON ERRAND BOYS--
WHAMM
--WHEN YOU CAN TANGLE WITH ME!
SKRRASH
GAHH!
DID YOU APPROVE OF MY APPROACH TO THE SCENE?
HNN.
MASTERFUL OVERACTING.
I BELIEVE YOU MEAN MASTERFUL IMPROVISATION.

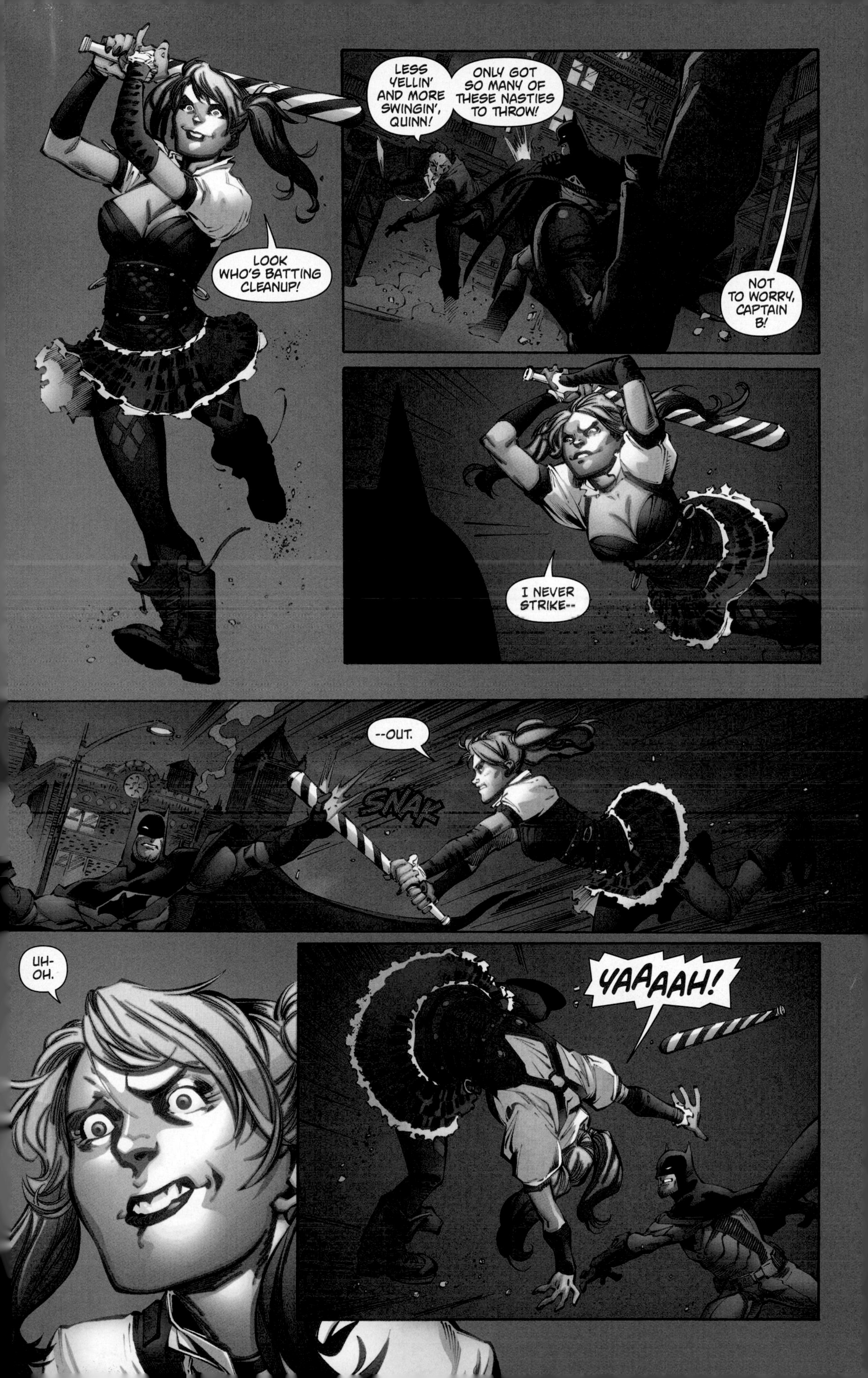
LOOK WHO'S BATTING CLEANUP!
LESS YELLIN' AND MORE SWINGIN', QUINN!
ONLY GOT SO MANY OF THESE NASTIES TO THROW!
NOT TO WORRY, CAPTAIN B!
I NEVER STRIKE--
--OUT.
SNAK
UH-OH.
YAAAAH!

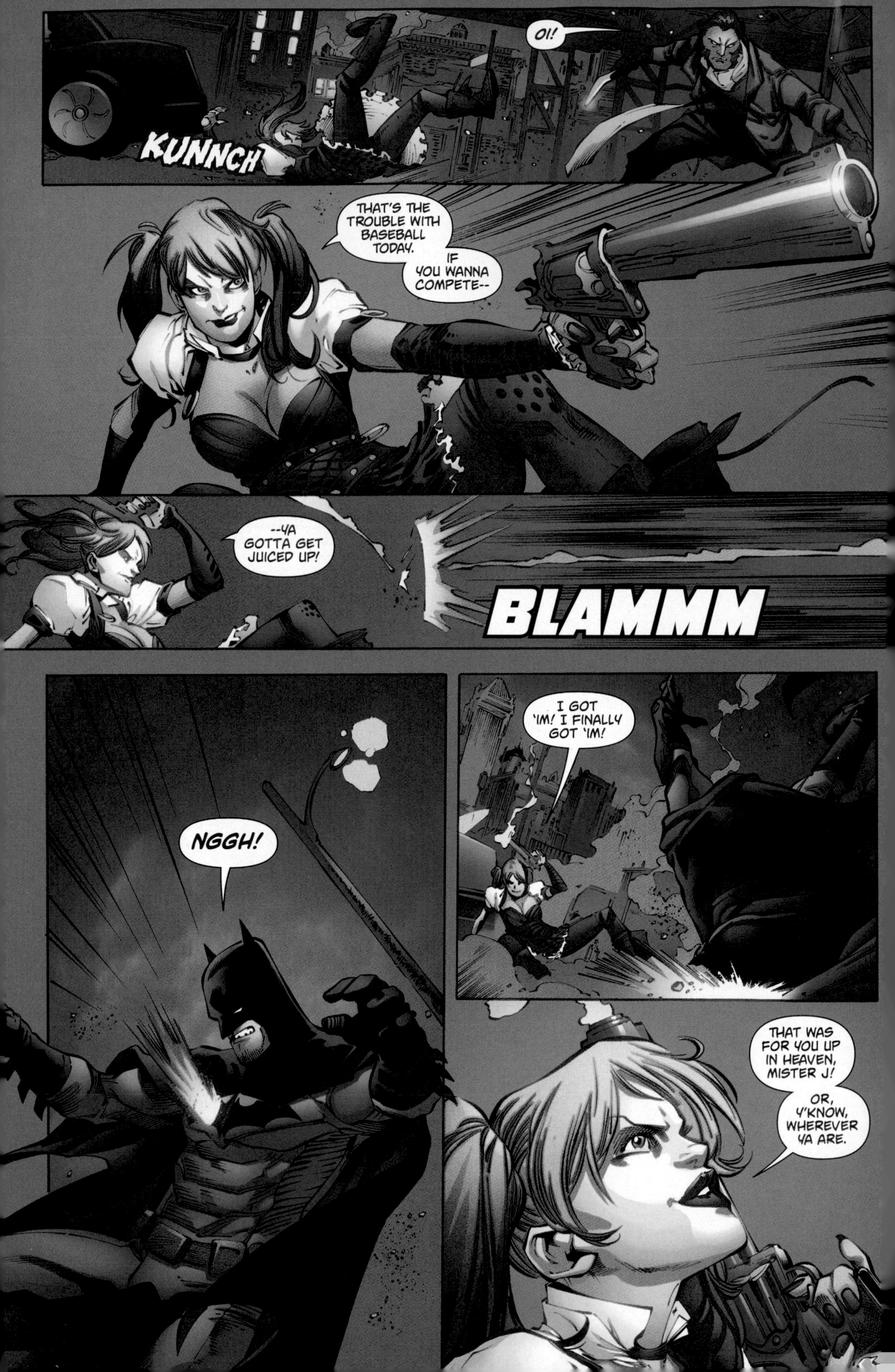
OI!
KUNNCH
THAT'S THE TROUBLE WITH BASEBALL TODAY.
IF YOU WANNA COMPETE--
--YA GOTTA GET JUICED UP!
BLAMMM
NGGH!
I GOT 'IM! I FINALLY GOT 'IM!
THAT WAS FOR YOU UP IN HEAVEN, MISTER J!
OR, Y'KNOW, WHEREVER YA ARE.

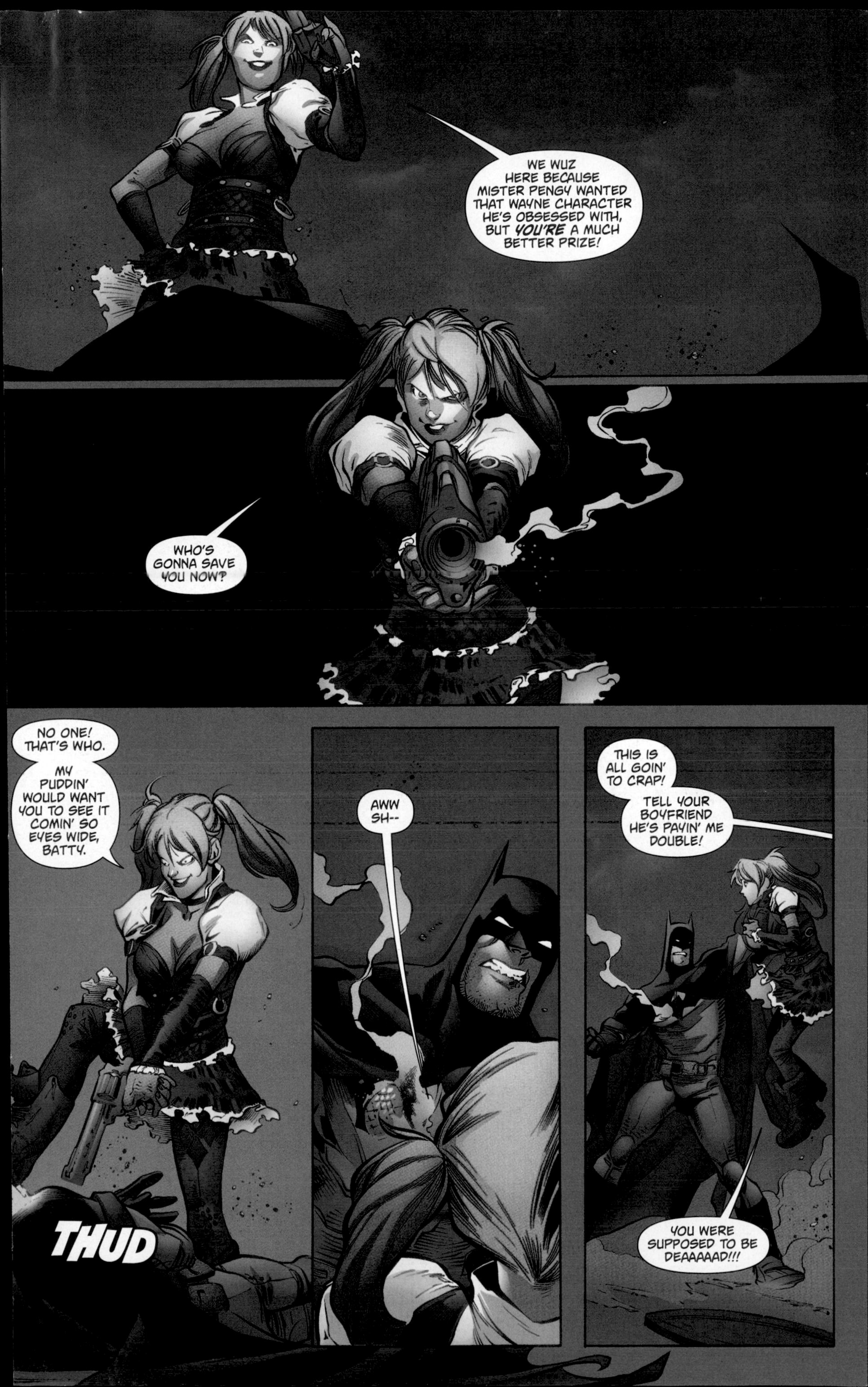
WE WUZ HERE BECAUSE MISTER PENGY WANTED THAT WAYNE CHARACTER HE'S OBSESSED WITH, BUT YOU'RE A MUCH BETTER PRIZE!
WHO'S GONNA SAVE YOU NOW?
NO ONE! THAT'S WHO.
MY PUDDIN' WOULD WANT YOU TO SEE IT COMIN' SO EYES WIDE, BATTY.
THUD
AWW SH--
THIS IS ALL GOIN' TO CRAP!
TELL YOUR BOYFRIEND HE'S PAYIN' ME DOUBLE!
YOU WERE SUPPOSED TO BE DEAAAAAD!!!

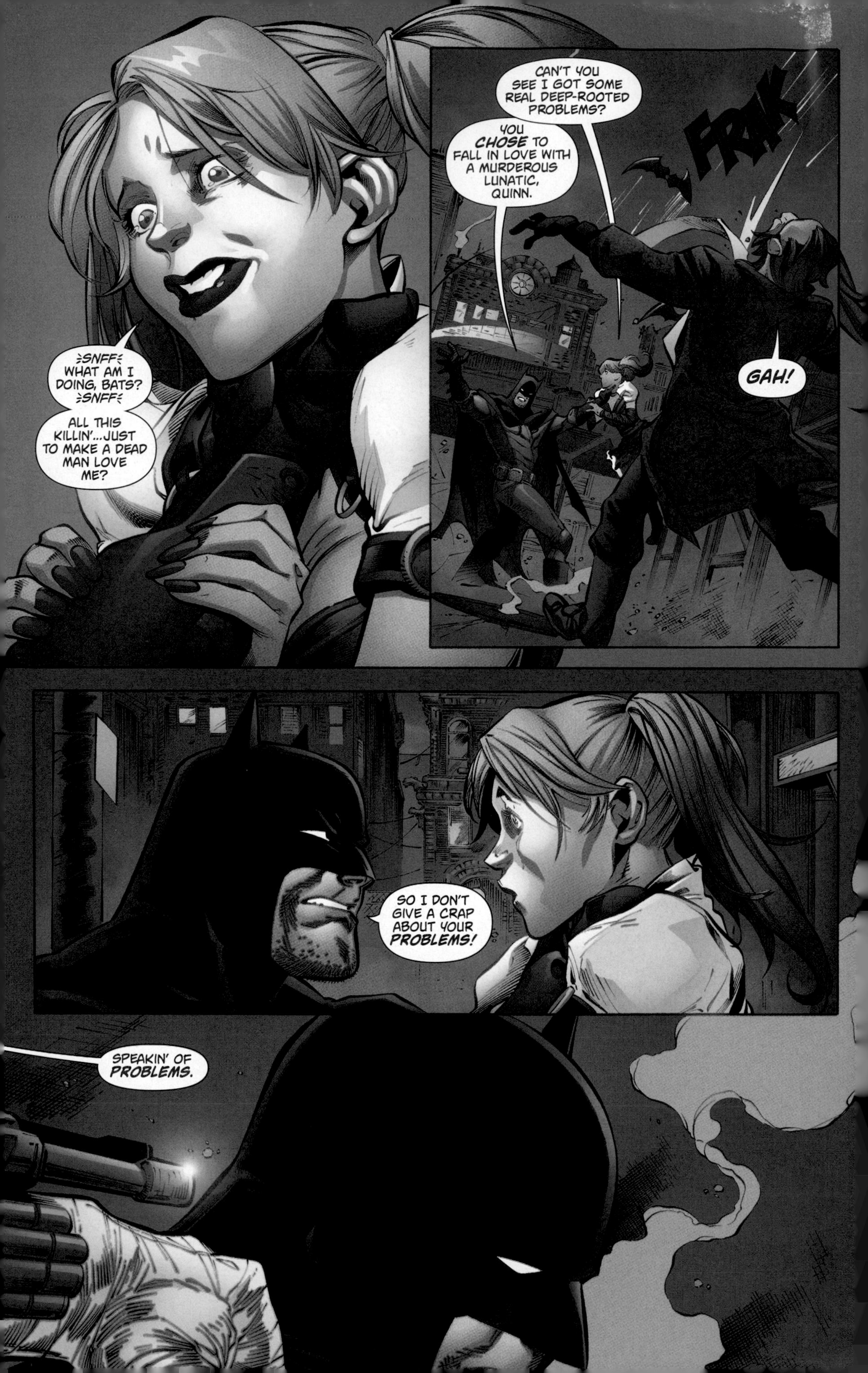

SNFF WHAT AM I DOING, BATS? *SNFF*
ALL THIS KILLIN'...JUST TO MAKE A DEAD MAN LOVE ME?
CAN'T YOU SEE I GOT SOME REAL DEEP-ROOTED PROBLEMS?
YOU CHOSE TO FALL IN LOVE WITH A MURDEROUS LUNATIC, QUINN.
FRAK
GAH!
SO I DON'T GIVE A CRAP ABOUT YOUR PROBLEMS!
SPEAKIN' OF PROBLEMS.

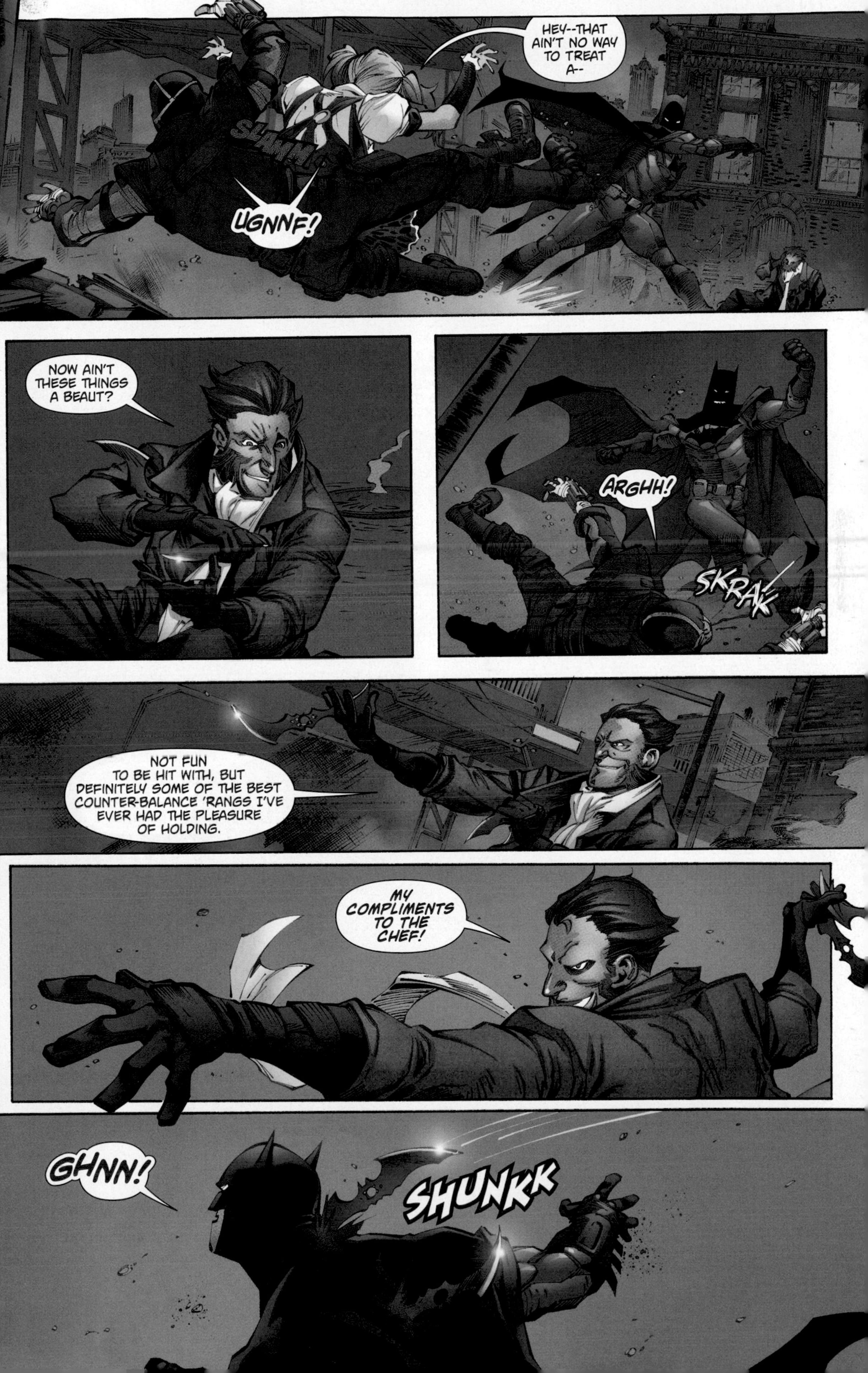
HEY--THAT AIN'T NO WAY TO TREAT A--
SLAMM
UGNNF!
NOW AIN'T THESE THINGS A BEAUT?
ARGHH!
SKRAK
NOT FUN TO BE HIT WITH, BUT DEFINITELY SOME OF THE BEST COUNTER-BALANCE 'RANGS I'VE EVER HAD THE PLEASURE OF HOLDING.
MY COMPLIMENTS TO THE CHEF!
GHNN!
SHUNKK

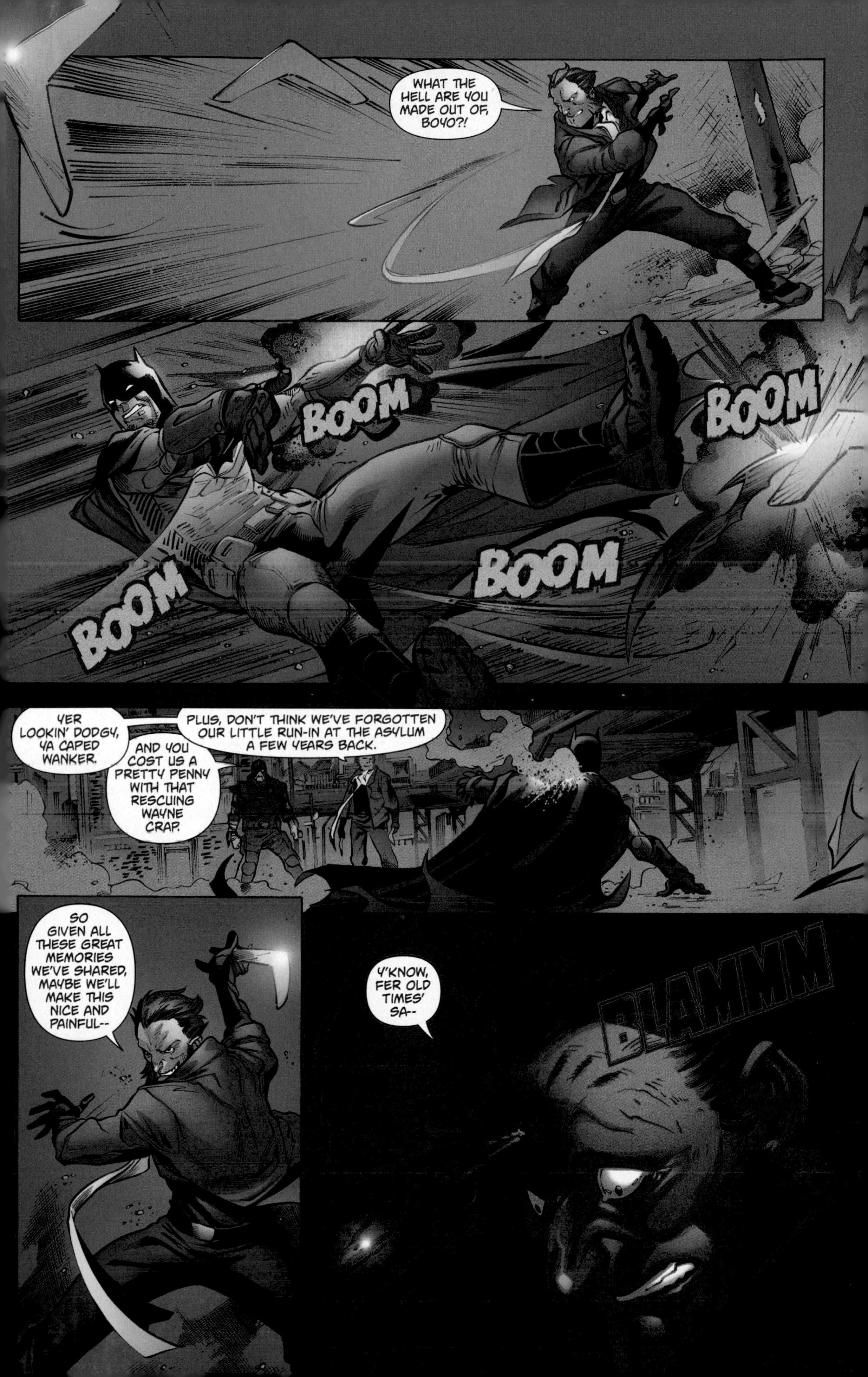

WHAT THE HELL ARE YOU MADE OUT OF, BOYO?!
BOOM
BOOM
BOOM
BOOM
YER LOOKIN' DODGY, YA CAPED WANKER.
PLUS, DON'T THINK WE'VE FORGOTTEN OUR LITTLE RUN-IN AT THE ASYLUM A FEW YEARS BACK.
AND YOU COST US A PRETTY PENNY WITH THAT RESCUING WAYNE CRAP.
SO GIVEN ALL THESE GREAT MEMORIES WE'VE SHARED, MAYBE WE'LL MAKE THIS NICE AND PAINFUL--
Y'KNOW, FER OLD TIMES' SA--
BLAMMM

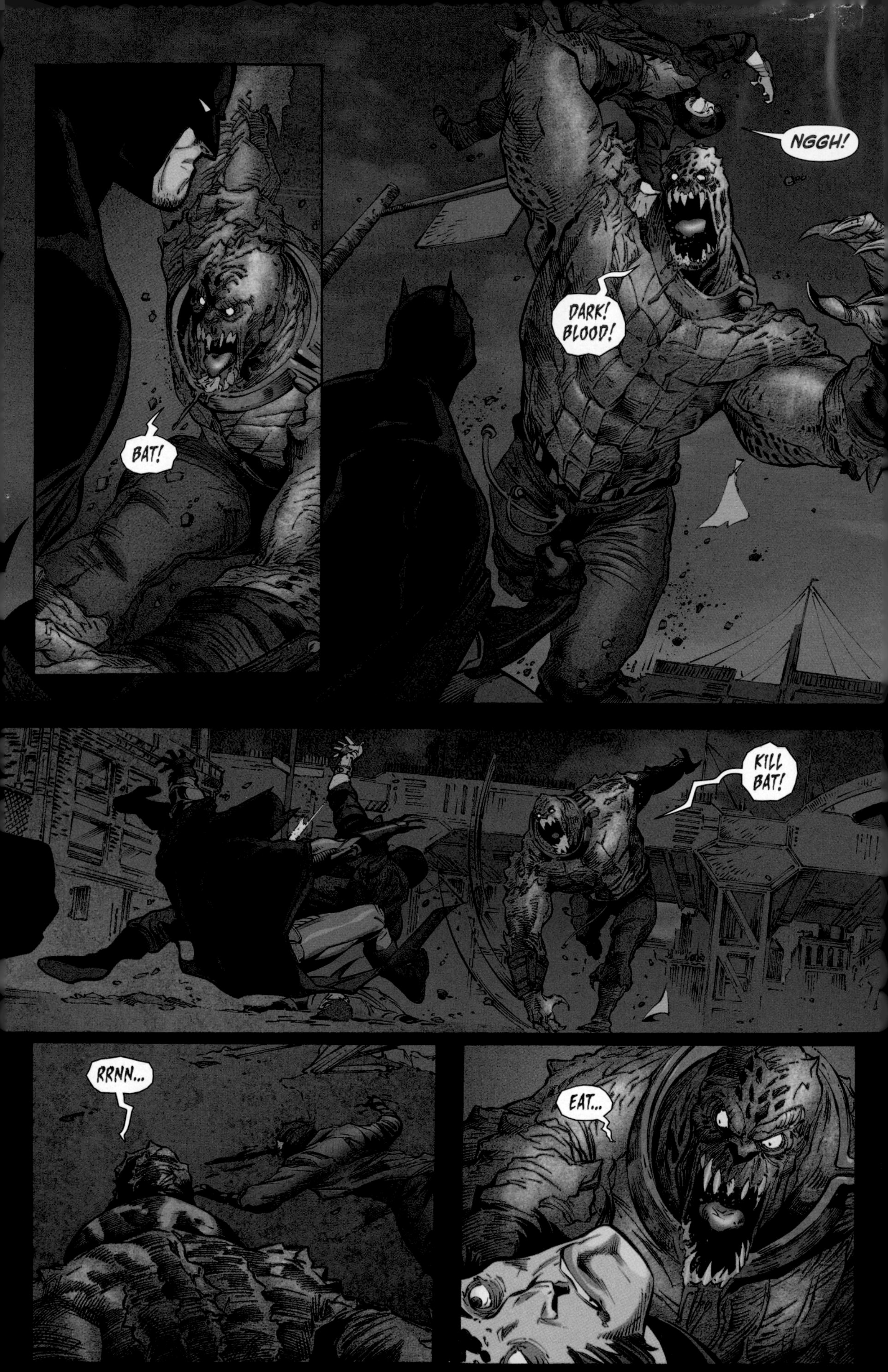
BAT!
NGGH!
DARK! BLOOD!
KILL BAT!
RRNN...
EAT...

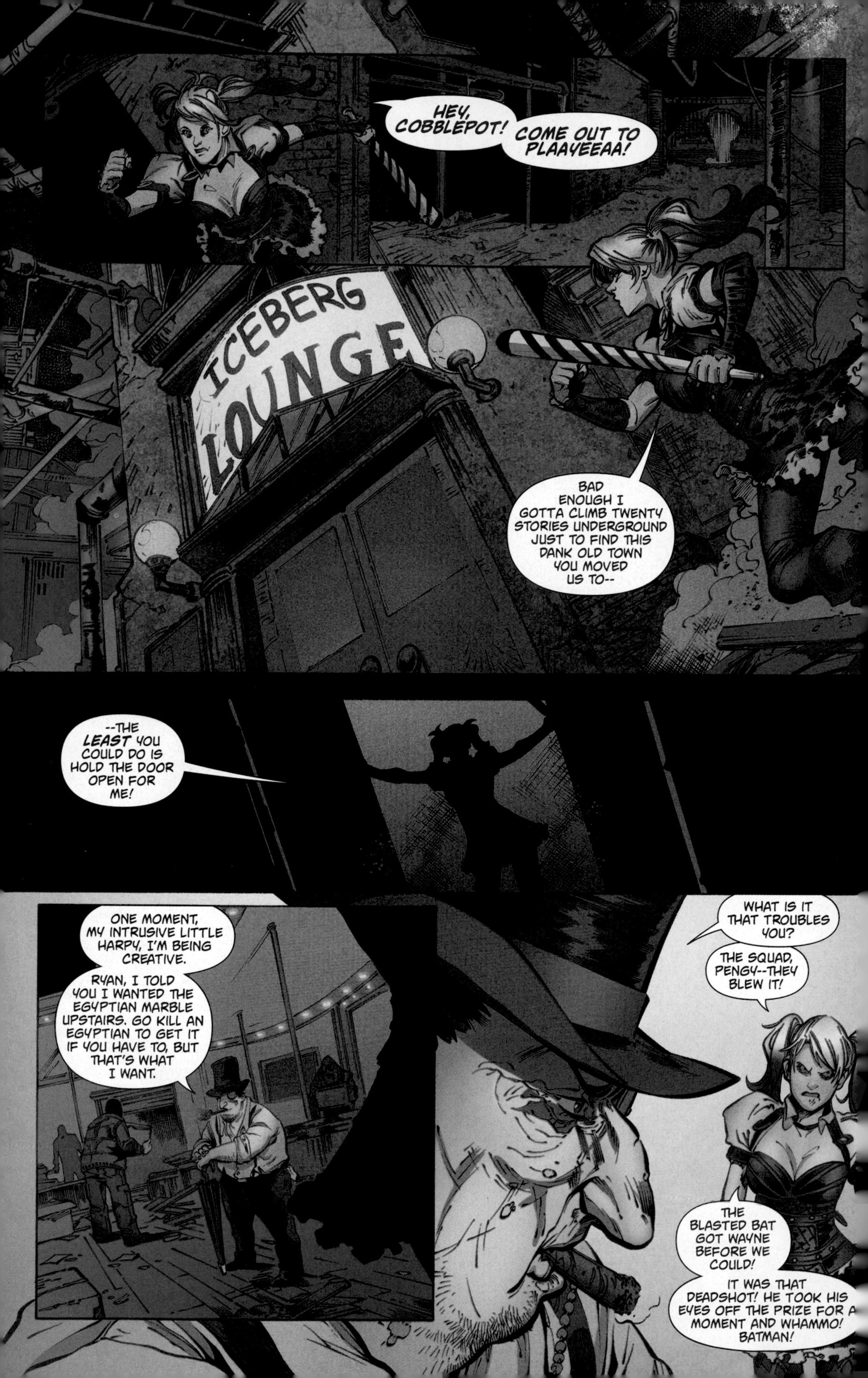

HEY, COBBLEPOT!
COME OUT TO PLAAYEEAA!
ICEBERG LOUNGE
BAD ENOUGH I GOTTA CLIMB TWENTY STORIES UNDERGROUND JUST TO FIND THIS DANK OLD TOWN YOU MOVED US TO--
--THE *LEAST* YOU COULD DO IS HOLD THE DOOR OPEN FOR ME!
ONE MOMENT, MY INTRUSIVE LITTLE HARPY, I'M BEING CREATIVE.
RYAN, I TOLD YOU I WANTED THE EGYPTIAN MARBLE UPSTAIRS. GO KILL AN EGYPTIAN TO GET IT IF YOU HAVE TO, BUT THAT'S WHAT I WANT.
WHAT IS IT THAT TROUBLES YOU?
THE SQUAD, PENGY--THEY BLEW IT!
THE BLASTED BAT GOT WAYNE BEFORE WE COULD!
IT WAS THAT DEADSHOT! HE TOOK HIS EYES OFF THE PRIZE FOR A MOMENT AND WHAMMO! BATMAN!

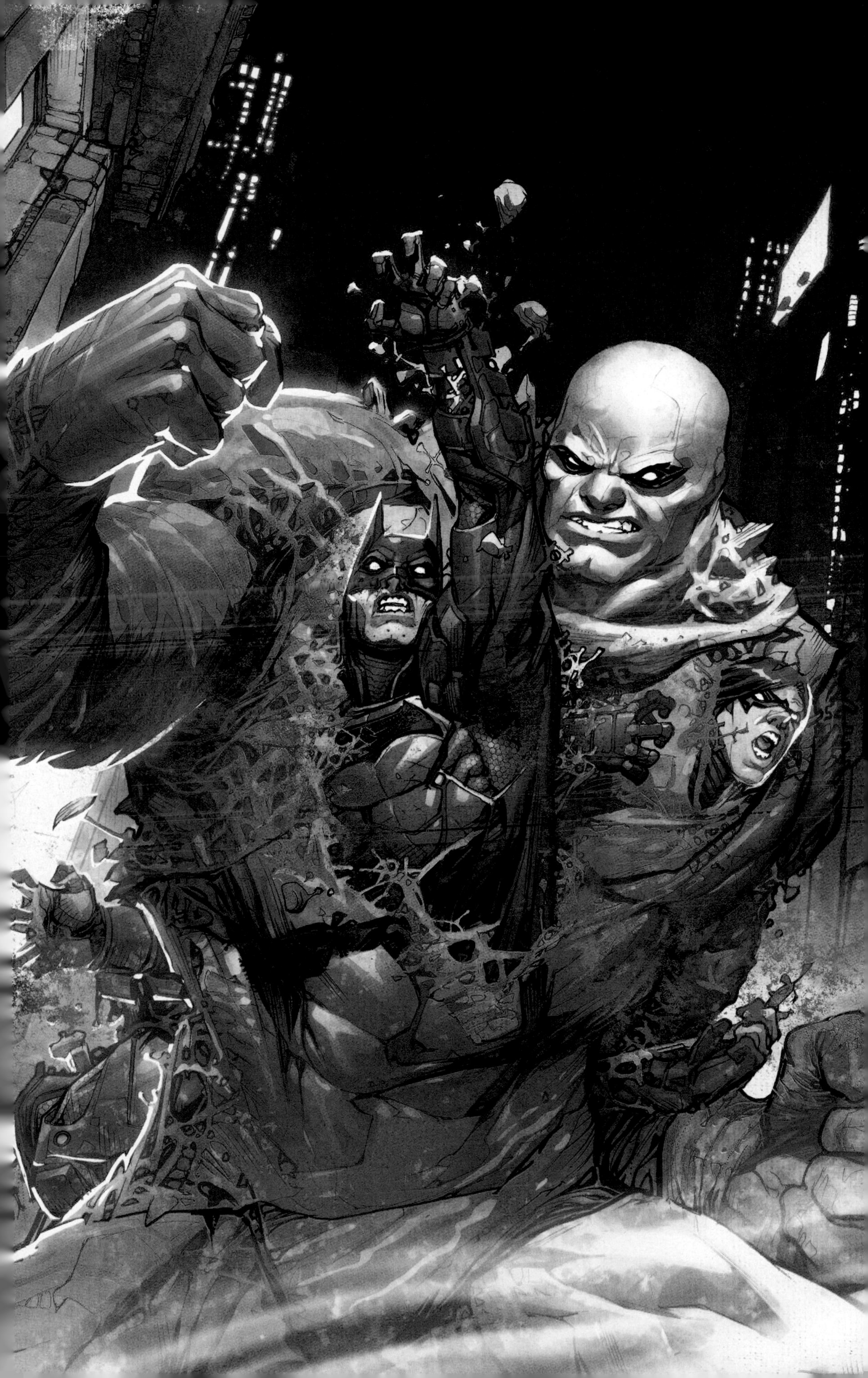

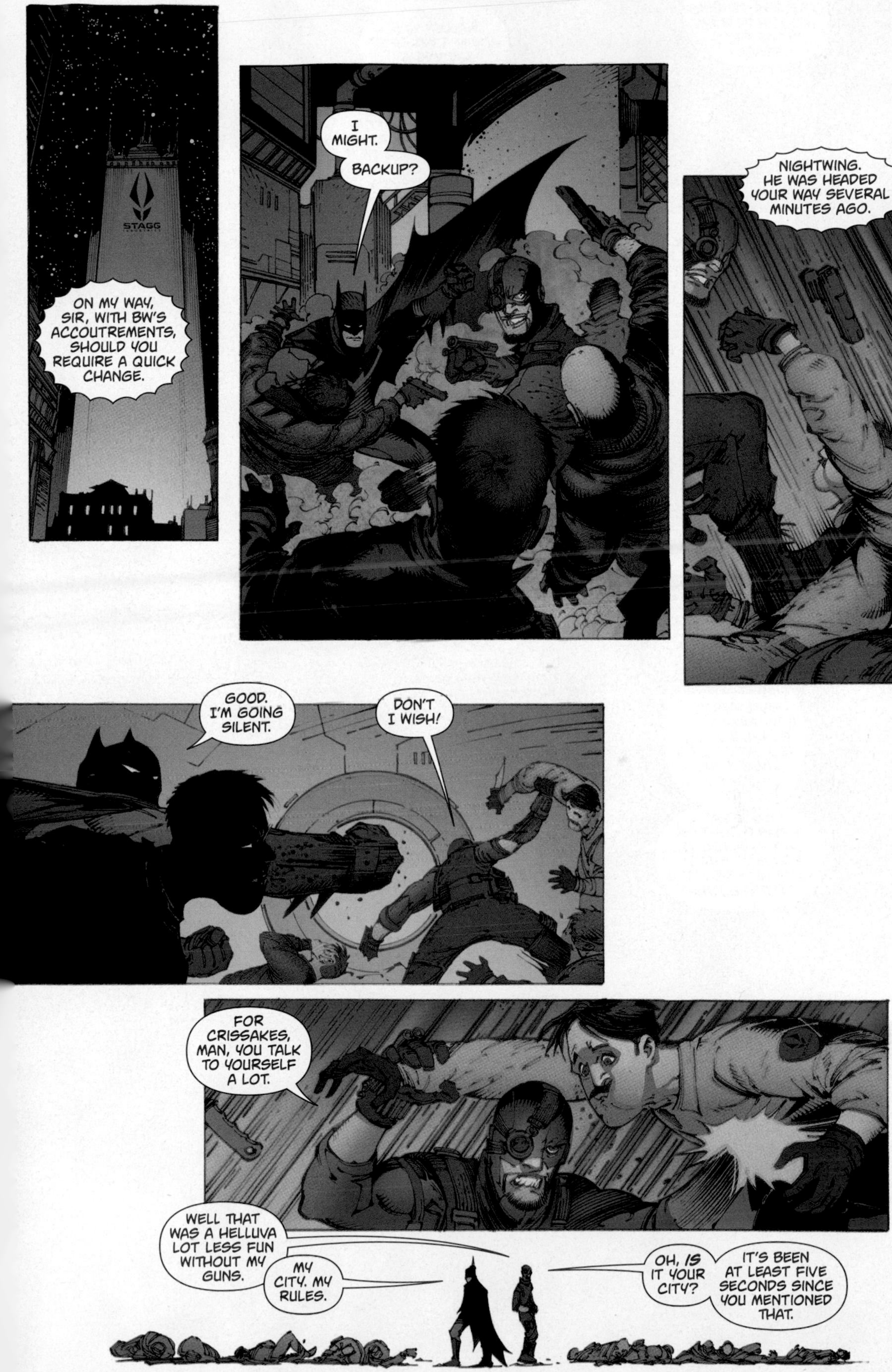
ON MY WAY, SIR, WITH BW'S ACCOUTREMENTS, SHOULD YOU REQUIRE A QUICK CHANGE.
I MIGHT.
BACKUP?
NIGHTWING. HE WAS HEADED YOUR WAY SEVERAL MINUTES AGO.
GOOD. I'M GOING SILENT.
DON'T I WISH!
FOR CRISSAKES, MAN, YOU TALK TO YOURSELF A LOT.
WELL THAT WAS A HELLUVA LOT LESS FUN WITHOUT MY GUNS.
MY CITY. MY RULES.
OH, IS IT YOUR CITY?
IT'S BEEN AT LEAST FIVE SECONDS SINCE YOU MENTIONED THAT.

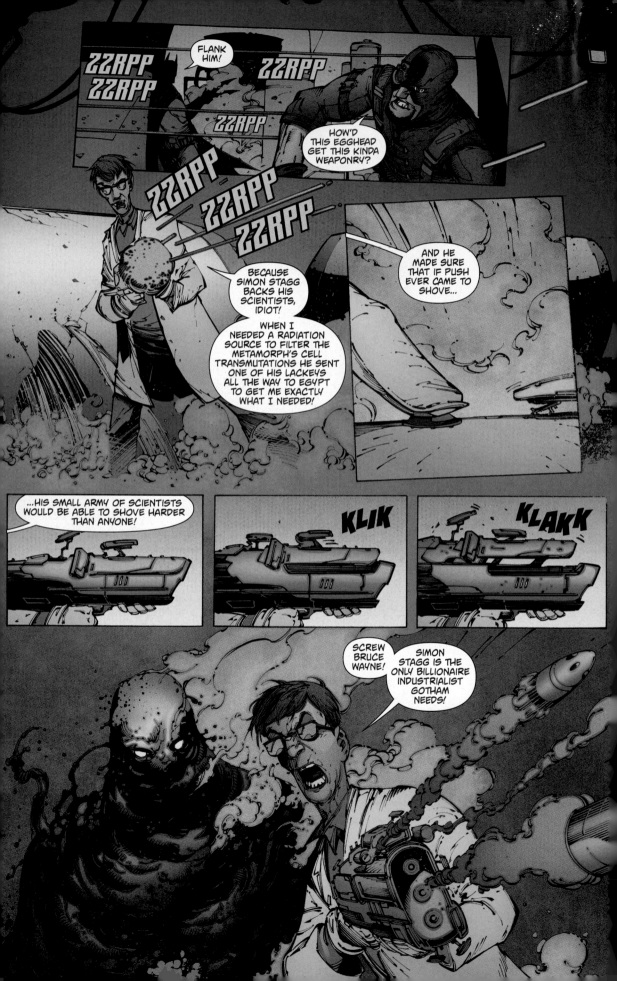

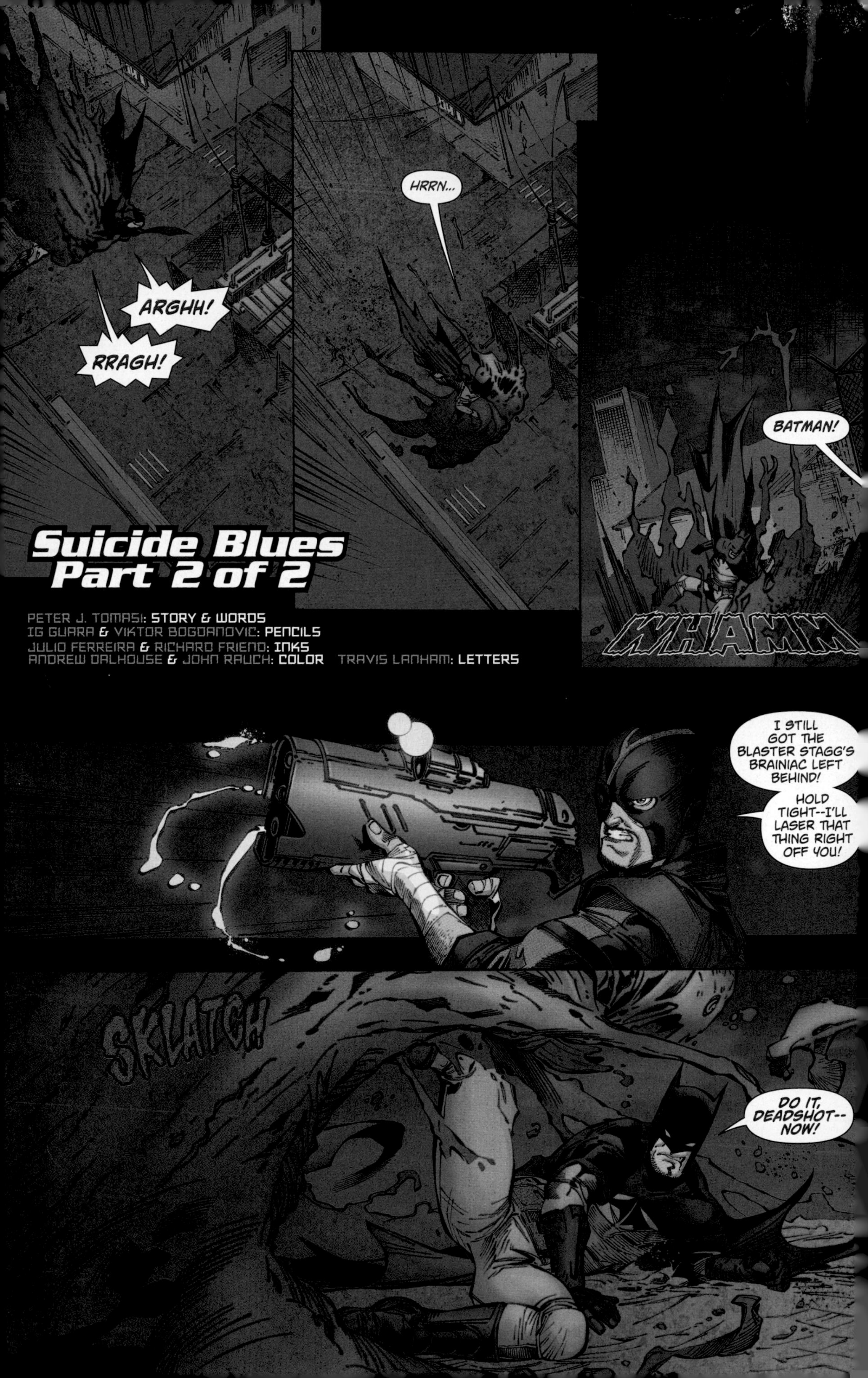
ARGHH!
RRAGH!
HRRN...
Suicide Blues
Part 2 of 2
PETER J. TOMASI: STORY & WORDS
IG GUARA & VIKTOR BOGDANOVIC: PENCILS
JULIO FERREIRA & RICHARD FRIEND: INKS
ANDREW DALHOUSE & JOHN RAUCH: COLOR
TRAVIS LANHAM: LETTERS
BATMAN!
KHAMM
I STILL GOT THE BLASTER STAGG'S BRAINIAC LEFT BEHIND!
HOLD TIGHT--I'LL LASER THAT THING RIGHT OFF YOU!
SKLATCH
DO IT, DEADSHOT--NOW!

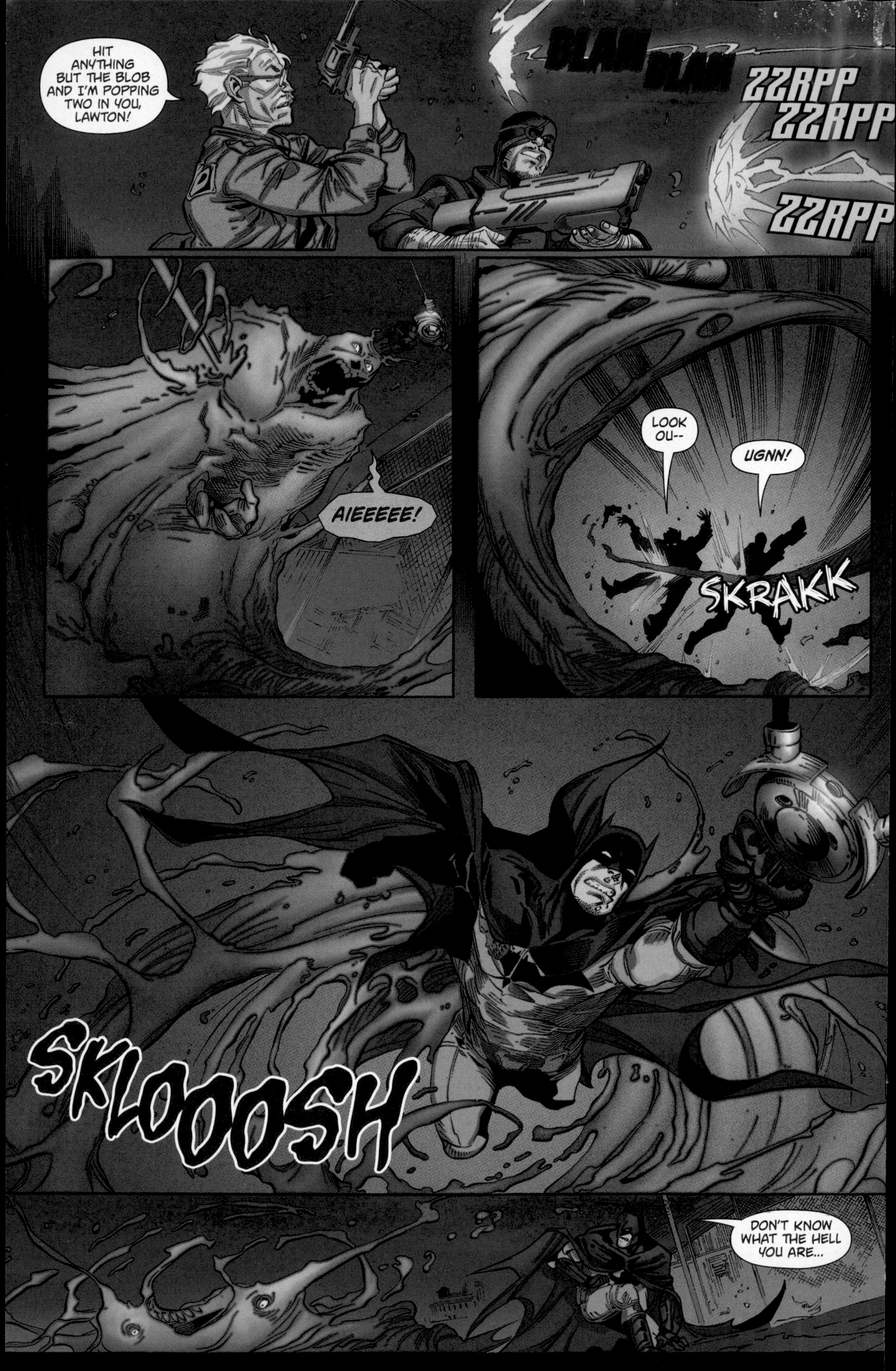
HIT ANYTHING BUT THE BLOB AND I'M POPPING TWO IN YOU, LAWTON!
BLAM BLAM
ZZRPP
ZZRPP
ZZRPP
AIEEEEE!
LOOK OU--
UGNN!
SKRAKK
SKLOOOSH
DON'T KNOW WHAT THE HELL YOU ARE...

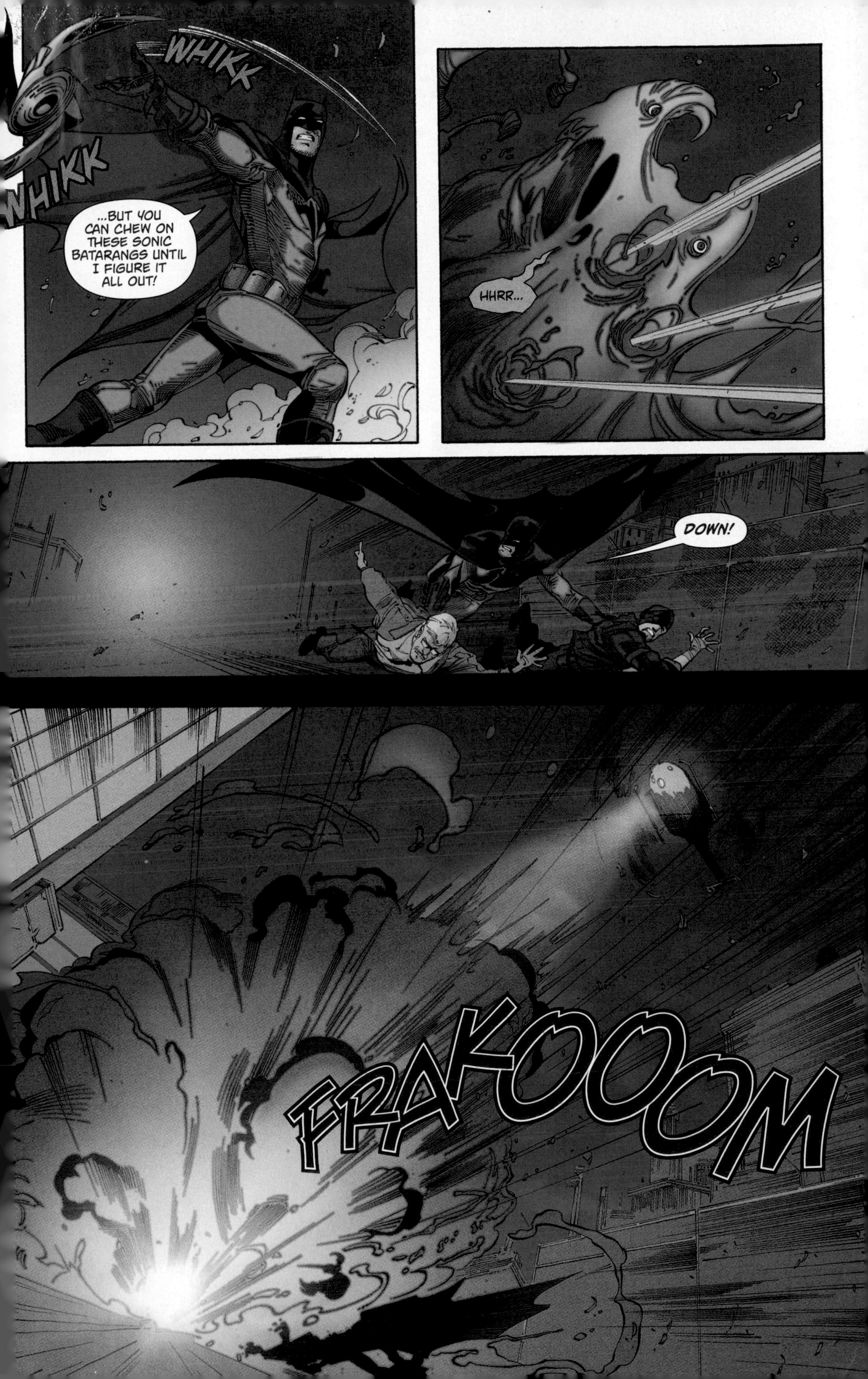
WHIKK
WHIKK
...BUT YOU CAN CHEW ON THESE SONIC BATARANGS UNTIL I FIGURE IT ALL OUT!
HHRR...
DOWN!
FRAKOOOM

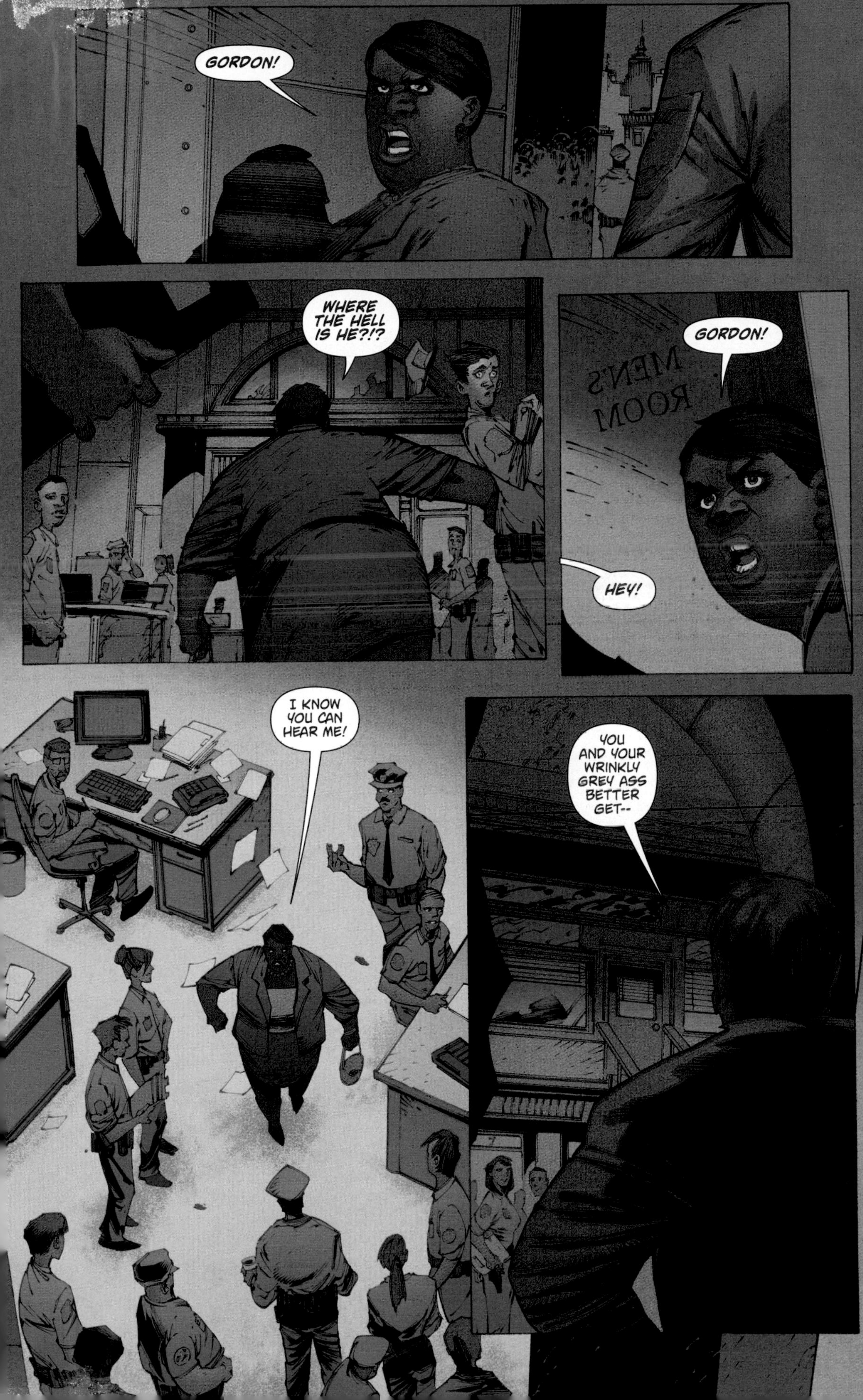
GORDON!
WHERE THE HELL IS HE?!?
MEN'S ROOM
GORDON!
HEY!
I KNOW YOU CAN HEAR ME!
YOU AND YOUR WRINKLY GREY ASS BETTER GET--

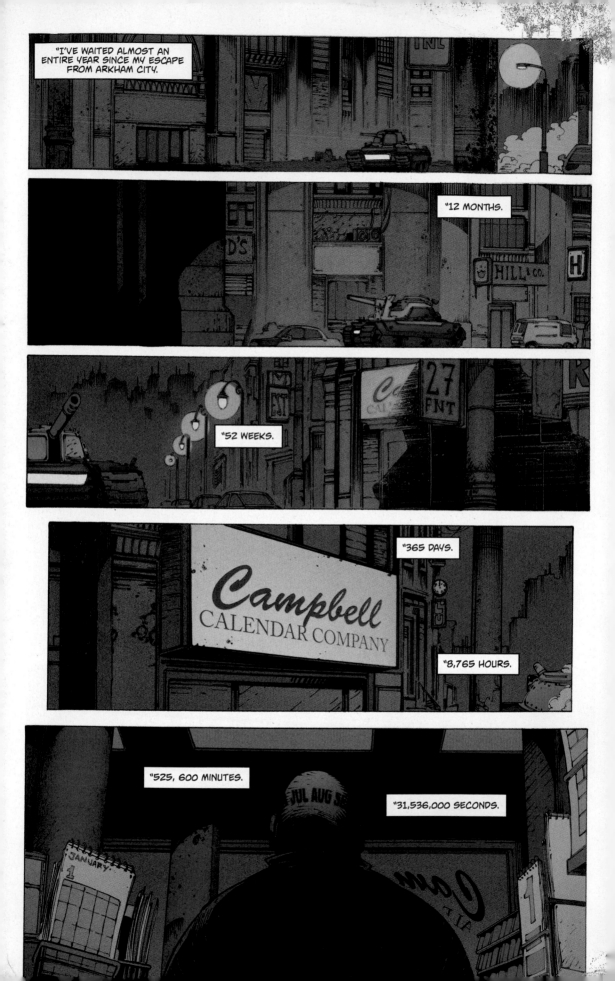

THIS KIND OF KNOWLEDGE COULD GET A YOUNG GIRL INTO A LOT OF TROUBLE.

MISS? AHEM... EXCUSE ME.

I'D LIKE TO GET SOME BOOKS.

MS. GORDON! CUSTOMER!

@Burnside_Boy88: Three creeps hanging from a street light outside my building this morning #busyBatman #Batmansighting

@TheRealTimDrake: He was in my hood too! The guy is everywhere! I wonder if he needs help...#Batmansighting

OH, SORRY! JUST CHECKING-- UM, LIBRARY STUFF.

WHATEVER. CAN YOU CHECK TO SEE IF THE STUFF I ORDERED CAME IN? *WALKER, DRURY.*

YOUNG PEOPLE THESE DAYS. ALWAYS UPDATING THEIR FACEBOOKS AND TWITTERS.

BATGIRL BEGINS

TIM SEELEY: SCRIPT MATTHEW CLARK: PENCILS WADE VON GRAWBADGER: INKS
ROB SCHWAGER: COLOR TRAVIS LANHAM: LETTERS MATTHEW CLARK & ROD REIS: COVER

SORRY, MR. WALKER. THEY HIRED ME TO HELP CONVERT ALL THE OLD MICROFICHE INTO DIGITAL FILES, AND I HAVEN'T GOTTEN TO THE BATMAN PRESS CLIPPINGS JUST YET.

BUT I CAN STILL CHECK OUT YOUR BOOKS FOR YOU. HOPEFULLY SOME FASCINATING MOTH FACTS WILL KEEP YOU BUSY UNTIL THE FILES ARE READY.

MOTH

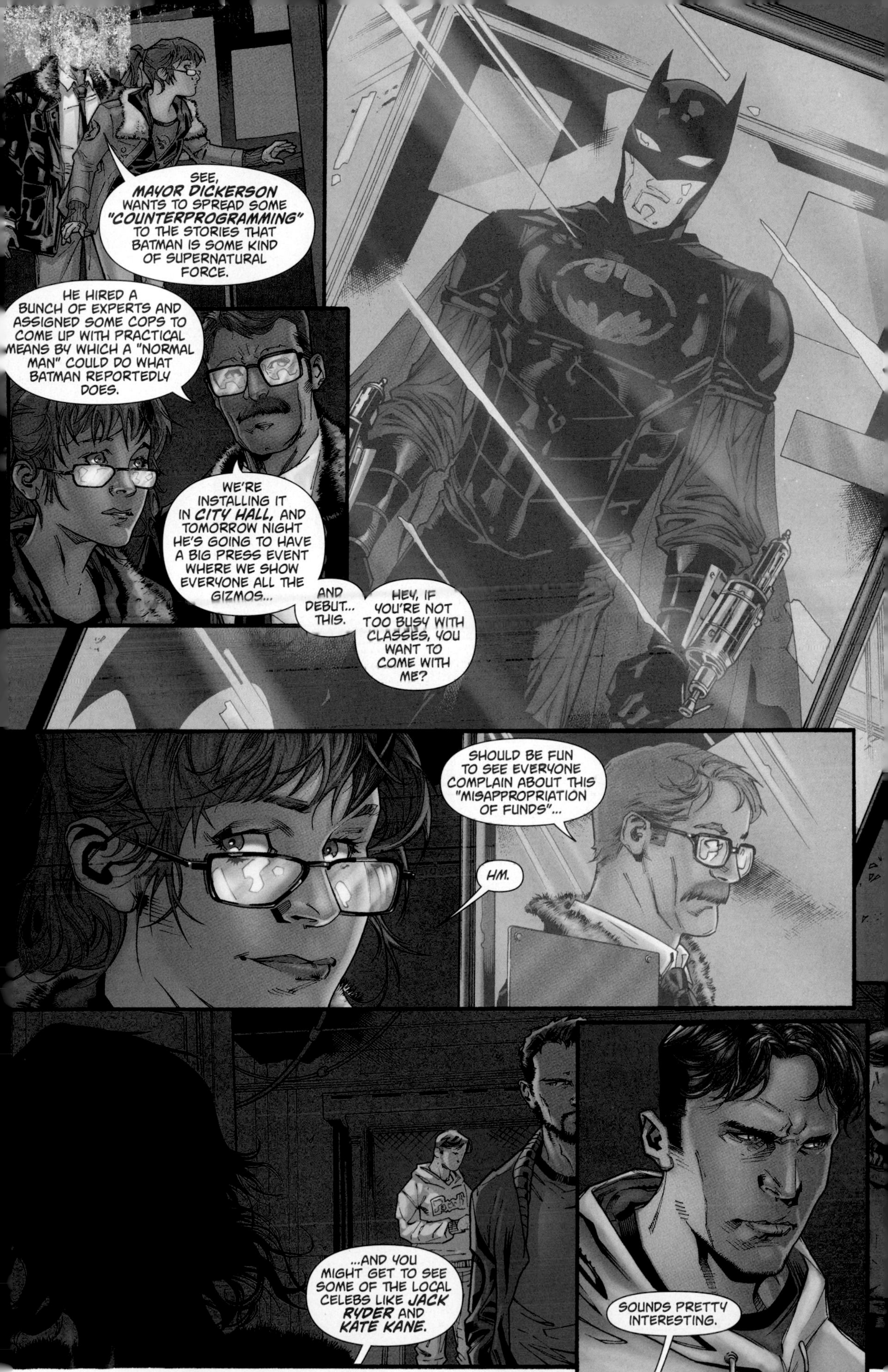

SEE, MAYOR DICKERSON WANTS TO SPREAD SOME "COUNTERPROGRAMMING" TO THE STORIES THAT BATMAN IS SOME KIND OF SUPERNATURAL FORCE.
HE HIRED A BUNCH OF EXPERTS AND ASSIGNED SOME COPS TO COME UP WITH PRACTICAL MEANS BY WHICH A "NORMAL MAN" COULD DO WHAT BATMAN REPORTEDLY DOES.
WE'RE INSTALLING IT IN CITY HALL, AND TOMORROW NIGHT HE'S GOING TO HAVE A BIG PRESS EVENT WHERE WE SHOW EVERYONE ALL THE GIZMOS...
AND DEBUT... THIS.
HEY, IF YOU'RE NOT TOO BUSY WITH CLASSES, YOU WANT TO COME WITH ME?
SHOULD BE FUN TO SEE EVERYONE COMPLAIN ABOUT THIS "MISAPPROPRIATION OF FUNDS"...
HM.
...AND YOU MIGHT GET TO SEE SOME OF THE LOCAL CELEBS LIKE JACK RYDER AND KATE KANE.
SOUNDS PRETTY INTERESTING.

THE BEGINNING!